646.77089 L962b

JUL   - 2011

A
BELLE
IN
BROOKLYN

A BELLE IN BROOKLYN

THE GO-TO GIRL FOR ADVICE
ON LIVING YOUR BEST SINGLE LIFE

DEMETRIA L. LUCAS

ATRIA BOOKS
NEW YORK LONDON TORONTO SYDNEY

ATRIA BOOKS
A Division of Simon & Schuster, Inc.
1230 Avenue of the Americas
New York, NY 10020

First Atria Books hardcover edition June 2011

ATRIA BOOKS and colophon are trademarks of Simon & Schuster, Inc.

For information about special discounts for bulk purchases,
please contact Simon & Schuster Special Sales at
1-866-506-1949 or business@simonandschuster.com.

The Simon & Schuster Speakers Bureau can bring authors
to your live event. For more information or to book an event,
contact the Simon & Schuster Speakers Bureau at
1-866-248-3049 or visit our website at www.simonspeakers.com.

Designed by Jill Putorti

Manufactured in the United States of America

10 9 8 7 6 5 4 3 2 1

Library of Congress Cataloging-in-Publication Data
Lucas, Demetria.
A belle in Brooklyn : the go-to girl for advice on living your best single life /
Demetria Lucas.
    p. cm.
1. Man-woman relationships. 2. Dating (Social customs) 3. Single
women. 4. Lucas, Demetria. I. Title.
HQ801.L823 2011
646.7'708996073—dc22

2011011689

ISBN 978-1-4516-0631-7
ISBN 978-1-4516-0930-1 (ebook)

For my grandmothers,
Comilla and Aletha.

A
BELLE
IN
BROOKLYN

INTRODUCTION

While I was writing this book in 2010, there was an onslaught of articles (*Washington Post, Economist, New York Times*), prime-time TV segments (*Nightline*—twice), books, and countless blogs examining "Why Black Women Are Soooo Single." It seemed that whenever a media source needed some sort of Nielsen ratings bonanza or to send their website's comments section into a frenzy, they'd trot out a horrific tale of no love and lots of loss. The plot was always the same: a single Black woman from a densely populated city clinging to a flavored martini, a Louis Vuitton Speedy, and/or a perfectly coiffed girlfriend wondering where all the good men had gone. (Go-to answers: dead, gay, unemployed, on the down low, in jail, or with a White woman.)

As I watched, read, and listened to the same story over and over, I wondered why "the problem" of singleness was being presented as a Black issue or even a female one. There are 96 million people in the United States who have no spouse, according to a

2010 study from the U.S. Census Bureau. That means 43 percent of all Americans over the age of eighteen are single. *So where are the news stories about White women and Latinas and Asian ladies who are desperately single and searching?* The closest I saw was "The New Math on Campus" in the *New York Times,* a story where White women at the University of North Carolina talked about their dating dilemmas and all the quotes sounded as if they'd been lifted from an early Terry McMillan novel.

What about the single men? Black ones and the ones of all other colors, too? If women are not getting married and we're supposed to be marrying them, shouldn't they get an equal number of stories? I've never understood how we're having an ongoing national discussion about the difficulty facing heterosexuals who want relationships and almost the entire conversation is about or aimed at women.

While *Nightline* had single Black women talking about crying into their pillows and throwing Black men-at-large under the proverbial bus, I couldn't help but recall that the most prominent tale of Dating While White, *Sex and the City,* featured women well past thirty shown practically high off new experiences, the carefree unaccountability of considering anyone else's feelings, and the thrill of picking through men like trying to find organic produce at Whole Foods. For White women, singlehood looked exhilarating and adventurous, not desperate, the way it is too often shown for us as a tedious but important exercise to make sure we don't end up alone. (See Pam from *Martin*, Regine from *Living Single*, or any character from a Terry McMillan novel for reference.)

As I tuned into *Sex and the City* each week or popped in the DVDs during the off seasons, I became increasingly frustrated. I knew plenty of Black women who were single and satisfied or single and searching but more optimistic than desperate. We lived full and adventurous lives, finding ourselves regularly sitting across from (and flirting with) attractive suitors with good conversation and pretty white teeth. It was a rare occasion that any of us sat home unwillingly for lack of a quality male option to happily plunk down his debit card after dinner and a drink. We still got giddy over meeting up with a new guy and exchanging witty banter at chic venues. And we knew there were a lot of cheerful single women like us who enjoyed dating, whose sole focus in life wasn't how to get a man to put a ring on it.

I began blogging in 2007 because Happy Black Girl stories weren't being told. I was sick of depictions of my Black and single life that made it look so burdened and heavy. I wanted everyone to know about regular Black girls and women with semidramatic adventures that were pretty painless and very amusing but resulted in extraordinary growth. I wanted everyone to know about the quality men in the world, the ones I met every day, that I *know* exist, but are rarely shown in the media. I'd been waiting for someone to tell that tale again since it had been years since Tracy Chambers (*Mahogany*), Nola Darling (*She's Gotta Have It*), and Nina Mosley (*Love Jones*) had a say. Then I realized that as a writer, I could just pick up my laptop and start typing.

At the time, I was in my third year as a book editor, working with bestselling romance authors and in my sixth year as a professional journalist, covering entertainment and lifestyles. My musings began on MySpace, quickly gained a following, and moved to a wider audience at HoneyMag.com, where my blog about my "hilarious dating misadventures as a Southern woman living too far above the Mason Dixon" became the most popular feature on the site.

As the audience grew, so did the number of letters in my in-box. Women from eighteen to sixty began thanking me for offering an alternative portrayal of Black life and for writing what they felt but couldn't find the words to say. That's when I *knew* I was on to something that was bigger than me and my girls.

Four months after my blog launched on *Honey*, I accepted a position as the relationships editor at *Essence* magazine, a job that utilizes my desire to debunk the negative depictions of single Black women, tackle our dating dilemmas, and help us live our best lives possible, whether our goal is to have fun or to have a relationship. I've also popped up in newspaper articles (I was dubbed "The Black Carrie Bradshaw" in a *Washington Post* feature article, which I have mixed feelings about) and on TV shows, both as a dating expert who teaches Sandy Denton aka "Pepa" from Salt-N-Pepa how to meet men on *Let's Talk About Pep*, and selecting a sexy man to be featured in *Essence* on *Being Terry Kennedy*.

Over the last four years, I've also completed thousands of interviews with men and women to gather information so we can close "the dating divide," hosted roundtable discussions where the sexes are provided a forum to hash out their issues face-to-face, searched for and offered up single men to the *Essence* audience, interviewed hundreds of experts about what we can all do better, became a life and relationships coach, answered thousands of dating and relationship questions on Formspring, and penned a monthly column for *Essence* that tackles current dating issues. Slowly but surely, I'm convinced, a dent can be made in the way we are portrayed, and the way we see ourselves. Together, we can close the gap between how women and men relate to one another.

In your hands, you hold my best attempt to make a difference. I've shared my life—mistakes and all—as well as the insights I've gained. My story isn't perfect, it's not always pretty, but it's honest, with ups and downs and many more highs than lows. Some details have been changed to protect the innocent (or guilty, depending on how you look at it), mostly names and physical descriptions but some places, too. I hope you can learn as much by reading about my trials and triumphs as I did by living and growing through them.

YOU CAN'T START THE PLAY
IN THE SECOND ACT

I went to Dream every Friday night to free my mind and hope the rest would follow. It was 2002, and the posh four-story super club in Washington, D.C., was newly opened. Dream was the only place to be after-hours in the city if you were young and/or fabulous or aspiring to be such. I was not fabulous. I was miserable, twenty-three, a recent graduate and stuck in Maryland when I desperately wanted to be back in New York. Calling my situation a quarter-life crisis would be an understatement.

I would show up to the club with Aliya, my best friend since junior high, around seven. We usually two-stepped until midnight and were safely and soberly, or relatively such, tucked in our beds before one A.M. One of those nights, I met a boy. He was . . . beautiful. No, scratch that. He was of such beauty that he appeared to be handcrafted by God herself. That's much more accurate.

I spotted him in the crowd on the venue's third floor, the one with the open-air deck. He was walking in my direction but not headed toward me. I smiled. He smiled back. I bit my bottom lip and looked away, pretending to be coy. But then I realized he could pass me by and I might never see him again. Something feisty in me kicked in.

I made eye contact again, pointed to him, crooked my finger, and yelled "You! Come here!" loud enough for him to hear me over the bass line of the classic Baltimore club track "How U Wanna Carry It?"

It worked. He happily and promptly obliged. I introduced my-self cheerfully, told him he was the cutest thing ever. I even stood on my tiptoes to ruffle his Maxwell-esque hair (the early years) with my fingers. As we chatted, I beamed. So did he.

We saw each other at the club every Friday for the rest of the summer. He would see me, give me a hug, buy me a drink. His boys would spot Aliya and me, and they would come up to tell me what floor Dude was on to make sure we could find each other in the massive club. Or they'd bring Dude over to me, and we'd just sort of stare at each other, smiling like dolts going, "Hey." Pause. "Hey." Blush. "Hey." Giggle. "Hey." I was smitten, but I didn't even remember Dude's name, much less know his number.

Three months of these Friday interludes went by. (I'd figured out how to meet men, not how to get them to ask me out.) In passing conversation, I'd pieced together that he was a senior at a local uni-versity and was a year younger than me and that our parents worked in the same industry. I'm sure more details were exchanged, but I usually couldn't hear him over the music. I knew the facts that mattered, though: he was cool and he had great energy.

One Thursday afternoon, I got a call offering me a position in NYC. I'd spent three hours a day for seven months scouring the Internet for job listings and applying for anything that sounded remotely interesting. This one was far from my dream job, but it was in New York, where I desperately wanted to be. Of course, I took it. I had to move and start working in two weeks, and for part of those weeks I had arranged to take an overseas vacation with my dad.

My summer of Friday-night partying came to an abrupt halt, as the next evening would be my last at Dream for the foreseeable future. In honor of my departure, Aliya and I decided to arrive at the club when the doors opened, dance to R&B, hip-hop, reggae, and house until we sweated through our dresses. We would not leave till the lights came on, at which point we would switch into flip-flops and walk to the parking lot arm-in-arm. After, we'd head to Adams Morgan for "big pizza"—a slice that's the equivalent of one-fourth of a pie. It was the only proper way to say good-bye to the city.

That night, Dude finally asked for my number, told me he'd like to call me sometime. But summer was almost over, and so was my stay in D.C. *What's the use? To be friends?* I already knew I didn't want to be "just" Dude's friend. With a deep sigh, I asked him, "Dude, why'd you wait so long? I'm moving."

"Moving?" He looked stunned. "What do you mean, moving?"

"I'm leaving. I'm going to NY," I said. "I'm out."

He asked for my number again anyway.

I asked him back, "What's the point?"

We hugged with no malice or love lost, but he didn't let me go from the embrace right away. I wondered if he was thinking about the could-have-been possibilities, too, like that old Pepsi commercial when the couple gets on the elevator and on the ride to the lobby their whole possible life together flashes before their eyes. I sighed. He said good-bye, and we went our separate ways.

Monday morning, I crossed the Atlantic, landing in Paris. I was in an ill hotel, much different from my last visit when I was still an undergrad and stayed at a hostel. After I settled in. I bought crêpes that tasted like gourmet delicacies from street carts. I took a photo in front of the Arc de Triomphe, then strolled through the surrounding streets once walked by James Baldwin, Josephine Baker, and Richard Wright. Dude crossed my mind more than once. I didn't know him, still didn't even know his name, but I knew enough about him to know I could dig him. I started to wish that I had more time in D.C., but I stopped myself.

I'd prayed every day to get back to New York. It was all I wanted in life. Just a job, any job, a chance to compete with the best of the best. And I had the opportunity I'd been begging for, literally, on bended knee. A great guy (or two) would be a small sacrifice to live a big dream. Me and Dude? I wished it could have been explored. *If it was meant to be, then it would have been, right? You win some, you lose some. Maybe next lifetime?* I told myself every clichéd platitude I could think of to keep from letting my mind wander to the what-ifs and possibilities. Then I got to my favorite: *If not this time, then the next time. And maybe that time will be the right time.* I'd watched *Love Jones* way too many times.

My second day in Paris, I saw the *Mona Lisa* at the Louvre (much smaller than you would imagine and barely visible behind all the bullet-proof glass), sat in a café on the Champs-Élysée and sipped espresso (which I don't even like, but it seemed like the Parisian thing to do), and people-watched for hours. I took the subway and reveled in the ability to take public transportation in a foreign land in a foreign language and not get lost.

That night, I took the elevator in the Eiffel Tower to the highest level possible (not the actual top) and looked out at the city. I was humbled by all the beauty stretched before me. The City of Love, or Light, depending on which travel guide you read, is a great something to behold.

When I got back on solid ground, I walked underneath the

structure with my head bent back, admiring its intricate construction as if I were seeing it for the first time. When I'd taken my fill, I walked across the street and peered at the Seine River to admire the gold-tipped statues adorning the archways that cross it.

I could have gazed for another hour, if not for the rumble in my stomach. I headed to a nearby street stall to get yet another crêpe, and I saw . . .

"Dude?"

He looked up, paused mid-chew on the first bite of his crêpe and his mouth spread in a huge grin. He had Nutella on his teeth.

I flashed all thirty-two, too. We were both smiling like idiots.

"Hey."

Pause.

"Hey."

Blush.

"Hey."

Giggle.

Hey.

Just like old times.

Dude and I talk for hours as we walk along the edge of the Seine. It's seventy degrees or thereabout—all of the signs are in Celsius, and I can't do the conversion to Fahrenheit in my head. It's breezy, and the sky is lit with a half-moon. Turns out our parents are both in Paris for an international conference, and God bless them, they both brought their kids along for the European getaway. It's his first time in France, and he doesn't speak French, either. His hotel is near mine. Today is his first day in the city.

Is this fate? Divine intervention? Luck? Destiny? Cosmos? I don't usually believe in such things, but running into Dude makes me wonder if I should.

I try not to keep looking at him as he talks, but I can't help myself. Until now, I've only seen him in collared shirts, tailored slacks, and hard-bottom shoes. A decent outfit can make any man look half-official. Tonight Dude has on a backpack, camo shorts, and a crisp white tee. Oh, and flip-flops. Dressed down, he is still certified.

Every time I look over at him, I catch him smiling at me. I bite my lip and stare all the way up at him.

"What?" he asks, grinning.

I shrug. "Nothin."

We're both stuck on stupid.

By the time one of us thinks to check a watch, we've wandered to the middle of God knows where and have no idea how to get to the nearest subway station. Not that it would make a difference, since the English-speaking couple we finally encounter tells us the subway closed an hour ago. I guess we could take a cab, but instead, we walk back to the Eiffel Tower, pull out a subway map, and figure the way to the hotel based on trains named after nearby landmarks. This should not work, but somehow it does. We both have an internal GPS apparently.

By the time we get back to my hotel, it's past three A.M. That's four hours after we bumped into each other. I feel as if I know Dude's whole life story—fears, regrets, ambitions, goals, passions, and shortcomings. I shouldn't be nervous to ask if I'm going to see him again, but I am.

"Well, this is me," I say. I wait for him to say he'd like to see me tomorrow. I do not want to seem too eager for his attention. *One Mississippi. Two Mississippi. Three Mississippi,* I count in my head. "So I guess this is good night," I hint.

He smiles at me again. It's like the only expression either one of us can make right now.

"I wanna see you tomorrow," he says.

I exhale like I'm in a Terry McMillan novel. *Thank you, God!*

"Meet you at noon?" he suggests.

"Here?"

"Yeah." Pause. Smile. Blush. Giggle. "Right here," he adds. "We'll get lunch."

I nod. Giggle. Bite my lip. "'Kay."

"'Kay."

Mutual staring commences.

Finally, he pulls me into a big hug and kisses me on my cheek. He hesitates a moment longer than normal, then lets go. We're just looking at each other again.

"I can't believe you're here," we blurt almost at the same time, then laugh. We're like awkward adolescents with our first crush.

"Get some sleep," he says, ruffling my hair, the same way I did him when we first met. I have a big, curly-fluffy 'fro just like his. Smile. Giggle. "It's late."

Giggle. Again. Bite lip. Again. "It is."

He waits for me to walk through the doors of my five-star hotel. I look back and see that he's gone. I feel like doing cartwheels across the marble floors on my way to the elevator. When the doors close to take me to my floor, I scream into my hands and do the Happy Dance, similar to, but actually much different from, the Pee Pee Dance. Belatedly, I hope there are no cameras in here.

Dude and I spend nearly every waking moment of the next three days together exploring and enjoying Paris. We walk through the Place de la Concorde one night, and he chases me around the Luxor obelisk the way Larenz Tate does Nia Long at Chicago's Buckingham Fountain. He has me close my eyes and point to a random destination on the subway map, and we take the train there, get off in Château Rouge, where we find Black people and African food. We fill our memory sticks taking flicks together while we hold our own cameras. (I have red eye in every pic.) He buys an English-to-French translation guide and teaches me how to say *"Où est la salle de bains?"* (Where is the bathroom?) and *"Comment puis-je me rendre à . . ."* (How do I get to . . . ?) in a terrible French accent. Later, we take the midnight Bateaux Parisiens cruise on the Seine to learn the history of the city and get a different view of its architecture. We go back to the Eiffel Tower *together*, and he kisses me for the first time.

Near dusk on day five in the City of Love (or Light), we are sitting in the travel guide aisle of a small, English-only bookstore, flipping through Paris guides. He is trying to find something exciting to do that we haven't already done.

"What are we doing tomorrow?" I ask him. I pretty much couldn't care less what it is as long as I am doing it with him.

"I dunno. I feel like we've seen everything. Twice." He sounds frustrated. "What do you want to do? Like, is there anything else you want to see?"

"In Paris?" I attempt to raise one brow, but I'm sure I raise both. I've never been able to do that properly.

He shrugs. "In Paris . . . or anywhere."

I look at the bookshelf and scan the spines of the books: *Amsterdam. Barcelona. Japan. London. Madrid. Paris. Rome.*

The theme song to *Mahogany* pops into my head: "Do you know where you're going to? Do you like the things that life is showing you?" I've wanted to go to Rome ever since I saw Diana Ross as Tracy Chambers. I fell in love with the scene where she's in the cab, staring at the city with a look of awe and anticipation as she passes by the ancient monuments.

We find an Internet café and book round-trip tickets on his card. We locate a relatively cheap boutique hotel near the Colosseum and put it on mine. This is totally not in my budget, but my grad-school professor once told me that if I was going to spend frivolously, I should do so on experiences, not things.

We are scheduled to leave the next morning at seven and stay overnight, coming back to Paris the morning after that to make our evening flights back to the States.

The boutique hotel isn't so close to the Colosseum after all. It is miles away, but after we check into our room, which is standard European size (i.e., the equivalent square footage of a large walk-in closet), we decide to hike to it, wherever it is.

On the way, we find a hole-in-the-wall restaurant with the most delicious aromas emitting from its kitchen. I eat the chef's special, a meatless pasta with cheese and tricolor tortellini. Neither before nor since will I taste anything as good. Dude eats all of his food, then scrapes my plate, before finally ordering an appetizer-size portion of what I had.

When we're back en route to the Colosseum, we pass a *gelateria* and stop in even though we're stuffed. *Caramel latte* (dulce de leche) for him, *stracciatella* (chocolate chip) for me.

We are walking along some winding ancient street, eating off each other's spoons, when he stops and says, "Oh, shit." I look up at him, then look in the direction he's looking. It's the Colosseum. It's one thing to see it in pictures or the CGI re-creation in *Gladiator*. It's another to see it in person. It's no surprise why some consider it one of the seven wonders of the world.

We take a tour of the structure, then wander to the Spanish Steps and take a seat to watch the street entertainers. Dude tells me his what-I-want-to-do-when-I-grow-up-slash-graduate-from-college story while we drink espresso so we can stay up through the night and enjoy every minute of our twenty-four-hour trek through the city. I tell him about my fear of moving to New York permanently. I wonder out loud about my ultimate goal, to write cover stories for magazines and land a job on a masthead.

"What if I'm not as good a writer as I think I am?" I ask. "What if I'm good in D.C. but not good enough for New York? What do I do if I don't make it?"

"You'll make it," he tells me as if it's a fact.

"You don't know that. You've never even read my work."

He pulls my head to his shoulder, smoothing back my hair to keep it out of his face. "You will."

Dude's image of me is what I hope someday to be. I kiss him to thank him for believing in me.

We find the Trevi Fountain (under construction) and the Pantheon. We make a quick stop in Vatican City to see the Sistine Chapel. He holds my hand as we gaze at the intricate paintings on the ceiling. We spend the next hour fruitlessly trying to find the run-down restaurant with the great food, and we get lost. Over a late dinner, we split a bottle of red wine. Somewhere around glass two, I realize this is our last night together. I get a little sad. Again, I wish I could put the move to New York off for a little while, take some time in D.C. to explore what direction life could take with Dude a part of it.

I shake off the thought as quickly as it comes. What kind of life would Tracy Chambers have had if she'd never left Chicago? And yes, I know she decided in the end that success meant nothing without someone to share it with and went home, but couldn't she have found someone to share success with in the city where she professionally flourished?

Life will take me to New York, and if that path leads back to Dude, then it will. And if it doesn't? Well, then, it just does not.

I tell as much to my mother when I call back to the States to assure her that I'm fine in Rome and haven't lost my mind by running off to a foreign country with a boy I barely know. I'm in the bathroom at the hotel with the water running in the sink. It's the only way Dude won't hear me in the bedroom/living room.

"Eh . . ." she says when I tell her I wondered *What if?* "Timing is everything. If you're a halfway decent woman, he'll be back. They all come back. Some sooner than others."

After I shower, I collapse onto the bed in my towel while Dude goes into the bathroom to get clean, too. Somewhere around the time he pushed the "Buy" button for our plane tickets and booked a hotel room with a queen-size bed instead of a double, I wondered if we should have sex in Rome. I usually take my time— months, plural—getting to know a man before I'll even consider it. I don't even know if I'll see Dude again, but I don't think I can pass this up.

To arrive at a final answer, I ask myself, *Self, when you are seventy-two and retired to the South of France, and you sit and reflect on your heyday while staring at the Mediterranean Sea from your penthouse, will you regret enveloping him, or will you wish you did?*

Dude comes out of the bathroom with his towel around his waist. It's the first time I've seen him shirtless. He is . . . chiseled perfection.

"Hey," I say, looking up at Dude. No giggles. No smiles. No blushing. This is serious business.

He responds with a kiss and discards his towel. He unwraps me and kisses every inch he can get access to, then flips me over. He starts on my neck, running his tongue across my tattoo, a profile of a black butterfly with her wings poised, ready to fly. He travels down my overly sensitive back until I get goose bumps and spontaneous shivers.

"You got a condom?" I finally ask between convulsions, my nudge that it is time to get things popping *safely.*

He leans back, and soon I hear the wrapper rip. I move to turn over, to welcome him to me, but he places a hand on my lower back, keeping me on my stomach.

Er?

I try to roll over again.

"D, stay still," he says, moving to cover me.

I freeze for a moment, thinking about the romantic week in Paris, the excursion to Rome, all the Fridays for the whole summer where I have lusted after this man, then finally had a chance to know him and found him to be deeper, doper than I imagined. I've spent the last week on vacation with Dude, roaming foreign countries with him, and I dig him. I try to comply. *Just be easy, D,* I tell myself. *Go with the flow. Live in the moment.*

But I can't.

There are rules to the dating game. And although I admit I have broken a lot of them and need to let go of some of them, I'm not letting up on this one. You do not start the play in the second act.

The first time you have sex with a new person whom you halfway respect and are not paying for their services, entry has to be face-to-face. Missionary, woman on top, woman on bottom with her legs spread in the air or tied to the headboard or placed on the man's shoulders or wrapped or cuffed around his neck, waist, whatever, are all fair game.

First-time etiquette doesn't dictate that the sex be in a bedroom or even in a private setting. Do it in the car, the movie theater, the restaurant bathroom. Do it in the park. After dark. At Rock Creek Park. Wear a bunny suit, role-play as a soldier coming home from the war, or be an ex-con coming home to one of his baby mamas.

Use food. Use toys. Pee on folks (but not me) if that's what gets you going. Get choked if that does it for you (don't knock it till you try it). Do anything consenting adults find freaky and pleasurable, anything at all—as long as you are face-to-face for the first few pumps. Anything else is just uncivilized.

"Uh, Dude?" I roll over, ignoring his stilling hand, and back myself up into a sitting position. The more I think about it, the more offended I am. "It's not gonna happen."

"Huh?"

"It's just . . ." Deep breath. Do you know how hard it is to be confrontational naked? "Uh-uh." I shake my head. "It's just crass. It's uncouth. It's just . . . no." Another firm shake for emphasis.

"What's wrong?" he pleads. "Did I do something wrong?"

He looks genuinely concerned. I can't find a way to clean my thoughts up and make them sound ladylike, so I sigh heavily and blurt it out. "You can't go around trying to fuck from the back the very first time."

He looks at me blankly and walks into the bathroom. He shuts the door. I hear the lock click.

He's in there forever. I can likely imagine what he's doing. I put on a tee and shorts and slip under the covers. By the time he comes out, I've somehow fallen asleep.

I wake up the next morning to find Dude dressed and packed, ready to go to the airport. He informs me that he'll be waiting in the lobby. I look over at "his" side of the bed. It's untouched. I guess he slept on the floor?

He doesn't speak to me beyond necessities on the ride to the airport, the wait in the terminal, the ride on the plane where we sit right next to each other, or the shared cab we take back to our respective hotels in Paris. I don't say anything, either. What is there to say? He was out of line. I called him out and spoke my piece. I don't have any beef.

I offer him a handful of euros when I get out of the cab in front of my hotel.

"So, um, 'bye," I say.

He won't even look at me.

"I don't know what else to say," I prompt, wanting him to say anything.

"You ain't have to play me like that, you know?" he finally says.

"Play *you*? Are you kidding me?"

We go back and forth, and nothing is resolved. The meter is still running on the cab, and eventually, he just says, "Whatever. Take your money back!" I slam the door on him without accepting it.

I return to D.C. the following morning and move to New York less than a week later. I love my apartment. I hate my new boss. I'm lonely. Most of the friends I made in grad school have moved on in my seven-month absence. Greg, my "gentleman friend," is all tied up with work this week and can't see me until the weekend. It's like starting over. I don't know if I made the right decision coming back. I know an opportunity to succeed was what I wished for. But maybe I should have been more careful.

My cell phone rings late one night. I assume it's Aliya or Tariq, a guy I dated for two weeks in college who has since become my best male friend, calling to check on me. They are the only people who call regularly, and they know I'm bordering on depressed.

"Hello?" I answer.

"Hey."

I recognize his voice immediately, though I've never spoken to him on the phone. I thought I would never hear from him again.

"Dude?" I ask, just to make sure.

"Yeah."

He tracked down my number through mutual friends. Not hard, since there are no more than two degrees of separation between all Black people who attended (or attend) a four-year college.

"So, what's up?" I ask once the pleasantries are out the way.

Pause. Pause. Pause.

"Hello?" I ask.

"Yeah. D, I just . . . wanted to apologize for what happened."
Pause. "In Rome. 'Cause I got back . . . and I talked to my boys
about it . . . and, uh, You're cool, and I hope we can still be friends.
So . . . I'm sorry. Okay?"

I don't think he meant to be disrespectful. I think he made an
honest mistake. And *maybe* I overreacted. I appreciate the apology.

"Yeah," I say. "Okay."

NEW BEGINNINGS

I fell in love with Brooklyn because of Nola Darling. She was the heroine of Spike Lee's first feature-length film. She was young, artistic, and Black, a single woman with a small harem of men vying for her affections. Instead of picking one and living happily ever after with a bunch of brown babies, she refused to commit, enjoyed the best each man had to offer, and put her wants before any man's. Her men made her laugh, played jazz for her on her birthday, or just looked good on her arm. She wasn't living to get married or even to get a man. Just to be happy. And she was. On her own terms. If this was possible in Brooklyn, I was moving.

I'd watched the movie on VHS the same weekend I'd lain on the living-room couch and read my mother's copy of *Waiting to Exhale* in an eight-hour stretch. Despite being the product of married parents, I reasoned by thirteen that singlehood was likely what awaited me, so I could do it like Nola, or I could hold my breath (and die desperate and alone) while I dabbled with broke men, married men, and gay men. I figured that would just make me bitter. Nola it was.

It took ten years between the time Nola Darling became my personal icon and the day I moved into my first New York apartment. It was a luxury one-bedroom off Wall Street that I shared with a roommate while I attended grad school. Technically, it was campus housing. I completed my second degree in three semesters, but by graduation, I had yet to land a job. The city had fallen into an unexpected recession when, in my last semester, the World Trade Center, five blocks from my dorm, tumbled to the ground. Getting a job was . . . difficult.

I'd moved back to Maryland with my parents to hash out a plan to get back to the city. It took seven months, but I'd reached my goal. I moved to Brooklyn on a Sunday. I'd started work the following morning.

The pay sucked. My bosses? I make a habit of not writing negatively about my employers and coworkers. The people were a cast of Tyler Perry TV characters, but the actual job wasn't that bad.

As the new girl in the office, I garnered a fair share of male interest. I realized this when my boss commented on the amount of time a few of my male coworkers spent at my desk. There was Nelson, whom I had cursed out already for telling me I had a "pretty tongue." Then there was Tony who seemed like the father-figure type. And Ethan, who was like a cool uncle. They'd taken a liking to me, spotting a completely naïve Southern woman too far above the Mason Dixon for her own good.[1] Evan, cute, but too old for me, ignored me. Finally, there was Jackie, a self-described pretty boy with hazel eyes and three-sixty waves. He dressed like an invest-

---

1 For clarity, I well recognize I am not technically Southern. No self-respecting girl from Maryland calls herself Southern *in Maryland*. We are a "mid-Atlantic" people. I only became "Southern" when I moved to New York and opted for being called "Southern" over "country."

ment banker instead of a city worker. We're talking a Rolex (not the "cheap" one), tailored Armani suits, and Hugo Boss ostrich hard bottoms . . . to a government job. I knew the designers, because he told me (and anyone listening) several times a day.

It was an interesting first week of work. And tonight was my first Saturday in the city.

I was meeting up with Dakar at the Shark Bar, a restaurant-turned-Black institution for managing to survive when so many establishments held their grand opening and grand closing within a year. We were getting together to celebrate my return. I would have preferred to hang out with Greg, but he couldn't see me until the next day. Dakar would do.

We initially met on the penthouse of the Park, an open-air space at one of the city's chicest restaurants, for the book launch of Russell Simmons's *Life and Def: Sex, Drugs, Money + God*, when I accidentally spilled my cocktail on Dakar's Wallys. I apologized profusely. He reached for a napkin and wiped his shoes good as new, then introduced himself. Dakar Jameson. I recognized his name immediately.

I was a *Vibe* magazine intern getting my master's in journalism from NYU; he was an established journalist and editor with a list of cover stories and high-profile jobs I could recite. We moved to a corner and talked about the future of journalism and hip-hop, and he introduced me to every boldfaced name in the room. I'd been poring through magazines for as long as I could remember, obsessing over stories written by dream hampton, Lola Ogunnaike, Kierna Mayo, Raquel Cepeda, Akiba Solomon, Margeaux Watson, Shaheem Reid, Harry Allen, Touré, Kevin Powell, and Joan Morgan. So when Dakar introduced me to some of them as "a budding young journalist with a lot of promise," I had to compose myself to keep from groupie-ing out and quoting lines they'd written in stories as if they were lyrics from *The Miseducation of Lauryn Hill*.

Dakar became my mentor, of sorts. When I eventually got my first byline for *Vibe*, a review of some artist who never became even a footnote in hip-hop, it was Dakar who read it over before I turned it in to my editor. He did that for every review and every profile and every anything I wrote until I was confident enough to do it on my own. When my internship at *Vibe* was up, he helped me land at *Time Out New York*. When I wanted to leave that internship early to go to London for a better summer job, he told me how to finesse it with the managing editor so I wouldn't be blackballed. When I came back from overseas and needed a fall magazine internship, he helped me land one at Russell Simmons's *Oneworld*. When I needed a real job, he called over to *The Source* and got me an interview. And when I was broke in Maryland, he hooked me up with *XXL* to start writing reviews and profiles for them, too. I owed my entire writing career, thus far, to him.

Of course, we spent our fair share of time on the rooftops and at the reserved tables of swanky venues. Anytime Dakar got an invite to a party, I was his official plus-one. There was a guaranteed good party every Tuesday when CDs dropped, and usually Wednesday and Thursday as well, when magazines celebrated their new issues and liquor brands launched new products. The events were always free, we never stood in line, there was always an open bar, and food was often served. As a bonus, the parties were early. I could go out with Dakar and be tucked into bed—alone—by midnight, early enough to make it to my internship or classes on time the next day.

People often assumed, incorrectly, that we were a couple. Dakar was cute—tall, wide, and solid. I had to be the only woman in New York who didn't want him, though. Women stumbled over themselves—and cut their eyes at me—whenever we walked into a room.

He hit on me once. Just casually put it out there one night when we were standing at the bar of Lot 61 to celebrate Outkast's *Stankonia* release. "You should make me your man," he said. He took a long sip of whatever was free at the bar and looked at me over the rim of his glass.

I'd known this was coming. My editor at *Vibe* had warned me about Dakar when she'd run into me navigating the city with him. Said he'd slept with nearly every female writer in the business. He'd confirmed as much, too. Whenever he would introduce me to a female writer, he would mention, "We used to date."

I shook my head and chuckled—not hard enough to bruise his ego, though. "Can't. You know my situation." I had a boyfriend back in Maryland who was finishing up his bachelor's degree at my alma mater. We'd been together almost a year by then.

"He's home. I'm here," Dakar said cockily. He was from Maryland, too.

"Dude! You're like my brother! Plus, you're old." He was well into his thirties. I was twenty-two. But that's not the only reason I wouldn't consider the idea, nor was my boyfriend, really. I had no delusions that he was forever-ever. I held back because my future was in journalism. I didn't want to get to the top of the masthead by humping my way up the ladder.

Dakar dropped it, never brought it up again . . . until he was sitting across from me at our celebratory dinner welcoming me back to the city.

"Whatever happened to your man?" he says when the waitress drops the first round of drinks on the table—something dark for him, something light for me. It occurs to me that this is the first time we've been out and actually paid for a cocktail.

"We broke up," I say bluntly. There's a long backstory, but I'm not telling it.

He nods. "Don't you regret not taking me up on my offer back in the day now?"

"It doesn't still stand?" I quip. I'm joking.

He smiles. "Nope."

We pig out on soul food, and Dakar declines my offer to split the bill. I'm thankful—I haven't gotten my first check from the new job, and I spent all my savings moving back to New York. If I paid, I would live on Ramen noodles and boxed mac-and-cheese until Friday.

After he pays, Dakar invites me to party with him at Bungalow 8. It's a newish club in the Meatpacking District. The venue is überexclusive, and you need a key to get in on weekends. Of course, Dakar being Dakar, he has one.

We hop into a cab and head south. On Fourteenth Street, Dakar jumps out and comes around to open my door and balance me on the cobblestone streets so I don't stumble in my heels. He's such a regular that the doorman doesn't ask to see his key.

I take a seat at a booth while Dakar heads to the bar for our drinks. He returns with two cranberry and vodkas. Mine is strong. I'm not buzzed, and I rarely get drunk, but I sip slowly anyway.

We've been here half an hour, laughing, talking about nothing and everything, including the décor—black-and-white striped banquettes. I look across the room and see two A-list actors and a singer having a night out in the city. They are being ignored because this is New York, and celebrity sightings are a dime a clichéd dozen. This, it occurs to me, is the life I missed when I left for seven months. The glamour! The exclusivity! The access! I'm in mid-revel of my good fortune when a hostess stops by to ask us to move.

Dakar reaches into his pocket for his key and dangles it in front of her.

"I'm sorry. You need another key to enjoy the booths," she says in a saccharine voice. What she means by "another" is *better*.

Dakar protests, she insists, but then the man with the better key who is responsible for us getting kicked out of the booth approaches the table. He insists we can stay. His accent is thick—Russian? Euro definitely—but I make out that he is buying a bottle of vodka and drinking alone. He wants us to keep him company for a while.

Dakar refreshes my cocktail for the first of many times. I get caught up in the modern-day fantasy my life has become—free drinks, fancy venues, fine men—while Dakar entertains the rich Russian who is supplying our beverages.

An hour later, I stand to go to the potty, my legs feeling like lead. In the bathroom mirror, I talk to the reflection, calling my own name and enunciating all four syllables in a pitifully sad attempt to get back to sobriety. Then I laugh at myself.

I concentrate on walking on steady heels back to the table. No one looks at me funny, so I tell myself I'm not drunk. Dakar and the Russian are taking shots. He holds one up for me, and I decline. I slide into the booth and pour myself a cranberry and orange with no vodka.

I've been sitting silently, staring off at the White girls dancing off-beat with their boyfriends and wondering why there are so few Black people in this privileged party, when Dakar asks if I'm ready to go. I look over at him in slow motion. It's so slow I know it's slow.

I'm done.

Dakar knows it, too. He tells me to get up, well, slowly, instructs me to grab onto the booth. When he slides up, he takes my arm and holds me still as he thanks the Russian and escorts me out.

On the sidewalk, my head is spinning. "D, I'm drrrunk," I slur.

He laughs. "How'd that happen? You ate. You never get fucked up." He shakes his head at me. "Kids," he says, and chuckles. "Stay here. I'll get you a cab."

I don't have the wherewithal to correct him. I am not a kid. I am twenty-three. And on my own. In New York. And I made it out of Maryland and D.C. And I have a job. And an apartment. And I. Am. An. Adult.

I stumble back and slump against the wall, lean my head back against the brick, and close my eyes.

Bad move. My head spins again. It's been a while since I've hurled from drinking, but it's a feeling you don't soon forget. It dawns on me that I don't know how to get home from here. I've been in my new Brooklyn apartment not even a week. What if the driver doesn't know how to get there? What if I throw up in the cab? Or pass out? Or . . .

I get my phone out of my Louis and call Greg without realizing it's two A.M. It's okay. He rarely sleeps, and he's probably out.

When he answers groggily, it doesn't register that I've woken him up. I just blurt, "I need you to come get me. Please." I get really proper when I'm drunk. For anyone who knows me, it's the sign that I'm a sufficient two sheets to the wind.

"Demetria?" he croaks. "Where are you?"

I tell him. And I tell him I'm with Dakar, whom he's met before but didn't particularly care for. He never did explain why.

He releases an exasperated sigh. "I'll come get you. Give me thirty." He's driving from the Bronx.

I don't have thirty. I'll be upchucking in the street by then. "Never mind, I'll be okay."

He pauses. "You sure? I'll come for you."

I shake my head.

"Hello?" he asks.

"No," I say. "I'm good."

I hang up as Dakar walks up to the sidewalk to give me a hand to the cab he's hailed. In retrospect, I will wonder what made me call Greg first before asking Dakar my next question. But in the moment, I don't think about it. Why can't foresight be twenty/ twenty, too?

"D, you got a two-bedroom, right?" I know the answer, so I don't wait for him to answer. "Can I crash with you?"

He shrugs, says "Sure," and slides into the waiting car beside me. I ask the driver for a plastic bag to throw up in before we hit the West Side Highway, a block away.

I wake up a while later—no clue how long I've been out—with Dakar's face between my legs. I thought I was having a wet dream.

I don't remember the ride to Harlem. I don't remember getting out of the cab and walking inside his building. I do remember him unlocking the door to his actual apartment, me stepping inside and asking where the guest room was. He told me down the hall. I found it and flopped face-first on the left side of the bed. I asked for a trash can, and when he brought it to me, I threw up in it before he could place it on the floor by the bed.

"Dakar."

He pushes harder into me.

I am on the right side of the bed on my back. My dress is hiked around my hips and my panties pushed aside. His tongue is inside me.

I realize all of this in slow motion. It's like pieces of a puzzle floating around in my head, then suddenly they snap into place and I get a complete picture of what is going on.

Oh. My. God.

"Dakar!" I shout. I push myself up and back, effectively pulling myself away from his face, lest he mistake my cry of horror for a pleasurable moan. I snap my legs shut, pull my knees to my chest, and pull my dress to my ankles all in one seamless motion. I swallow back the terrified lump in my throat. I'm suddenly sober and very, very scared.

How did I get here? *Cab.* How did I get up here? *No clue.* How did he get between my legs? *Blank stare.* Did anything else happen? *I dunno.* I can't even let my mind go there right now.

I look down at Dakar, who is lying on his stomach on his bed, gazing up at me with glassy, puppy-dog eyes.

"Where's my purse?" I snap.

He dutifully rolls off the bed and grabs it from a chair in the corner. I snatch my Louis from him when he holds it out to me and immediately search for my phone.

It dawns on me then that I need to get away from him, off the bed, out of the bedroom. I leap up and head into the hallway. In the dark, I can make out another open door. I walk inside the room and run my hand along the wall for the light switch.

I fumble for a few seconds, then find it. I'm in an empty room with no furniture, no closets, and a gigantic pile of clothes in the middle of the floor—jeans, tees, button-downs. I wonder if they are clean or dirty. *This is the second bedroom? Where's the bed?* I close the door, lock it, and slump against it. I'm no match for Dakar if he tries to get in, but it's an attempt to stay safe.

I punch Greg's number into my cell.

"I need you to come get me," I say as soon as the phone stops ringing. I'm as calm as I can manage. I don't want to alarm him, don't want him to know what foolish thing I've gotten myself into. "Come get me *now*."

"Where are you?"

I don't even know where I am, only that I am at some building in Harlem. I can tell by looking out the window at the tops of trees that I am on a high floor. I cover the phone and yell through the door, "Dakar, where am I?" And for the record, yes, I know I'm pitiful.

He gives me his address, I give it to Greg, who says he is leaving right then, and hangs up the phone.

I look up at the ceiling as if the crown molding is going to provide a way out of here, then close my eyes, trying to stave off the tears. *No sense in crying*, I tell myself. *That's not going to solve anything.* I debate going outside, if I can get there, but what awaits me in the middle of Harlem at—I look down at the time on my phone—three-thirty A.M. could be worse than what I encounter in here. Maybe I should take my chances. How could I be this stupid?

I'm startled when Dakar interrupts my self-loathing. "What'd you call Gregory for?" he asks through the door. He sounds as if he's still in his bedroom.

I don't answer him. My mind is whirling, thinking of how to get out of this apartment without further harm coming my way. I don't think Dakar would attack me, but he has already, hasn't he? Because I know him, my mind can't make the shift between the guy who's always looked out for me and the guy who just violated me. It's just all so creepy. If I woke up to his penis inside me, I'd at least get it; he gets something out of it, even if it's nothing more than feeling empowered since a passed-out drunk girl can't be all that pleasurable. But giving me oral while I'm asleep? I don't get it. It's just . . . gross. Who does that? Better yet, who is Dakar? This is not the man I knew, I've *known*.

An involuntary shiver passes down my back, and I squirm as if something yucky is on me, then finally adjust the bunched crotch of my panties back to their proper position. I desperately clutch my cell phone, my only lifeline to the outside world, and I jump when I feel it vibrate in my hand.

I look at the screen. It's Greg.

"Why am I coming to get you at three-thirty in the morning from Dakar's house?" he blurts into my ear when I answer.

I can't tell him the truth. It sounds silly. I'm freaked out because a guy licked me without my consent? "I just need you to come get me," I plead. "Are you on your way?"

"Demetria!" he demands. "Why am I coming to get you at this time of night?"

I start to answer the question, and I can't. I try again, and I can't say the words.

I know I'll fall apart as soon as I do. "Are you on your way?"

"Yes." Then he's silent, waiting for the answer to his question.

I sigh. "I don't know . . . I think . . . Dakar . . ." I try to say it, and that's when the magnitude of what's happened hits me. I reel back, brace myself on the wall to keep from falling. I can't pass out again now. I'll have to tell him at some point anyway. "I dunno. I think he might have been about to rape me, but I don't really know." There. I said it.

I take in a long breath, and my eyes burn as my mascara and liner run down my cheeks. I don't bother to wipe my face. I choke back a sob and close my eyes in the dark, feeling pathetic and stupid and like the child Dakar accused me of being earlier.

It seems like forever before Greg says anything. "Where are you now?" he asks calmly.

"In his other bedroom. I locked myself in," I squeak.

He exhales heavily. "Can you get out of there, D?" he asks more urgently. "You have to get out of there. Now."

I nod. "I'll think of something."

"I'm on my way. What apartment are you in?"

"I don't know."

He lets out a very frustrated sigh. "Get out, and call me when you're in the hall or outside, okay? Get out." It's a command, not a suggestion.

"Okay."

I hit the end key and wipe my face, taking a moment to compose myself before I unlock the door, step into the hall, and stand in the doorway of Dakar's bedroom.

He's still on the bed, now on his back, hands behind his head, chilling as if he's staycationing on a Brooklyn rooftop in summer.

"I need my purse and my coat," I demand.

He rolls over slowly, grabbing my Louis from the floor. I tense as he approaches me to hand it over, then plods past me down the hall. He flicks the light switch, and I turn to watch him take my jacket from the closet at the end of the hall by what I assume is the exit.

How did it get in there? When did he take it off me? There's no time to worry about that now. I walk down the hall as he chivalrously holds up my jacket to put it on me. I look at him like he's crazy, snatch it from him, and unlock his front door in one motion.

He looks at me curiously. "What're you doing?"

I ignore him as I step into the hall. I don't even know where the elevator or steps are. I don't remember how I got up here.

"Going outside," I say.

"It's not safe. I'll come with you."

I don't know why he chooses to wait with me.

Dakar pulls the door shut behind him, and I have to fall back to let him lead the way. I follow him down the hall, down the stairs. I couldn't have found my way out without a search.

I observe that his building is filthy. There's dirt caked into the grooves of the floor tile. I'm afraid to put my hands on the stairwell banisters because they are just that grimy and, frankly, I already feel disgusting enough. I teeter on my heels, which are *clack-clacking* against the floor, then echoing off the walls.

When we get to the building's lobby, I see a small wood desk and chair in the center. This dump has a doorman?

I sit on one side of Dakar's wide stoop, and he takes the other. We sit in silence. Neither one of us has said anything since we left his apartment. I call Greg to tell him I'm outside, then I look up at the lamp illuminating the night sky above wherever I am in these Harlem streets and wait for Greg. I just want to go home. And not Brooklyn home. *Maryland* home. I'm not cut out for this city.

Greg's car speeds up and jerks to a stop in front of us ten minutes later. I rise and scamper to his vehicle as he unexpectedly gets out of the car.

"Are you all right?" he demands, giving me a probing once-over. He searches my eyes.

I nod obediently. "Yeah."

"Get in the car."

I sit in the passenger seat and put my safety belt on, put my head down, and start to shake. I sob into my chest and let the tears fall. *How could he do this to me? How could I let this happen?* I cry so hard I begin to dry-heave. I open the door so as not to hurl on Greg's leather interior.

I can hear him yelling at Dakar, but my mind's too far away to make out what he is saying. But the sound is getting louder, closer.

"Is that what you do? You get women drunk to fuck them?" Greg yells.

Dakar gives a muffled reply. I look in the passenger-side mirror and see Greg slam Dakar against the back of the vehicle before I actually feel the impact.

"Where'd you learn that?" Greg yells at him.

Greg jerks Dakar around to my side of the car and opens my car door. "What'd he do to you, Demetria?"

"Greg, let's go. Let's just go," I plead without holding my head up. "Please, Greg."

"What'd he do?" he demands.

"He . . . Greg?" I finally look at him, and he just glares back at me, waiting for an answer. His stare is blank. He's looking at me but seeing through me. "He . . . I . . . I woke up, and he was . . . he was between my legs. His tongue . . ." It's all I can manage before I break down in tears again.

"That's the type of motherfucker you are?" he shouts at Dakar, his voice laced with disgust.

"I thought she wanted it," Dakar offers by way of excuse.

I pull the car door shut and cry harder, as if that is possible. I feel dirty and used. I trusted someone I shouldn't have. And I can't trust myself to make good decisions.

I can hear the guys tussling in the distance. Something—no, *someone*, Dakar—is being slammed against the car. They are loud.

I worry, in a moment of clarity, that a neighbor will call the police. I've already made this night bad enough by getting drunk, getting into this situation, causing this whole dramatic scenario. The last thing I need is for Greg to get arrested for beating someone over me. I don't deserve the effort.

I unbuckle my seatbelt and get out of the car. It's quiet. Dakar is lying in the street, his body curled and breathing hard.

Good, I think. *Greg didn't kill him.*

Greg is standing over him. I can see his chest heaving with the exhausted effort of their confrontation. I don't want to know what happened. I don't much care.

"G, get in the car. Let's go. Somebody's gonna call the cops on us," I say.

We look at each other for a moment. He wipes his hand down his face, rubs the sweat on the side of his jeans. He walks past me to the driver's side, and I follow his lead and get into the car.

Inside the vehicle, Greg leans over, grabs the back of my head, pulls me gently to the middle of the armrest, and places his forehead against mine.

"You okay?" he whispers against my nose.

I nod. My head feels heavy. I'm tired. Exhausted, really.

He sighs deeply, kisses my frontal lobe like Taye Diggs did to Nia Long in *The Best Man,* and starts the engine. As we pull off, he grabs for my hand.

"You want to go to the police station?" Greg asks, taking a too-hard, too-fast left.

"Just take me to your house," I say.

I put my seatbelt on, lean my head back, and thank God the night is over. I'll deal with the aftermath in the morning, probably for longer.

THE ROUND TABLE

Sometimes I question whether I am built ever to be in a relationship. Here's the deal society has given man: By virtue of being bestowed with a penis, he is to be a leader. He is to be head of the household. That's it. Possession of a penis, working or not, gives a man the upper hand when it comes to common sense, logic, and guiding the way.

So if he, male, possessor of the all-knowing and almighty penis, is to lead and head, what am I supposed to do?

Follow? FOH!

I posed this question to GVG, a.k.a. the Mayor of Black Brooklyn, a.k.a. the Great Blaxby, a.k.a. one of my best male friends above the Mason Dixon. He's received his accolades not just for knowing (and introducing me to) everyone who's anyone throughout Brooklyn but for making sure they know him, too. And he's got a way of summing up male thought pretty concisely.

GVG and I met in an atypical and ultimately classic New York way. I was riding the train in the city, likely headed to SoHo to shop. I was in grad school, and it was a bad hair day. Instead of getting it done at the Dominican shop, I'd pulled my hair back into a low bun and added an off-white kufi to keep the frizzies to a minimum. I'd have preferred a white one to match my outfit, but they're hard to come by, even in New York.

"I like your kufi," said a man from above.

I looked up from my seat to find a brown stranger. He was wearing a kufi, a white one. I asked him where he got his, and he snatched his off his head and offered it to me. "I'll trade you," he said.

We exchanged kufis, but not numbers, before I got off the train.

Two and a half years later, I was leaving an artist showcase and spotted a familiar face in the let-out. The guy smiled. I smiled back. He crossed the street and asked, "Excuse the randomness of this question, but did you ever give a guy a kufi on the train?"

We became instant friends.

Today we're having brunch at Madiba, a South African restaurant on Black Melrose Place. If you look at a map, the venue is on Dekalb Avenue in Brooklyn's Fort Greene neighborhood. It's a collection of beautiful brownstones and chic restaurants and the epicenter of the borough's bourgeois weekend and holiday life. (And it's also where Nola Darling's loft was located.)

GVG takes a bite of his Durban bunny chow while he contemplates the answer to my question regarding the roles of the sexes. "Real men don't follow," he says, immediately sussing out what I'm aiming for.

"So what are women supposed to do?"

"Follow a man who knows how to lead."

"And from your male POV, when do women get to lead, exactly?"

He looks up at me from his curry dish. He knows that I know his answer, I'm just waiting to hear him say it. Again. "When they're single."

I stare at him, allowing my food to get cold. He sighs and drops his spoon on the side of the dish so it clanks.

"You don't want to follow a man? Don't get into a relationship, D," he says. "Problem solved. You don't have to defer to anyone. But just so you know, no real man is going to let a woman lead him. You don't want the type of man who lets you lead. And if you don't trust a man to lead you, why are you dating him, anyway?"

Point taken. But that's not the point I'm going for. I want to know why men feel qualified to lead. What makes them "natural leaders"?

I've had this conversation with many a man, and many insist I should just let the laws of nature, biology, and/or the Bible be. They don't have a valid reason but insist it's the only way to make a relationship work. No one seems to recall that Ephesians 5:21 talks about husbands leading wives. There's nothing about boyfriends leading anybody anywhere.

I took the question to the grown folks, two married coworkers at my government job. They were around my mother's age and had been wives for twenty-five years each. I asked them if their husbands were the leaders of their relationships or their households.

They laughed. Hard. Thought it was the most foolish idea I'd ever introduced at the lunch table. Their response was best summed up by Selene, who rhetorically asked, "How in the hell is someone going to lead me somewhere? I'm a grown woman. The only person I follow is God." She added that most people get the Bible verse screwed up. Wives are to follow husbands. Husbands, in turn, follow God. "Every Black man you know spits that verse, but how many you know that go to church?" Rakia scoffs.

That said, they both conceded that their inability to follow blindly was a source of great contest in their households, but they both preferred the idea of co-leading and arguing to following any man. Occasionally, they let their husbands think they were leading just to keep the peace.

"Make up your mind what you're going to do, then ask him like his opinion matters," Rakia suggested. "He'll feel like he made the decision, and you can go on and do what you want to do without him getting in the way."

The men I spoke with at my office preferred this method also. They wanted to feel like kings in the house, even if they were only akin to court jesters. "Let me think I'm in charge even if I'm not," Tony told me. "It makes a man feel like a man."

Sounds like the strategy of the oppressed or the underclass. While I may be considered that by some for being Black and female, I can't see myself playing that role in my own relationship.

I talked to another coworker—someone I considered a sensible soul. Ethan had been married—"happily," he said—for fifteen years, and he told me that a large part of his happiness was that he and his wife were equals in their relationship.

This! This was all I was asking for. I don't need to lead a man, but I want equal say. I want to be an equal partner. Why is that so hard for men to fathom?

Then he added that he still considered himself the head of the house, and only once in a decade and a half of marriage has he "pulled rank" on his wife.

Rank?

I questioned his sensitivity after that.

He shrugged when I pointed out that a man who pulls rank does not really consider his partner equal.

"It's fifty-one/forty-nine in my favor," he said. "There's no such thing as exact equality in a relationship."

Perhaps that's why I'd rather date than be in one.

My already somewhat cynical view of relationships was deepening the more I broached this conversation. Every time I asked, "Why can't there be two leaders?" I was hit with some cliché like "Ships don't have two captains." "Cars don't have two steering wheels." "There's only one quarterback per team."

I have this seemingly rare and utopian idea of making decisions *with* my partner. We just communicate and negotiate until we reach a decision *together*. And at the very least, we divvy up all of the responsibilities as equally as possible and I make the call on my assignments, and he makes the call on his. Is that too much to ask?

I was fretting over the issue. So much so that on a bus ride back to New York from D.C. on the King holiday, I turned to my traveling companion, Parler, a well-known DJ friend and fellow Marylander who'd recently left for points North of the Area, too, to ask what he thought.

"P, when you get married, do you have to be the head of the household?"

He paused the *Wire* DVD we were watching on his laptop. "Is this a trick question, D?"

He knew me too well. I gave him my most innocent look. "No." I added a slight shake of my fluffy-haired head for good emphasis.

He didn't believe me and asked me to explain where I was going with this. I laid it all out, including the "What's a woman supposed to do? Follow?" line.

He thought for a moment. "You both lead."

A man who didn't expect to lead alone? They exist? Or was he just saying it because it sounded good?

I challenged his comment. "Can you have two leaders in one house, though? That won't get tricky? Who sits at the metaphorical head of the table?"

"Think of it like sitting at a round table. That way, everyone's equal." He punched the play button as if the matter was done.

If only it were that simple.

MALE BAGGAGE

I was in Miami vacationing with my dad and Aliya on a random spring weekend. He was on another business trip, and Aliya and I tagged along to crash his suite at the Loews Hotel. We were walking up to Nikki Beach for its Sunday brunch when my dad launched into a pep talk about things we should know about men. This was the first time in my entire life he'd brought it up.

On the top of his list was "Men need to feel needed."

"Wanted is not enough?" I countered.

"No, needed," he insisted.

"And if I don't need a man?" Aliya chimed in.

"If you want one and you want to keep one, act like you need him."

The oracle waited until we were all seated to share his additional insight: "Men are insecure, too."

It was as if a light bulb had gone off. But in retrospect, I don't know why that was such a revelation. I guess because so often, insecurity is made to seem like an intrinsic female trait. It's so common that when you meet a woman who's comfortable with her weight, doesn't buy expensive clothes or accessories she can barely afford, or doesn't define herself by her relationship (or lack thereof), you actually notice.

But with guys, it's not talked about often. Very few people point out that hypermasculinty and its accompanying I-must-hump-any-woman-with-hole bravado and you-can-buy-whatever-you-like spending sprees of TI proportion are a cover-up for insecurity just like women in too little clothes, too much makeup, and "too many" sex partners.

I am walking to Century 21 on my lunch hour, debating an upcoming vacation. I want to go back to Miami. It has been almost two months since my last trip. I can't get free until Memorial Day, and there's no way I'll step foot near South Beach that weekend. It's practically a Hood All-Star convention. I like Vegas, but lying by a wave pool won't do. I need a beach bad. In my adult life, I've never been this pale. Maybe Trinidad? Antigua? Cuba if I can fly to the Bahamas first?

I'm shaken from my ponderings by the boom in a male voice. It says, "Wow, you look really good."

I look over to find a chocolate specimen. Flawless skin, Chiclets-white teeth. Tall, nice build. A little thin for my taste but would be workable if he was a little older. I'm flattered as all get-out. I'm in a sweat dress, low-heeled boots, and no makeup. I wasn't thinking about meeting a man today.

I smile and say hi as I keep it moving, appreciating his compliment, especially when I don't feel it's deserved. He spoke. I spoke. No harm, no foul, right?

"You must got a man," he calls after me. "But you wouldn't fuck with a nigga as Black and ugly as me anyway, right?"

Skip the needle on the record. I am caught so off guard by his comment that I stop on the crowded Lower Manhattan sidewalk, something only Ground Zero tourists do, turn, and yell after him a very baffled "What?"

I'm not offended about the implication. Nothing could be farther from the truth. My dating track record includes a long list of chocolate cuties to prove otherwise. I am actually curious about what level of self-hate a young Black man could have that he would blurt that to a woman on the street.

That incident reminds me of a scene from *School Daze*. Not the musical number when the light-skin and dark-skin girls face off over complexion and hair texture but the less-discussed scene when Rachel and Dap, played by a young Laurence Fishburne, are in his dorm room and she points out his animosity toward Blacks of a particular hue. "I'm beginning to think you're color-struck," she tells him. "You definitely have a thing against light-skinned Blacks."

"It's them, not me," Dap quips. "I adore octoroon, quadroon mulattoes. They're so unpure."

I remember the scene because it's the only time I've ever recalled Black men's color complexes toward one another being discussed. But I've dated or encountered enough Black men[1] affected by it to *know* it exists. Abundantly.

Once I dated a very chocolate man whom I adored for his personality, but it was his hue and build—tall, wide, strong—that attracted me across the room. Months into dating, I would stop clicking away on my laptop when he walked across the room shirt-

---

1 This is not an indictment of all dark-skinned men. Just an issue I noticed among some (okay, like 50 percent) of the many I have encountered.

less to . . . well, watch him walk, enjoying the way his muscles rippled beneath his unblemished ebony skin.

Despite how beautiful I found him, he didn't see it in himself. He was opposed to taking pictures of any kind and always complained, like Biggie, of being "Black and ugly as ever" (he was a god, I tell you, a god). On occasion, he'd say something along the lines of the dude in the street about how he didn't see why I was dating a man "as Black as" him and wonder out loud why I didn't "go out and get one of them pretty niggas with good hair."

I didn't get it. Or I didn't until he told me about his childhood. I was doing my best to build his confidence, showering him with compliments and pointing out the way women fawned over Mekhi Phifer, Tyrese, and Terrell Owens, but it all fell on deaf ears.

"I'm 'chocolate' *now*," he pointed out. "I used to be burnt, crispy, tar, or darkness."

While I was in elementary school, dodging accusations of being stuck-up and thinking I was "better" for being light-eyed and light-skinned, he was catching hell for being too dark.

"There was nothing good about being dark-skinned when I was growing up," he recalled matter-of-factly.

Another ebony-hued honey had told me the same. At twenty-eight, his clock was ticking loudly, and he talked about wanting kids constantly. Occasionally, he'd say something along the lines of "If I had a son as light as you or a daughter as dark as me, I'd oh my God die."

"What's wrong with a light-skinned son?" I asked. In my head, I was thinking, *Mofo, what?* But I wanted to get the logic before I went in. Maybe *I* was missing something?

"Oh, my little nigga won't be a yellow bitch," he says, his voice dripping with disgust. "What does that look like?"

"He's a bitch because he's, quote, yellow, unquote?" (I ignored the part about calling his would-be son "nigga" because I can only fight one battle at a time.)

I'd heard this line of thought before, too. Until recently, I kept a picture of a friend on a table in my foyer. He's all Black, looks part Asian. He's about my complexion and has a wild mane of curls. Nearly every brown or darker guy who's ever crossed my threshold has asked some version of "Who's the *pretty* boy?" as if it's ingrained in chocolate men to feminize lighter-complexioned guys.

My date must have thought my question was rhetorical because he didn't respond. Or maybe his lack of response was all the answer I needed.

The final straw with him came when we were on a classic Brooklyn date, walking along the promenade and looking at the view of Manhattan. We passed by a group of three friends, girls, yukking it up on a bench. The only thing I noticed was that they were women in their early twenties.

"She better get out of the sun," my companion quipped out of nowhere.

"I'm sorry, what?" I blurted.

"The Black one. I know she doesn't want to be any darker."

I turned around and looked at the girls. There was a darker one. She was the same color as my date's mother and sisters, the women he showcased proudly in picture frames in his living room.

I had to point that out. "You know, your mom—"

"You're trying to say my family's ugly?" he snapped, cutting me off. "They're dark but *not like that*."

I looked back at the woman on the bench as if I was the one who was crazy. Nope. They were all the same color.

That's when I realized his insecurities ran too deep for me to compliment the source of them into nonexistence. I dropped the subject and, eventually, him.

DEAL BREAKERS

People tell me random things they usually don't tell others. It's always been this way. I think that my normal speaking voice is soothing like a phone sex operator's has something to do with it.

I went to my very good friend Penelope's birthday cocktail party on Black Melrose Place. Penelope and I met when I walked up to her at some industry event at Lemon on Park Avenue and asked, "Who are you? I see you everywhere." She's from LA, moved to New York for undergrad, and can't see herself living anywhere else either.

At her celebration, I found myself at the bar sipping Ethiopian honey wine and holding court with several gentlemen while they complained about how hard it was to meet someone they wanted to date for any length of time. Seems the ladies aren't the only ones having a hard time.

One of the guys, Devin, told me about a woman he met at the club. She wore a long (good) weave, a tight dress, makeup, and high heels. In a relatively sober state, Devin exchanged numbers with her early in the night. The next week, they talked on the phone, and he deduced she was "cool." When he finally met up with her for drinks at Ava Lounge on the rooftop of the Dream hotel, she had on flats, her hair pulled back, a cute casual shirt and jeans and was wearing little makeup. She'd just come from the office. They hung out for the night, but he never called again.

"She was a visual liar," he explained. And he then began a rant about women and all the lies we tell that don't come out of our mouths, including our makeup, hair, heels, push-up bras, contacts, acrylic nails, and Spanx, too.

I looked at him like he was stupid.

He looked at me accusingly. "You're lying to me, too, D," he said, studying my made-up face, beat hard to ensure that I looked my best in the photos that would be splashed all over social networking pages. "Your cheeks ain't that rosy!"

Another man complained of a woman he admitted "was really cool" but he'd unceremoniously dismissed from his roster, too. I asked why. Damn my curiosity.

"Fat girl tendencies," he said. Once they'd gone to Saturday brunch at Essex on the Lower East Side. She'd ordered an omelet, French toast, and a side of grits. She ate it all, then ordered toast. She was a shapely size eight, but he was convinced she'd double her size as soon as he put a title on it, so he cut his losses early. Oh, and she had fat ankles and thick arms. He swore those were telltale signs that she was going to blow up.

"I don't want a fat girlfriend," he said.

The third gentlemen stopped seeing a woman because she had a boob job. He gave a general description, and I realized he was talking about someone I knew.

When I met her, her boobies were riding high like a Chevy on twenty-fours. It wasn't a good breast augmentation or even a subtle one. At least DDs. Surprisingly, he had no idea they were fake until he saw pictures of her from years before on her MySpace page.

His whole perspective on her changed. He decided he could never wife her. "I wonder what kind of self-esteem issues she has that she'd be willing to go through all that pain just for bigger breasts. A boob job just screams *I'm not happy with myself*. I'm sure she's a lovely woman, but I'll never take her seriously."

The first guy chimed in that this was the logic for why he didn't date women who were too "fancy"—hair done, nails done, everything did. "It's not only about what you are hiding but why," he added.

I'd heard most of these complaints before. Ever since I'd started hanging with GVG, most of my friends had been guys (except for Penelope, my unofficial therapist, who has diagnosed my all-male inner circle as a craving for protection in the Dakar aftermath). I was privy to all sorts of random conversation. But what the guys said next actually shocked me.

"You want to know what the worst is?" one of the men asked rhetorically. "When the sex is bad. Automatic deal breaker."

The other two men nodded vigorously in agreement. "It's ever been so bad you have to fake it?" one asked.

I assumed he was joking until the other two men agreed.[1]

"You all fake it?" I blurted way too loudly just as the music died in preparation for Penelope's birthday toast.

As Penelope's friends wished her another year of wealth, health, and happiness, I wondered what would cause a man to pretend to have an orgasm. I mean, they go through so much trouble to get the "va-jay-jay"—spending money and time, spitting "game," hunting—shouldn't they want to enjoy the act for as long as possible?

---

1 In a 2010 *Essence* survey, 37 percent of Black men admitted they had faked an orgasm.

Usually yes, but sometimes no.

"Va-jay-jay can be that bad?" I asked bluntly.

Devin was baffled that I thought it was all good.

"So what makes it bad?" I posed my query to the trio.

"Dryness," one blurted.

"She just lays there like a log," announced another.

"Bad rhythm," the last one said.

We were wrapping up the night when the topic was broached. I would have followed the crowd to the Five Spot, a nearby soul-food restaurant that morphed into a club on weekend nights, to probe the guys further, but I had to rush home to write my first feature story. It was about a rapper who'd just got out of jail on an assault charge. He'd punched a man so hard that he broke the guy's eye socket. Our interview had lasted two hours, and I still hadn't transcribed the tape. I thanked the guys for the enlightening conversation and headed to Penelope to say good night.

A couple days later, when my work was complete, I had the time to think about bad va-jay-jay and faking it. Were the guys for real, for real, or was that the liquor talking? I hit up my boys, a group of twenty or so employed, mostly single, educated, and articulate Black men, to get their thoughts on the matter. Women can philosophize about the meaning of what men do all day, but the best—and quickest—way to find out what a man is thinking is just to ask another man (or a woman who interviews them all day and hangs out with them all night). I'd met all of them about the same way I'd met the guys at the bar: Randomly talking. I jokingly referred to them as my Male Mind Squad.

"Are men really faking it?" I asked in a mass e-mail. "Or are my dinner companions just weird? And can va-jay-jay be bad?"

In a nutshell: Yes, men fake it. No, the guys I met weren't weird. And yes, "pussy" can be bad since "real" men don't call pussy "va-jay-jay."

On Why They Fake It

"I have been so bored sometimes, I would do anything to get it over with." He added that faking it was a last-resort measure, only done when "thinking about another chick doesn't really do the job."

From another man: "It was after multiple sex acts during the course of the night. She took it personal if I didn't 'finish' each and every time we did something. I was sleepy, it was six in the morning, so I faked so I could go to sleep."

On What Makes Bad Va-jay-jay

Lack of rhythm/bad technique

"Some women just don't know what to do or how to move their body. For example, riding doesn't just mean going up and down, it's about hitting different angles because each one feels different. Not to mention it's boring to stay in one spot continuously."

"The pussy itself isn't bad, it's the woman attached to it. Bad pussy is a woman who doesn't know how to work her hips, ride me properly, and runs from me during back shots. If she doesn't have rhythm, then it's difficult for us to work together."

"Some girls just don't know how to position themselves. In the 'doggy style' position, your back should not be rounded. The arch should be concave from the guy's point of view, not convex."

No response

"I had a girlfriend who was utterly silent throughout the entire experience. A man wants to hear from his woman that he's doing a good job. Any absence of feedback is pretty bad."

"Some girls don't know how to relax. It's like they want to have sex, but still perform like it's their first time. When a guy is on top of you, why not wrap your legs around him? Why just lay there?"

Dumb talk
"Women who call me 'Daddy' and use other cliché corny terms."

Dryness
"Bad pussy is subjective, but for me it's 'clam pussy'—super dry and sandbag like." (He asked that you "please excuse the *40 Year Old Virgin* reference.)

"Pussy can be bad if there are no juices and berries, basically if it's just dry. You can start fires like that, especially with all the friction and pubic hairs."

Lack of feeling
"Pussy can be bad if there is not an emotional connection. Sex and orgasm may happen, but after, you either feel empty inside or like you just raped someone."

Smell
"Uh . . . she wasn't fresh down there. So it ruined the moment."

And finally, nothing
"Bad pussy is like bad pizza. As long as you're eating it, it's pretty fucking good."

THE CONDOM CONUNDRUM

"What do you think of a woman who carries a condom in her purse?"

I was at my favorite Mexican watering hole in Brooklyn with one of my male besties, Kenneth. I had met him when I was at a party in the Meatpacking District, and my drink—thankfully clear—spilled on my ruffled dress. I was cursing my misfortune when a handkerchief appeared like the twenty that Billy Dee Williams held for Diana Ross in *Lady Sings the Blues*. The hand holding the hanky was Kenneth's.

Before we met up for guac and chips, I'd been tinkering around online and found a Centers for Disease Control stat that said the rate of HIV for Black women was 15 times as high as that of White women. The site suggested that women prevent HIV by carry condoms so a guy didn't have any excuse for not using one. It made sense. Anybody having sex should be expected to arrive at any sexual encounter prepared to protect themselves, if not their partner.

The response I was expecting from Kenneth was something along the lines of "We're grown. I expect her to." But instead, he sneered and said, "Ugh!"

Then he told me the story of a woman he dated briefly. She'd gone home with him after dinner and drinks at the Mandarin Hotel with its panoramic views of Central Park and the Manhattan skyline. He hadn't expected her to ask to stop by his place, and when things were about to be on and poppin', he realized he didn't have a condom. He was prepared to make a run to the *bodega* when Qiana spoke up.

"That's okay," she offered. "I do." And then she reached for her purse.

This is what I call being responsible, and I applauded her smarts.

Kenneth had an entirely different take. He immediately lost interest. "What kind of woman carries around condoms?" he wondered. "Like, how often is she having unexpected sex?" Without intercourse taking place, he asked Qiana to leave.

I took the question to the Male Mind Squad. I had to know what the reigning consensus was on women carrying condoms. Was Kenneth's outlook unique?

I presented them with Kenneth's scenario: "First time with a new woman at your house. You don't have a condom, and she offers one up. What do you think?"

Turns out they understood Kenneth's reaction, although they wouldn't necessarily have deaded the evening.

The menfolk were cool with one condom in the purse and agreed that it reflected the woman's responsibility level, although a woman would not lose "points" for not having one. "I would think she was grown about her shit if she had one," a gentleman said. "And I'd see it as an ego boost, like *Oh, she was prepared for me.*"

However, each man, without any prompting, added that more than one condom in the purse was an ominous sign. Breaking out a three-pack or offering him a variety of choices—ribbed, extra lube, extra large—was a no-no.

"I'd see that and think, *Do you plan on fucking unexpectedly often?*" one of them said. "How many unplanned sexual encounters are you having?'"

Yet another added, "A variety of condoms makes you look like a promiscuous woman, and no man wants his woman to be promiscuous. I'd probably have sex with her. But I would reserve any type of emotional attachment."

He acknowledged that this was a double standard. "It's not right, but women get free dinner, so deal with it."

The limit on the number of condoms in a woman's possession apparently doesn't apply to just those kept in her Gucci bag, but it applies to her Goodie Drawer, too. (You know, the one where grown folks keep their toys and lubes and such?) I thought it could be seen as considerate and prepared for a woman to give a man some latex options. Maybe a woman could luck out and have a brand he preferred?

Bad idea. Very bad idea.

More than a three-pack of condoms in her stash, and the man she's about to envelop might be thrown off. Too many condoms evidently imply a lot of sexual encounters, and as we've discovered, that's not a good sign if she's looking for a man instead of a jump-off. Overwhelmingly, the gentlemen said they'd think the woman was getting it in too often. "I'm immediately wondering how many men have been in this bed," one man said.

Another added, "That says to me that she's stroking more than Clarence Carter. I'm thinking I might not want to see the inside of her."

The same man flipped the scenario on me: "If you were at my house and saw condoms galore, you'd think, *What the hell is that?* right?"

Touché.

One more gentleman suggested the best way to avoid the headache of sending the wrong signals to her suitor was just not to let him see what's in the drawer. *You* reach in, pull out a condom—separate, do *not* pull out the whole panel of them—and get it on. "The drawer should be a mystery," he added. "Men like mystery."

Finally, I wondered what not having a condom in the house implied. The men were confused. "No drawer? Everyone over twenty-five has a drawer!" was the common response. When pressed further, they hypothesized what this could mean, as they hadn't encountered a woman without one in quite some time.

The good: "Perhaps she was in a long-term relationship and didn't use them?"

The bad: "Maybe she just ran out?"

The ugly: "I'm going to have to brush the cobwebs off her pussy."

MEN: THE MANUAL

I don't claim to know everything about men, but a lifetime of people telling me things they wouldn't tell many, has taught me more about the species than most women would know. This is because almost my entire inner circle is guys and I pay attention to them. And also because I ask a lot of questions and I listen pretty well. Blame it on being a journalist. Or maybe I'm just nosy.

I've compiled a list to help women understand men better. The opposite sex tends to think about things entirely different from how we do. And that's okay. They're not women, so don't expect them to act like us. Oh, and they're not monolithic: There will be variations from man to man, but the following are pretty universal.

1. Men talk about relationships constantly. Just not with the woman they're dating. When they talk among themselves, it's all action-oriented. They don't talk about feelings.

2. Despite rarely ever talking about feelings with their boys, men have them. Lots of them. And the more alpha males are more sensitive than the most feminine women. Most men have been taught not to express their emotions since somewhere around age three. You have to look for the symptoms of feelings to figure out if something is wrong. Giving off heat when upset is an obvious sign.

3. If they're remotely interested in you, they want to do good. Yes, like superheroes. They want to make you happy and honestly don't know how sometimes. You have to tell them what you want. And damn near applaud when they try, even if they mess up, if you want them to try again at that or anything else. If you have a man who is trying, stop the battle, you've won the war.

4. They don't give a damn about your salary, where your degrees are from or how many you have, or what you do for a living as long as it's not immoral, illegal, or a drain on their finances. It's a nonfactor in their decision to consider dating you, marrying you, having sex with you, treating you well, or replacing you.

5. Men don't need to be reminded of our strength. Most know women are emotionally tougher. They just don't want it thrown in their faces. It makes them feel weak or resentful when you do. Woman up without telling them (or, worse, reminding them) that you're doing it. They'll respect it (and listen) a lot more.

6. They think about sex more than we can ever imagine. Pretty much everything they've ever done since they hit puberty—from wearing cologne to washing daily to going to college to buying a car to taking out the garbage, and so

on—has been in some form about getting more access to sex. Note: because he wants sex does not always mean he *only* wants sex.

7. Sex can be just an act, like eating a sandwich or going to shoot hoops. That doesn't excuse cheating, of course, but that also doesn't mean that because he has sex with you, he feels anything for you.

8. They worry about how they look and perform in bed. Everyone is vulnerable without clothes on. He worries that his chest is too birdlike or that his stomach is not a six-pack or that his biceps are not big or hard enough. Ever notice how whenever you swat a man, he steels up? He also worries that his penis could be too small or that he will cum quick. Or that he will not satisfy you and you will talk bad about him to your friends.

9. They like to see you in sweats sometimes. The idea is that (1) most men just think natural beauty is prettier; and (2) if you look good in sweats and Timbs, you'll probably look amazing in a dress.

10. Men like monochromatic colors. When our clothes look less busy, they aren't distracted from our bodies and faces. White seems to be their favorite color. Maybe because it's virginal? Probably because it's often sheer.

11. Sports are male soap operas or reality TV for men. Think about it. Do it now. I'll wait.

12. They like to protect you from the big bad world. I've been crossing the street by myself for more than two decades, but suddenly, when I'm with a man, he must become a barrier between me and oncoming traffic. I have no idea

exactly what I am being protected from by him walking on the outside, but it seems to make men feel manly. It gives them purpose. Fine. Whatever.

13. Men like confident women; at least, the good ones do. If you don't have confidence, fake it. A male friend once shared an e-mail a woman had written him. She explained why a man like him would never stay interested in a woman like her. Eventually, he'd leave her for someone more worthy of him. He adored her before he read the e-mail. By the end, she'd convinced him that she wasn't that great after all, and he lost interest. If you can't see your greatness, he probably won't, either.

14. Most men don't like makeup. Or at least they think they don't. I've found when men complain about makeup, what they're really whining about is foundation and eye shadow. This is also what tends to stain white tees and button-downs and, as one man told me, furniture.

15. Men like to use their imagination. They will look, of course, if you're parading the streets in an outfit best suited for a model in a *King* layout, but what *really* seems to do it for them is just enough of you to inspire their minds to wander. For *years*, Tariq, my bestie, talked about a woman he saw at Georgia Avenue Day in D.C. She had on an ankle-length skirt with side splits up her thigh. When she danced, he could see a good chunk of leg . . . but only for a second. The words he used to describe her were "enticing" and "mesmerizing." He talked about that woman for literally ten years.

16. They don't bond best by talking. Two men can work on a car and grunt, or play one-on-one and grunt, or go to a bar, watch a game, or drink some beer, barely communicate verbally and feel as though they have bonded significantly.

17. Men often say women talk too much, but what they mean specifically is nagging or women who say dumb ish that they don't want to hear. I did a survey of men once, asking how they liked to be romanced. I wondered, what would make a great evening? Every man mentioned something about good conversation. They don't mind us talking—in fact, they like it a lot—when we're saying something of intellect and interest.

18. They hate being doubted or accused of anything they didn't do. To us, it's being inquisitive, trying to play detective harmlessly. They interpret a casual inquisition as a character assassination. Tread lightly—unless you've got solid evidence.

19. They like compliments. A lot. They respond like dry plants to water when you tell them they look nice, smell good, did something well. Once I texted a guy who was preparing for a big meeting, "You are phenomenal. You will make me proud." He *still* talks about it, and calls to tell me.

20. They always tell us we think too much, but they think a lot. Video games are a distraction from all that thinking. (They're still thinking, though.) So is driving while listening to music made before they were born or before they graduated high school. And they do a lot of thinking in the shower and while aimlessly watching movies. I don't know if men know how to be spontaneous. They think about everything. Trust me.

AN A/B CONVERSATION

There are a million fancy, black-tie parties in the city, but frankly, I don't feel like going to any of them. It's New Year's Eve, and the same club I could get into for free and drink at for free any other day of the week will want to charge a hundred dollars just to get through the door and double the usual price of drinks. Plus, I don't want to put on a cocktail dress only to have cheap champagne spilled all over it by people who literally and figuratively can't hold their liquor.

Greg might come by later, but for now, I plan to stay in and do something constructive like paint my walls, which I've been talking about since I bought the colors and the rollers months ago.

My buzzing phone stops me at ten o'clock as I'm on the way to pull the plastic canisters from my storage closet. It's Penelope.

"Be dressed for twelve-thirty. We're going out." She always knows what's going on. "And don't give me that bullshit about you not going. It's New Year's. And don't get all dressed, either. It's a house party, D."

I sigh in her ear solely for the dramatic effect. "Fine. Who's driving?"

The car honks from downstairs, fifteen minutes late, which is fine because I wasn't fully dressed until five minutes ago. I've got on jeans, heels, and a frilly top that's cute and I can sweat in.

Penelope gives the livery cab driver the directions to the next destination.

"Who's throwing it?" I ask.

"A DJ. Friend of a friend. We should be able to find it. I have the cross streets."

"Um, you don't have the address?"

"Relax," she assures me. "We'll find it."

Not even ten minutes later, the cab turns onto the street we're looking for and slows to a crawl. Penelope and I peer out the windows looking for a crowd outside a brownstone, or just a couple of people who look like us headed to a party.

The sign comes in the form of music. We're halfway down the block when we hear the deejay looping Biggie's infamous best-borough shout-out, "Where's Brooklyn at? Where's Brooklyn at?" at top decibel. It's coming from the house on the corner.

We pull up, split the fare, and hustle up the steps eagerly to get out of the cold and also to find what awaits inside. Brooklyn house parties only come in two types: a bang or a bust.

I'm only just inside the foyer and can already tell this is a bang. Penelope's cracked the second entrance door, and from behind her I see what looks like that party from Biggie's "One More Chance" video. It's all beautiful women with freshly shaped Caesars or big, fluffy 'fros—some bigger than mine—that bounce and move when the diva they crown does. Others have newly twisted locks pulled high off their necks or left to flow in loose ropes that sway when they walk. A few fresh blowouts indicate the Dominican salons were busy today. It's hot, and most of the ladies are down to wife-beaters, tees, and cleavage-baring tops that show off their caramel, butter pecan, and chocolate deluxe hues.

The men are fine and tall, in vintage or one-of-a-kind tees and expensive jeans. They casually lean against the perimeter walls, observing the women passing by and showing off crisp cuts and fresh Air Force Ones. They entice passing ladies with flashes of pretty white teeth or the cocky borough swagger they adopted whenever it was they arrived in New York City proper. The smell of trees lingers through the air as a cutie exhales a dragon's puff of smoke from his tinged lips, watches it rise through hooded eyes, and holds up the spliff for his man's and them to pull.

I place both hands on Penelope's shoulders to keep up as she makes her way through the room. She shouts back at me over the music.

"What?" I lean in to hear her.

"The bar," she repeats, louder this time. "We gotta find it. We're like the only sober people in here."

I follow Penelope through the doorway into the main room. The music is at a deafening level, blasting Jay-Z's "I Just Wanna Love U." There's a fog of weed smoke hanging over this room, too. I can see it by the naked bulb hanging over the DJ booth. Other than that, the room is pitch black.

"Liquor?" Penelope yells to a guy holding up the wall, and he points to a doorway in the back. We snake through the crowd, meeting its rhythm as we shimmy by dancers who don't want their grind interrupted.

We take the stairs to the basement and find what can best be described as the liquor room but is actually a kitchen. There's a stove and a fridge, of course, but there are liquor bottles—empty, full, and half of both—over and under every surface. And not the cheap stuff. There's a case of Clicquot still holding unopened bottles sitting on the stove.

Penelope hands me a big red cup and grabs a bottle of expensive champagne to pop in celebration of this fabulous fête.

"To the good life," I quip after she's poured my cup to the brim, then filled her own.

"When the Clicquot is in the system, ain't no telling will I hump 'em or will I diss 'em," I chant, remixing the lyrics as we lap the room. We're easing our way through the crowd, looking for cuties and familiar faces.

Some tall dude in a royal blue Yankees fitted over locs wrapped into a messy Mr. Cheeks bun pulls Penelope to him, and she giggles and turns in to him for a dance. I recognize him as an A&R for a record label. He holds a blunt in front of Penelope, offering her a pull. She takes it and holds it out to me. I shake my head and leave her to her own devices since she knows him.

I walk as best I can through the gyrating bodies on the dance floor. The farther away I get from the DJ booth, the less I can see. With all the boys towering over me, I can barely make out anything. I get the same feeling I had when I woke up to Dakar doing what he did. This happens sometimes when I feel out of control. I panic just a little, even as I assure myself that I have nothing to worry about. I'm in a room full of people. Nothing will happen to me here.

Still, I turn back in the direction I came from, toward the light where it's also less crowded. The bodies seems denser, thicker than before. I breathe deep, calming myself as I sidestep through, trying to get around the people.

I head back to the foyer and plop onto the brownstone's steps leading to the second floor. I knew I should have stayed home. I break out my phone to text Greg to come get me, but I'm interrupted by a bass-filled voice.

"What are you drinking?"

I've met him before, but I don't remember where. Cute. My type. But I'm not in the mood to holler.

"Clicquot," I say, taking another sip from my plastic cup.

He sits next to me without asking, tells me he's drinking rum punch. He holds out his cup for me to taste. "It's good," he promises. "I'm good."

Not sure how many cups were in his system, but he was in the mood to talk. "You got a boyfriend?" he asks.

Trick question. Greg and I are Greg and I. I need anything, I call him. Technically, I'm free to date other people. I don't, mostly because I have no desire to. So much for Nola Darling living.

"I'm seeing somebody," I say, giving the vaguest answer possible.

"Well, there are some things you should know about men," the guy, not technically a friend, not really a stranger, begins.

This, in a nutshell, is what he tells me: The people you seriously date only come as As *or* Bs. Anything else, like a C through Z, is a time killer. It's not the real thing, so why put forth the effort?

An A is the nice man your parents would like to see you dating or married to. He is reliable, rational, dependable, honest, humble, considerate, and goal-oriented. He courts you. You know how he feels about you; you don't question his motives. He is consistent. You don't worry that he is cheating or lying. He does what he says he will do. Within reason, he does what you ask him to. Everyone you know likes him. He is good to you and for you. Basic common sense and all rational thought indicate that you should marry and live as happily as possible ever after with this man. A is boyfriend/husband material. A rescues princesses from disastrous situations in fairy tales.

A is for Aidan (for all you fellow *Sex and the City* fans).

B? There's just something about a B. You can't ever really put your finger on why. He doesn't do half of what A does, but you will do twice as much for him. He's not really reliable. He's definitely inconsistent and usually not *entirely* honest. He might not be conventionally attractive, but he's hypnotized you into believing he is the finest man you will ever encounter. He is, however, drama.

Around B, life gets way more interesting. Your emotions run the full gamut; you are a wreck operating in a near-constant state of stereotypical PMS or menopausal symptoms. You might coast with a variation of forty to fifty mph with A, but B is zero to ninety in six seconds flat. You know full and hell well it's disastrous just to be around B, much less be with him. But if loving B is wrong? Fuck it, you don't want to be right. And the sex! It's not *just* about the sex, of course, but with all that emotion, could it be anything other than mountain-moving? It's not the kissy, lovey-dovey, nice only-in-the-bedroom sex you have with A; this is Pinky-Cherokee–Italia Blue pornographic. And you love it!

Fairy tales are not made about B. The concept of happily ever after does not rationally exist with him. The best you can hope for with B is seven days without tears, without hanging up on him, or without breaking your BlackBerry in a fit of rage over the *most recent* stupid thing he did. For all his dysfunction, you'll want to spend the rest of your days with him. But if you have any sense, B, at best, is a one-night stand on vacation. B is the dude you cheat on A with if that's how you get down, but by God, you don't leave A for him.

B is for Big.

At this point, the drunk guy adds the real kicker: The odds of finding an AB combination are about as likely as Lil' Kim's comeback. So you're going to have to settle. Men don't come in packages that are dependable, drama-free, gentlemanlike, sensitive but also aggressive, swagged-out, and passionate, driving your emotions and your body haywire. Those are all the traits that women say they want in a man, but they don't exist well all in the same man. You're going to have to choose which one you want.

I've dealt with an A, and God knows, I've dealt with a B. I've tried to make an A more B and a B more A, and it did not work.

But then there's Greg, who is all of those things this guy says one man can't be, and he blows this theory out of the water.

"You can't have it all. Not in one person," the stranger promises.

I ponder his assessment as I wander back to the kitchen for a refill of bubbly. Is Greg the exception to the rule?

Maybe I'm lucky.

Maybe not.

CAN'T BE FRIENDS

"There are people in the world that have the power to change our values. Have you ever been with a girl who made you want to quit the rest of your life?"

—John Mayer on Jessica Simpson, *Playboy*

Back in 2000, I had a boyfriend. I lived in New York. The boyfriend lived in Maryland. We were good. And then I met Greg by accident.

I was new to the city, moved here to go to grad school, knew no one. I befriended a guy, Jonathan, who lived in my dorm. Jon was a New York native I met in the elevator, one of the only Black guys in the building. He dutifully agreed to take me, a naïve Southern belle, under his wing and make sure I got a sense of the city without getting myself maimed in the process. We hung out most weekends, and that's what we were doing on Saturday night at Nell's, a legendary New York nightclub. We were supposed to be meeting up with his cousin.

I'd just followed Jon to the basement when I spotted a man. Not my type. I was into pretty boys back then. I had a pretty boyfriend back home. Said stranger looked over at me. I smiled; he smiled back. I don't know what came over me, but I walked up to him, and we began to dance.

After a few songs, I was compelled to do my girlfriend duty and blurt over Biggie's "Hypnotize," "I have a boyfriend, you know?" There it was on the table. I'd let him know I was not on the market.

He looked directly into my eyes as he spoke more into me than to me. My monogamy censors went crazy at this clear threat as he responded, "It gets cold in New York." Then he smiled, a perfectly imperfect thing that made my heart go *thump-thump*.

Three hours later, I left the dance floor. I'd sweated out my dress and my unpermed hair. I didn't want to be caught looking crazy when the lights came on. I hadn't even asked the stranger for his name, and we hadn't had any real conversation other than my declaration that I was unavailable to date. But I knew I wanted to know him, likely in the biblical sense. I thought about my boyfriend and decided it would be best for my relationship if I carried myself home without having a way to contact this new, smiling, dancing man.

I thanked the stranger for a wonderful night, excused myself, and followed Jonathan to the door. Then my song came on. It was "One More Chance." I scurried back to the floor for one more dance with the stranger, then left as soon as the song was over. Jonathan was waiting, after all.

Standing on the corner of Fourteenth Street with him, looking for a cab with its light on, I asked about his night. I hadn't seen Jon since we'd walked into the club.

"Did you see your cousin?" I asked.

"Who? Greg?" He laughed. "I saw him. Didn't get a chance to speak with him, though."

"Huh?"

"He was busy," Jon explained.

"Oh."

Jon laughed again.

"So why didn't you say anything?" I prodded.

"You wanted me to interrupt you?"

It took a moment, but I got it. *Ohhhhhh!* That would be the sound of light dawning above my fluffy-haired head.

He gave me the you-cannot-be-that-naïve look. Oh, but I was.

Greg and I became the greatest of pals. Hung out every weekend at the movies and restaurants around SoHo and Harlem (he took me for my first visit, a nondate, to see *Bamboozled* at the Magic Johnson theatre), the Village, Chelsea, and every other part of Manhattan because he was determined to introduce me to *his* town. We talked on the phone most nights, mostly about nothing, sometimes just breathing into the phone while we did other things.

The only giveaway that we weren't completely platonic was his greeting, a hug that was a little too tight, then a smack of his lips right on my cheek that lingered a little too long and was a little too close to my mouth to be just a friend. Me? I had to bite the insides of my cheeks to keep from grinning with all thirty-two every time I met up with him.

Because I was convinced that I wasn't doing anything wrong, I told my boyfriend about Greg, my newfound New York friend. Of course, he wasn't too happy to hear about it, but I assured him, "There's nothing going on." It was the God's honest truth.

For seven or eight months, it stayed that way. Greg and I did no kissing, generally no touching unless we were on the dance floor, and not even a hug at the end of the night when he would walk me to my door and stand all up in my personal space to say good night and call me by my full government name. He'd smile that perfectly imperfect thing; I'd temporarily die from an unfulfilled longing, and I'd bolt away from him, trying to remain that good girlfriend I'd promised myself—and my boyfriend—that I was.

One night, Jon and I met up with Greg at a warehouse-turned-club for a Black Diamonds party on the West Side. The venue had a gigantic Buddha sitting in the middle of it. When we met Greg at the bar, something was different about him. He did his usual I-ain't-trying-to-be-your-friend greeting, but this time his energy intertwined with mine more strongly than usual. I ran to the bathroom to escape it.

Eventually, I made my way back to the bar and found he'd disappeared. Maybe Greg had finally given up on me. Jon was gone, too. I spent the next hour trying to get a phone signal—pointless—and searching for Jon. I knew he hadn't left me.

I was looking over a railing at the crowd below, contemplating heading home, when someone grabbed my elbow from behind and jerked me around.

"I've been looking for you all night!" Greg yelled over the chorus of Jay-Z's "I Just Wanna Love U. "Stop running from me!"

I was a split second from bellowing some bright feminist retort about who Greg thought he was, putting his hands on me uninvited, but I didn't have a chance. He simultaneously yanked me to him and shoved me against the railing. He planted his lips on mine, slowly sucking my bottom lip first, then sticking his tongue square in my mouth like it belonged there. I didn't even think about pushing him off me.

We kissed until I realized we were not alone and in a very public place. I pulled back and looked up at him with star-struck eyes. Something in my consciousness had shifted. Like the first time I had an orgasm, and realized what all the fuss was about. Yes, it was worth all the work, and the world is a better place because that feeling is possible. I also wanted to kick myself for waiting so long.

Greg looked back at me, his eyes equal parts confused, searching, and taunting. I had to know if I imagined what I felt. I stood on my tiptoes, grabbed the back of his bald head, and pulled him down to me. I know, I know, I had a boyfriend. But I wasn't thinking about him at that moment. Plus, I'd already messed up. What was another kiss?

I recovered my common sense at the end of the night, when Greg walked me to a cab. Jon had long since left. I told him I wasn't ready when he said he wanted to go. Greg assured him I would get home safely. Jon looked at us and shook his head, told me to call if I needed anything. At all.

I was already inside the car, but Greg was holding the door open, waiting for an invitation.

"Demetria Lucas, do you want to take me home with you?" he asked. "I will go if you want me . . . to," he added when I didn't answer for a full fifteen seconds.

I was someone's girlfriend—not his. And just because I slipped down a slope didn't mean I had to go tumbling down a mountain.

"No, I'm good," I said, shaking my head. I didn't mean it, but I tried to say it as if I did, if only because it was the right thing to well, say. Sometimes that's half the battle.

He smiled.

Thump-thump went the traitor in my chest.

He said, "Oh-kay," but what he meant was *I'll accept that for now, but I'll be trying again later.*

If later was sixty seconds, I was screwed, literally and figuratively. I reached for the door handle and pulled it shut before I changed my mind. As the cab pulled away, I had to stop myself from looking out the back window with longing.

Back at my apartment, safe and sound on my living-room couch *alone.* I did the same thing I'd done the night I met him: stayed up until daybreak thinking about my boyfriend . . . and Greg. I listened to Donell Jones's "Where I Wanna Be." On repeat.

Greg called, and I answered, before the weekend was over (i.e., the next day). We didn't talk about the Incident, just pretended the whole thing never happened. Perfect. We could go on as usual, as "just" friends. When I recapped the night to Aliya, I blamed it on the alcohol, but neither one of us had a drink that night.

I decided not to see Greg for awhile, although I didn't tell him about my vow. And to his credit, he didn't ask me to see me. And I didn't call as much. Neither did he. I thought about him, though. Constantly. Went to visit my boyfriend one weekend and drove to his apartment blasting Luther's "If Only for One Night": "I won't tell a soul, no one has to know . . ."

I did more pleading than singing.

I took the train home from the Bronx for a class assignment and played Frankie Beverly and Maze's "The Morning After." On repeat: "I know you think this is right, but what happens after tonight?"

Same general theme, but Frankie made me think of the consequences.

But then I saw Greg again. He took me to Battery Park City to show me the Statue of Liberty, and it began raining on the ride over. He pulled a golf umbrella from his trunk, and we walked along the waterfront.

I needed more than consequences to stop me. By then, I didn't give a damn about karma's boomerang.

I switched to Mint Condition's, "What Kind of Man Would I Be?": "If we lay down tonight, it won't justify throwing love aside . . ."

It appealed to my sense of personal decency. It was all I had left.

That worked—for another month.

I broke up with my boyfriend.

And I began dating Greg.

I realized I was in over my head when I didn't look both ways to cross the street. It's a small thing but a very big one to a proudly independent woman who likes to be in control. The logic goes: I only trust you not to mess up because I trust me to look out for myself. Unless I'm with my mother, I look both ways before I cross the street. I trust her to keep me safe. Unless I am with my father, I always carry his credit card. I trust him to take care of the bills. Anybody else? I'm looking right, then left, hard, like I'm at a stop sign while trying to pass my first driver's exam. And I'm keeping my daddy's credit card on me at all times.

But I stepped out into the street on autopilot, without a care in the world. The sun was shining. I was in SoHo with Greg, with a MetroCard, a driver's license, and a five-dollar bill in my pocket. I didn't even have a Louis. The energy we created together made the world a better place. Or at least, that's what it felt like.

He'd come over the night before to watch a movie. I'd fallen asleep on his lap, and when I awoke he was gone. I had a pillow under my head, and he'd draped his jacket over me to keep me warm. I woke up feeling like I'd been cloaked in an armor of love. If he stepped into the street, then it must be safe. There was no need to look. I believed he would never let anything bad happen to me when I was with him. And he never did.

He held me down . . . and sometimes together. When I landed a job in London one summer in grad school and debated not going so I could stay close to him, he told me to go. He took me on a driving tour of New York the night before I left and promised he'd be there when I returned. (He was.) He e-mailed me almost every day I was gone. When September 11 happened and my dorm was closed, I stayed with him until I could figure out where to go next. When my plans to stay in New York after grad school fell through at the very last minute, he talked me off my mental ledge and sat up with me while I cried until seven in the morning, assuring me that I'd make it back to the city. When I came back to visit New York, he saw me as often as possible. I came up for the day once for an interview. He couldn't spend time with me because he had a presentation at work. He met me at Penn Station to see me for five minutes to say hello and good-bye before I left the city. And when I couldn't make it to New York as often as I liked, he drove down to Maryland. When I moved back . . . and Dakar . . . and . . . Greg made sure I was safe.

I would do anything for him. The difficult I'd do right now. The impossible would take a little while. But I'd do it, because he would do anything for me. That's why I wasn't caught off guard when he called me during the first week of spring to ask me to meet him at the Brooklyn Museum. We usually saw each other on weekends, since the drive (for him) and the ride (for me) to and from the Bronx could be brutal. But occasionally, he would make the long trek to see me on a weeknight just because.

I meet him on the steps at the fountains at seven o'clock.

"You look like hell," I say before hello. He has terrible allergies.

He turns his head up instinctively, and I greet him with a kiss on the lips.

"I feel fabulous," he quips sarcastically.

He's not usually sarcastic. "What's wrong?" I ask.

I take a seat next to him and lean on his shoulder. Right up on him where life is best lived.

He sighs deeply. "I'm moving."

I sit upright excitedly and face him, stopping myself from clasping my hands together like a child. "To where? Brooklyn?"

"Charleston."

"North Carolina?!"

"South."

It's a job transfer. More money. Lower cost of living. A pension.

I nod, waiting for him to get to the part where he asks me to go with him. But he doesn't.

"How long will you be gone?" I ask, as if he is going on a business trip.

"I don't know. But I'm coming back," he offers.

I stare at the ground blankly. My pride won't let me blurt, *What about me?*

"You can't leave New York, D. You came here to be a writer," he adds. "You can't do that there."

I look up, not bothering to hide the tears in my eyes. "I can write from anywhere." It's a plea. *Take me with you. Don't leave me. I don't know if I can make it here without you. I want to quit my life.* "All I need is a laptop," I add weakly.

I have a few bylines, no cover stories yet. I have never been on staff at a magazine. I would find a new dream if it meant I wouldn't have to look both ways to cross the streets again, if I could still wake up cloaked in an armor of love.

"You should stay here," he says firmly.

He doesn't want me to go.

"What about us?"

Another heavy sigh. "You'll be fine . . . without me."

He doesn't want me anymore? I don't get it.

"Did I do something wrong?" I practically beg. I try, but I'm not *always* the easiest person to get along with. "What did I do?"

He shakes his head. "It's not you . . ."

The wind's been knocked out of me. I feel like I'm going halfway crazy. I gasp for air, I bury my head in my chest, and I watch as my tears fall from my eyes onto my jeans. "I'll fix it," I plead. "What did I do?"

"It's better for you here," he says.

There's an ache in my chest where my soul is tearing in half, separating his from mine. If there was ever a moment to lose it, this is it. I don't know what else to do.

"Well, fuck you, too!" I yell loudly enough to be heard by the children playing on the steps and the mothers and nannies watching them. Everything goes silent, like the power's blown at a block party. "Fuck, fuck, fuck you, Greg!"

I march down the concrete steps, and he doesn't come after me. I walk the avenues back to my apartment, bawling the whole way and not even bothering to wipe or cover my face. No one disturbs me.

At home. I flop onto the living-room couch and put on *Lady Sings the Blues* to keep myself from lying in the dark. I'm numb. The tears have stopped; my eyes are burning. I make it as far as the end of the opening scene, when Billie's in a strait-jacket and locked in a cell. She's throwing herself against the padded walls in a withdrawal-fueled fit, then stares at the ceiling aimlessly, directionless, hopeless. I feel how she looks.

I turn the TV off, ball up on my couch, tucking myself in as tightly as I can, because it feels as if my chest is splitting. I am literally trying to hold myself together.

I cry so hard and so long that my eyes are swollen shut the next morning, and I have to call in sick to work because it looks as if someone has beaten me.

For years, I'll think of him when I listen to Stevie Wonder's "If It's Magic." I'll think of him every time I pass the Brooklyn Museum in a cab on the way home from a party. I'll think of him when I hear Nina Simone's "I Get Along Without You Very Well" and every time my iPod Shuffle, well, shuffles to Jill Scott's "Cross My Mind."

I know what you're thinking. Why don't you just pick up the phone and call, D? He hasn't called me. And you don't go chasing men who walk out on you.

CRY FREEDOM

My boss is wasted. Like White girl wasted. We've been at this dive bar around the corner from the office for less than an hour. We're here to celebrate Evan's departure. He's the only Black guy in senior management at my job, and as long as I've been working here, he's barely said two words to me, acts as if I don't exist.

But back to my boss. While I've been nursing a glass of cheap-wine since five-fifteen, she's been doing shots of tequila with her work husband. It's nearly seven now, and I just shoved her back onto the bar stool she nearly slipped off of.

"Um, are you okay, Liz?" I ask.

I haven't liked her since the day after the first day I straightened my hair, and she, not Black, with curly hair that's worn straight, asked me, "How do *you* keep your hair straight? Do you put cream on it at night?" I guess she doesn't think Black people use a blow dryer or a flat iron, too. Anyway, I'm genuinely concerned about how she's going to make it back to Staten Island in this condition. I suppose the people on the ferry have seen worse, though.

"Lizzie is fine," she says, referring to herself in the third person.

I nod and take a sip of white wine as I check my watch. I'm only here to look like a team player. I'm leaving by seven-thirty.

It's Friday night, but I have to work later, although writing doesn't feel like work. I would do that for free. I'm freelancing for a few magazines right now. *Black Enterprise* assigned me a profile of a pair of twins who design upscale men's clothing. The interviews are done, but I need to transcribe the tape (story of my life), write the story, and turn it in on Monday. I'd easily rather be home doing that than here doing this.

"D!"

I turn my head to ID the male voice calling my name. It's my coworker, Jackie. He waves me over. I happily leave Lizzie to her own drunken devices and head to his table.

"Get a real drink," Jackie says as soon as I'm in nonyelling earshot.

"I'm a lady. I'll have my wine," I insist, plopping onto the seat across from him. I have my reasons, you may recall, for not drinking hard liquor.

He rolls his eyes. "Have another. It's on me." He looks at me pointedly.

I give him the same look, tip my almost empty wine glass to my lips, and swallow what's left. "I'll have another Chardonnay."

He shakes his head, mutters something about "prissy country girls" under his breath, and calls for the waitress. He's an actual New York native, sometimes hard to find in the city. He thinks everything outside New York is country.

While we wait for the next round, I do my best to attempt not to look bored and fail miserably. I know I should be playing the game, socializing and schmoozing and such, but I can't. I only took this job to get back to New York, and now that I'm here, I'm looking to leave as soon as possible.

A tap on my shoulder interrupts my brooding. I look up and back to see Evan. He's looking down at me, smiling. I stare back blankly.

"You came to see me off," he says, ignoring my expression.

"Yup," I respond dryly.

He smiles wider. "I'm glad you're here. May I?" he asks, indicating the seat next to me.

Now he wants to talk? This conversation right here? It's more than he's said to me in the entire time I've worked here. He doesn't even respond to my e-mails. Forwards them to his assistant, and *he* responds.

I look at the seat, look back at him. "It's empty."

He nods, still smiling. He's got even teeth and a dimple in his left cheek. He's cute. Too old for me, though. Got me by at least eight years.

Evan waits for me to scoot over into the booth, then slides in beside me, blocking my exit. I notice things like that now.

"What're you drinking?" Evan asks, noticing my empty glass.

"Oh, I got her," Jackie interjects. "What do you want?" he asks Evan.

Evan goes for a cognac and Coke—the seeming drink of choice for Black men from the block to the boardroom—and Jackie flags down the bartender.

"If you need anything else, just let me know," Evan offers to me.

I look at him curiously. "It's your party. You shouldn't be buying drinks."

He grins, pushes his glasses higher on his nose. "I know. I'll make an exception . . . for you."

That's when I realize he's flirting with me.

Evan spends the whole night by my side, despite it being his party. He's attentive (or trying to get me drunk), reordering when my Chardonnay runs low again and sharing so much about his background that I imagine this is how the head of any HR department feels interviewing a prospective hire.

He went to Brooklyn Tech, which seems to be the school attended by everyone from Brooklyn who ever goes on to do anything of substance in life. He went away to college and recently finished his MBA. He's godfather to several children, and he loves kids, but doesn't have any. All of his friends are married or engaged. But he's single, completely free, and interested in a relationship. Oh, and he's thirty-two, i.e., too old.

I nod, sipping from my new glass, taking it all in. He seems nice, mature, old (did I say that already?). But I don't get giddy the way I used to anymore when I meet a guy. I'm more cautious now, still not sure I can trust myself.

We have pleasant conversation long past seven-thirty when I said I was leaving. The room gets louder as my coworkers get drunker, and Evan and I are in the corner booth, practically yelling in each other's ear to hear above the noise. A few people stop by briefly to wish Evan well, but most offer a quick congratulations and move on as if they're interrupting something important.

By nine P.M., I've switched from wine to water and can no longer suppress my growling stomach, which I can feel but luckily can't hear over the dull roar of '80s rock music. I decide that when my boss finishes slurring her good-byes to Evan, I'm heading home, or at least for food. I've been craving a falafel from a spot in the West Village. I ate there twice a week in grad school.

"You look bored," Evan says after an apology for chatting so long.

"No apology necessary. It's your retirement party."

He laughs. "I'm not that old."

Now I apologize. "My bad. I'm hungry. I can't think straight. I'm getting ready to head out."

"Where are you going to eat?"

I shrug, tell him about the falafel spot.

"Why don't you let me take you out instead?" Evan counters.

"Now?" I check my watch. It's not so late. And he is nice. And I don't have real plans . . . "But what about your party?"

"I'm more interested in you."

Oh. Okay.

Evan says his good-byes, and no one seems to mind his departure. He's the excuse for the party, but he's not the center of attention.

He walks me to the car, keeping on "his" side, the one closest to the street. We drive to Blue Ribbon, a seafood bistro in SoHo. I've never heard of it. Its fancy, the type of restaurant my parents used to take me to when they came to visit me in grad school. It's a change from what I'm used to here. When I go out, it's to cheap, trendy-chic places like Spice or Café Habana. This is a place for real adults. Like Evan.

He's sitting across from me, talking about his new job and his five-year plan. I feel like I'm on my Ps and Qs, the same way I get when I go out with my dad and his business associates. Suddenly, I feel very immature and inexperienced. Evan's moved on to talking about some college tale, and I realize it was ten years ago for him. It was less than three years for me. I can still remember the names of all the buildings my classes were in.

At the end of our evening, Evan offers to drive me to my house. On the ride, we talk like we've known each other forever. I decide he'll be a great friend.

When we pull up in front of my building, he asks for my number. I rattle it off, and he punches it into his phone.

"I'm not looking for a boyfriend," I tell him, because it's the right thing to do. He's a nice guy, and I don't want to mislead him. My father told me when I started dating at sixteen, "I will be the only man ever to spend money on you and not expect anything but just your happiness in return."

Evan nods. "Okay."

I can't tell what that means, but I thank him for taking me to dinner, offer another congratulations on the new job, and jog up the steps to my building.

Evan and I are . . . cool. Sometimes we meet for lunch at a Thai spot downtown that's midway between our jobs, or we grab falafels from the stand in the park by where the World Trade Center used to be. He insists on paying for me, so I insist on going to cheap places. I'm pretty sure he likes me as more than a friend, and I don't want him to think I'm taking advantage of his generosity or misleading him, which, truthfully, I probably am by hanging out with him. But he's nice and funny . . . and safe.

We keep up our routine for months, lunch at least once a week, dinner weekly, too, including my birthday, when he sends long-stemmed roses to my job, takes me to a fancy restaurant and then a candlelit dessert in the Village. When I finally land a new job as an assistant editor at a book publishing company, he comes to the party and takes my closest girlfriends and me out for a private celebration after.

Evan's really cool. This is what I'm thinking about to keep myself awake in a marketing meeting at the new job. We're brainstorming ideas on how to package upcoming book releases. The team is presenting ideas for the bestsellers, none of which is on my list yet. I'm only here for the experience. And I'm bored.

Thinking about Evan is the only thing keeping me alert. He's panning out to be one of the nicest guys I've ever met. He's cute, funny, and definitely stable, safe, and secure. I can set a clock by him, which isn't a bad trait in a man.

I hone back in on the presenter just as the lights flicker low, return to normal, then go out completely. I hear the sucked-life sound of all of the office computers powering down simultaneously.

The associate publisher nervously quips, "I'm sure we paid the light bill," then sends her assistant to find out what the trouble is. He comes back moments later to announce that the whole building has lost power, and we—as in, the whole building, not just the people on our floor—are being evacuated.

I gather my papers and purse, grabbing my flip-flops and switching from my heels to walk down the seventeen flights of stairs. There are no emergency lights in the stairwell, so a gaggle of us hold up our cell phones to light the path.

Once outside, my senior editor and I realize it's not just our building that's lost power. There are people everywhere. All of the buildings nearby are dark. My first thought is, *not terrorists. Not again.* Like the rest of the city, I have mild PTSD, a holdover from September 11.

I tamp down the lump in my throat and focus on the task at hand, finding out what's going on. I try to dial Evan on my cell phone, but there's no signal. *Weird.*

We head west toward Times Square, and before we hit the end of the block, we overhear that our trek is pointless. Times Square is dark. I cover my mouth and gasp.

"Miss," I interrupt, speaking to the woman I eavesdropped on. "Times Square?" I can't even form the words.

"Not just Times Square," she says. "All of New York City."

I blink in disbelief.

"What?" my coworker finally asks, breaking the silence. We turn back to the office building. On the corner we decide we'll go our separate ways. On foot.

I barely know my way back to Brooklyn above ground. I don't drive in the city. I can get anywhere on the train, though. I walk south from Midtown with a large crowd of others to the Manhattan Bridge.

It takes me two and a half hours to get to my block. I have

sweated through my shirt and pants by the time I reach my Brooklyn building. But staying inside the house in August without the benefit of the AC is not at all an option.

I boil water on the gas stove, throw in some linguine. When the noodles are done, I put half in a bowl and pour still-chilled spaghetti sauce and a bunch of pepper over them. *Voilà!* Dinner is served.

I'm uncorking the bottle of red wine from the fridge when I hear . . . music?

Are the lights back on? I flick the switch in the kitchen. Nothing.

I gather up the wine and food and a fork and head downstairs to the front porch.

"These little town blues, are melting away. I'll make a brand new start of it in old New York . . ." Frank Sinatra's "New York, New York" is blaring from speakers outside. A set of turntables are hooked to a generator for an impromptu block party.

There are tons of people outside who weren't there twenty minutes ago. I laugh wildly and from the gut. I love Brooklyn!

I'm sitting on my porch to eat, singing along to the DJ's Jay-Z set, when Evan unexpectedly rolls up to my gate—literally. He's got on Rollerblades, basketball shorts, and head gear.

"What are you doing here!?" I exclaim with glee. I'm happy to see him, as unexpected as it is.

He looks more relieved than happy to see me. "You didn't answer when I called to make sure you were okay, so I came by."

Told you he was safe. I offer to get him a bowl of pasta and a glass of wine, and then we sit on the porch and sing along to whatever the DJ spins until his generator dies.

Evan stays over for the first time. On the couch. It isn't safe for him to roll home without the streetlights to guide his path.

This is also the night he asks me to be his girlfriend. I say yes.

TWO YEARS LATER

Evan is downstairs with the men, drinking Heinekens, playing Spades, and talking ish. I'm upstairs with the women and kids.

It's Labor Day, and we accepted an invite to his college room-mate's house—mansion, really—in New Jersey. We rode an hour and a half out of the city with a just-married couple and arrived to find six other pairs.

We only hang out with couples. They're all Evan's age, about ten years older than me. I get perpetually bored listening to everyone talk about 401(k)s, mortgages (Evan just bought a condo), kids, and, worse, the glory years of their mid-twenties, when they acted crazy before they met the One and settled down.

I'm in my mid-twenties, and I don't act crazy. While my friends my age run off to Atlanta or Miami for the holiday weekend, I'm sitting in a kitchen, awkwardly bouncing a fidgety baby on my lap while his mom prepares dinner. He's cute as all get-out and likes lots of attention, which keeps him from crying. I'd rather give my attention to him than intrude on the grown folks' conversation. These women all know one another and have things in common. Me? Not so much.

"Demetrius, do you and Evan want kids?" a mother of two asks. Her children are in the play room with the other kids.

I don't bother to correct her pronunciation of my name. I'm counting down the hours till we can leave. I pause, trying to fig-ure out a way to tell her, *I haven't thought about kids, much less marriage.*

"Um . . . sure," I lie.

"How many?" she asks sweetly. Everyone in the room is looking at me.

"One," I say. That's better than none, right? That's what I want to say. I don't know if I'm built to be a mom, if I can handle the responsibility.

Everyone chuckles and squeals at my response. I get the indication that I've said something wrong.

"Just one? Won't she get lonely? She needs someone to play with!" the woman exclaims.

"Oh . . . um, I'm an only child," I offer by way of explanation.

The baby on my lap must sense my increased awkwardness. He begins to cry instead of whimper and attracts the attention to him. I would do something great to thank him for the distraction, like stop the cause of his tears, if only I knew how. I don't know much about babies.

His mother takes him off my lap, and mere seconds pass before I excuse myself to the basement.

I find Evan at the card table. Surprise, surprise. He and his boys are recounting a story from when they used to live together just after college in a dirt-cheap house they were renting for next to nothing. They all had well-paying jobs and spent their money on women, parties, and last-minute vacations.

"Twenty-five was the best year of my life," Evan recounts.

I reach over his shoulder and take a swig of his beer. I hope to God—i.e., pray—as I sip that this is not the best year of mine.

By midnight, we are back in Brooklyn. I'm snuggled next to Evan on the couch at his condo, glad that it's just the two of us again. One old person I can do. A room full? Uh . . . I'll pass.

"So," Evan begins, "did you have a good time?"

"It was . . . cool."

"You don't like my friends?" He's very intuitive.

"No. I mean, yes, I like them, but . . ." I try to figure out how to say *but everybody's just so old* without saying it. "I didn't feel like I had much in common with them," I say, cleaning it up. "Everybody's talking about mortgages and careers and kids, and I'm just not in the mind-set, you know? Your friends are all established and married, and I'm getting started, and you're my boyfriend."

He nods. "I figured." He leans back on the couch and looks at the purple walls of his new condo. "I was thinking," he begins, "about you moving in. Would that put you more at ease?"

I don't mean to blurt this, but I do: "Huh?"

"Just that. . . . We always hang out with couples, and they're married. And we're not. But I want you to know that I'm serious about you."

Do I want to move in? I don't know. "Whoa. Okay," I say, stalling. "Let me think about it."

"I figured," Evan says. "Take your time."

As soon as Evan closes the cab door to send me back to my house the following afternoon, I call Aliya.

"Evan asked me to move in with him!" I blurt right after she says hello.

"Uh . . . okay. Do you want to move in with him?" she asks without missing a beat.

Here's the deal: I think I want my freedom. But as much as I think I want to run around the world and live it up at twenty-five like Nola Darling and like Evan and all of his married friends and their wives did, there's a part of me that wonders if I'll be hustling backward, gambling on the long shot that single life stays fun or even further against the odds that I can find another Evan when I'm actually ready to settle down if ever that happens. Maybe this yearning to be free is just a phase I can wait out.

"If you're not sure, don't do it," Aliya advises. "Stay still until you have a definitive answer. Don't rush into anything."

I think it over for less than twenty-four hours. The next day at work, I get a call from my friend Bonnie, who technically lives across the hall but practically lives in Miami, since she spends every possible weekend there. She's recounting all of her adventures from the previous weekend—VIP in Opium, rooftop parties, celebrity pool parties, three-dollar overproof shots at Wet Willie's, all of the guys she met there who live here . . .

As she's talking, I realize that is the life I want. I want to live it up and ride out singlehood till the wheels falls off. Dance on tables, holler at men for sport, no obligations, be selfish and think about me, me, me, then maybe settle down when I've got all the partying and playing out of my system, whenever that is. Thirty-two? That's when it got out of Evan's.

My mother calls unexpectedly that afternoon. She asks about me, then Evan. She's been head over heels for him since I took him back to Maryland last year for Thanksgiving. It was the turning point in our relationship. Every relative who came by looked at me, looked at him, then looked at my ring finger and asked, loudly, "No ring yet, huh? Just be patient." When they assumed I wanted to get married, that's when I realized I didn't. I'm thankful Evan hasn't brought that up.

"What's new?" Mum asks.

"Evan asked me to move in," I tell her.

"And you said?" she leads.

"I told him I'd think about it."

She reminds me of what she told me about "shacking"—yes, she still calls it that. Her rules are that a smart woman does not live anywhere where her name is not on the deed or the lease. "He tells you to get out, then what?" she's drilled into me.

"Is he putting your name on the deed?" she asks.

"I dunno. We didn't get that far."

"Well, maybe you should," Mum says.

I realize she has just given me the out I'm looking for. I can tell Evan that I need my name on the deed. This should be a headache that he should not want to undertake. I don't even know if he can take it. He just bought the place. There's got to be some rule about changing the contract so soon. It's a New York City condo. Every-thing is complicated. He will be disappointed, but this will give me time to slow our train down and exit gracefully so that I can still come back if the green grass I'm seeking isn't quite so green after all.

The next time I see Evan, I tell him that I can't move in without my name on the deed. I tell him the logic of having my name on it, too. That it's a gamble for me. What if things don't work out? I'm giving up my apartment and my stuff to be a girlfriend in someone else's house, and it just doesn't feel secure. Why would I live like a wife if I am not a wife? He recites what I thought he would about being unable to change the deed without a legal hassle.

He broods for a moment, then has a eureka moment. "This is easy. We can solve this so easy." He chuckles, smiling as if he has it all figured out. "We could just get married!"

I smile because he looks so happy and I don't want to crush his idea. I don't say anything, and he takes my silence as shock in a good way.

After I haven't said anything for a full sixty seconds, he asks, "You want to do this, right?"

I nod. Because that's what you do when a man who loves you and whom you really care about starts planning the rest of his life with you . . . right?

Evan has a list. We're at Chelsea Brewing Company on the deck watching the pink sunset over the Hudson River. It's one of the last days of summer.

"So I have the names of my guests," he says.

"I'm sorry, what?" I say.

"My guest list. For the wedding."

I go through the motions, pushing myself to rattle off my prefer-ences, listing which relatives are essential in the audience. While I talk to him, I try to talk myself into the idea of getting married. The man sitting across from me is amazing. He would do anything for me. I don't know how many men there are in the world like him. And despite the age difference, despite my inner cry for freedom, we are well suited in disposition and demeanor. We never argue, hardly disagree; he's funny and kind, loving and protective and safe. What is there not to love?

He's not Greg.

I don't know where that thought comes from. But it's like a roll of thunder, and I want to cry. It's the truth I've been trying to avoid and talk myself around. If it were Greg sitting across from me, there would be nothing to debate. I wouldn't want to run off and explore the wide world, I'd want to sit here and make a list of people who could witness me pledge my life to a higher purpose than myself.

Evan sees me back to my apartment safely. At the door, he asks to come up, and I agree. We're sitting on the couch watching TV in a silence I think is awkward but hope Evan finds companionable.

"What's wrong?" he says.

I don't answer him. I can't.

"Demetria?" he prods.

"I-I-I can't do this," I blurt. "I'm so sorry. I'm sorry. I'm so, so sorry." I reach for his hand, and he snatches it away. "Evan," I plead.

"You can't do what?"

I sit silently with my head bowed. I can't face him.

"You can't do what? You're not ready to get married. I can deal with—"

He makes me say it. "A relationship. I can't do this. I'm just not ready. I . . ." I ramble on about the reason, wanting to dance on tables, and all the crazy freedom he had when he was my age that he took for granted and how I want the same thing. And I apologize a million times more.

When I'm done, he yells at me about wasting his time and growing up and misleading him and making a mess of everything. I lock myself in my bedroom and he keeps yelling through the bedroom door even after I begin to sob. He's never yelled at me before, and I am terrified, not that he will hurt me but because I've hurt someone I genuinely care about.

I cry, too, because I am scared of what comes next. Between Evan and Greg, I've never been on my own in this city. The one week I was, a disaster happened. Since then, I've always had a safety net in the form of a man, and now I've snatched it from under myself.

"You'll never find someone as good to you as me!" Evan yells. I can hear the hurt in his voice. I cry harder.

He goes quiet. I hear his heavy footsteps in the living room, then the foyer, then I hear the door slam.

Can you make it on your own? the voice in my head asks me. "I guess I'm about to find out," I answer.

MY FATHER CALLED ME
A PARTY GIRL

Unless it's a "detox week," i.e., the seven days after Draft Week, Fashion Week (fall or spring), or MTV's Video Music Awards, when the city explodes with invite-only parties in very chic places, I go out more often than I stay home. In my ideal week, which I've been having a lot of as of late, I'm out every night Monday through Thursday, never clubs per se, usually industry parties, open-bar jaunts sponsored by the biggest name brands or musicians previewing their products in hopes of spreading the good word to what Malcolm Gladwell calls Connectors.[1] There are also the requisite birthday parties for all of the fabulous people who live and/or work in or run this city and then the obligatory "Black professionals" happy hours, although no one really calls them that. They're called networking events, and a surprising number of business contacts are actually made.

---

1 It's a reference from Gladwell's *The Tipping Point.* In short, they are the people who bring the world together and disseminate information quickly.

In a good week, without a major event hitting the city, there are no fewer than six parties worth attending. I usually make it to all six. When I'm not party-hopping, you'll catch me in SoHo, grabbing margaritas or sangria with my friends or a "special friend," maybe hitting a Broadway show or just meeting in the park and chatting over Jamba Juices. My philosophy, stolen from a tour guide my cousin met in Australia on holiday, is to make the most of every day I have.

I rest on Fridays, making a regular stop at my favorite Mexican restaurant where the waiter knows my order—blood orange frozen margarita and a plate of fish tacos—without me having to ask. Saturdays are for running errands (or hitting the beach in the summer). I rev up again for weekend nights, hitting a Brooklyn house party or, if it's the first of the month, the Brooklyn Museum for Target First Saturdays, when a thousand or more Black people pack the museum for a DJ-spun fête. Sundays I do church at Emmanuel Baptist, as much for worship as for socializing (its nickname is "Club Church"). If you hang out on Saturday night in Brooklyn at Deity, Five Spot, or South Paw, you're likely to see half the partygoers at the non-denominational noon service the next day. After church, there's brunch at Chez Oskar or The Spot, with its all-you-can-drink mimosas till four P.M., and after that, I head to DUMBO for a day party hosted by well-connected friends who offer an alternative to the Black Melrose scene, which is becoming overpopulated.

With rare exceptions, usually a close sister-friend's birthday party, I do not take shots. I am known to have a taste or two on a weeknight and then side-hug an attractive stranger or two. I reserve dancing on tables for excursions to Miami or overseas locales where none of my relatives live. In New York, both feet stay on the floor at all times. I am always fully clothed at events and remain so throughout the night. In fact, I can still count on one hand the number of dresses I own that do not brush my knees (I rarely wear pants). I also do not take anyone home with me, unless it's an exhausted sister-friend like Penelope who doesn't feel the urge to trek to her own home after dropping me off. By my estimation, I go to parties pretty often, yes, but I am not a party girl.

My parents, especially my father, do not agree.

Since I practically forced Evan to break up with me, I've reverted to my old ways, from the old country.

My first semester of college, my mother recalls me remembering what time the sun came up when I was on my way home from breakfast after the club. She was sure I was failing all of my classes because all I did was party. (I actually only went out Thursday through Sunday, college nights, because I didn't have a 21+ ID until two months after graduation.)

When my grades came in over Christmas break and I'd managed a 3.6 GPA, she shook her head. "You'd have a four-point-oh if you actually studied instead of partying," she told me.

"You're probably right," I said. "But I want to see the world, not just read about it."

She rolled her eyes. I went to take a nap. I hadn't really slept in weeks.

The last time I went to D.C. to visit my parents, I went out every night, as I usually do when I go home and get up with my high school and college crew.

On the last night of my visit, my father saw fit to sit me down in the living room for a "talk." We had not had an official talk since Miami, almost three years before when he told me about insecure men. Before that, it was when I left to go to grad school at NYU, and that talk was something about avoiding money pyramids, as if that was the biggest danger lurking in the most populated city in the country.

Our latest awkward conversation went something like this.

Him: "I, uh, am seeing some things I don't like. Uh, some things you need to change."

Me: "Hmm. Really? Like?"

Him: "Well, uh, I see you, uh . . . doing some things that you don't need to be doing at *this age.*"

Me: (*again*) "Hmm. Really? (*long pause*) Like?"

Him: "Well, you, uh, you're always at the parties, and, uh, you know, no man wants *to marry* a woman who's always at the parties, uh, uh . . . a party girl. A man might like to party with the party girls, but, uh, you know (*longer pause*) no one takes a party girl seriously in that way."

Me: "Huh?"

So, like, because I'm out where some guy also is four nights a week, I can't be taken seriously? Can he be taken seriously if he's always out where I am? I mean, if I'm out and he's out, why can't he and I party together for the foreseeable future in bass-driven bliss? If a woman likes to party, evidently a man who could label her as a "party girl" does, too, being as how he's seeing her out and about so often that he can apply the label. Shouldn't that just mean that the man and the woman have something they enjoy in common—at least, one thing he doesn't have in common with the boring girl he thinks he wants but will be leaving at home all those nights?

And who ever said anything about wanting to get married? When I brought Evan home for Thanksgiving, my dad was the only person who told me I had all the time in the world to think about marriage. This year, I should be hitched? What changed?

These are all questions I should have asked Daddy. Instead, I just sat on the La-Z-Boy, one of the four in the living room since my parents don't like couches, trying to form a coherent thought. I'm sure I had some sort of perplexed look on my face. He officially ended our talk with a quick "Good night," then turned the overhead light out on me and left me basking in the glow of the flat-screen TV.

I still can't figure out if I'm most offended that:

(A) My father has implied that I'm too old to be going out. What should I be doing? Baking muffins? Producing babies? Knitting scarves?

(B) He thinks I should actually care what some men I don't know and am not interested in knowing (especially if they have a problem with a woman who doesn't sit in the house) think about what I do.

(C) Although I have never expressed any desire whatsoever to get married, he thinks marriage is or should be somewhere on my horizon *now*.

(D) He actually thinks I'm a "party girl," a label so disdainful that he sputtered all over the words the same way a good Southern Baptist grandmother would respond to hearing the f-word.

(E) All of the above.

E. Definitely E.

GET OVER MR. EX

I was beyond drunk. It was my official birthday party and my unofficial Get Over Greg party. There are pictures to prove what I did, and the stories of what I said and did filtered in from friends for weeks afterward. I didn't dance on any tables, and I didn't manhandle any male suitors . . . well, no one that didn't want me to. All things considered, I think I was well behaved when I had every excuse to act a fool.

I invited a very attractive man, Isaiah, to party with me that night. If all had gone according to my weeklong, ish-talking plan, he would have been my birthday gift to myself.

The plan was to gauge Isaiah's interest and, if he was indeed up for it, invite him over to my house for an after party in which he would strip me down to my birthday suit, then grant me access to all six feet of his chiseled Panamanian self. I'd ask him to stop by the *bodega* to pick up a three-pack of Magnums (two for the night, one for the morning), put on R. Kelly's *TP-2.Com* (every Black person still has *TP-2.Com* on their iPod), and we'd act out scenes from a mild porno.

He showed up at 60 Thompson late enough to make an entrance and looking delicious as always. When he walked, he moved in slow motion. Yes, he was that fine. We met years ago at an artist showcase at the Canal Room. We were there to see an up-and-coming rapper, Kanye West. Since we knew each other, when Isaiah took a seat on the couch next to me to offer his *feliz cumpleaños* and conversation, it was comfortable, as it always was.

When I got up to dance, he joined me on the floor, and when I backed my booty up on him, I made no pretense that this was "just dancing." I reached my arms behind me, rubbing the back of his smooth bald head as I wound up against him to a reggae song.

When I finally turned to face him a couple of songs later, I fumbled with the buttons on his shirt, trying to undress him right there on the dance floor. God bless Aliya, who was in town for the weekend. She saw my impaired motor skills and came over to help, then placed my hands on Isaiah's chocolate chest. As soon as I felt that firm line that sat squarely between his pecs, I froze. God is a woman. A man could never make something as lovely, as beautiful, as perfect as that.

Evidently, he got the message I was sending, because he took my hand, the one on his chest, and slid it, slowly, lower until it was below his belt.

I looked up at him, biting my bottom lip, and I didn't move my hand as I waited for what came next.

"You know," he began. A huge smile spread across his face. "I would love to fulfill any needs you might have tonight and for the future." He said it with a conviction that left me with no doubt as to his sincerity.

Hot damn! This is what I've been waiting for.

But what did I do after a few chocolate martinis and a couple of tequila shots? (And yes, I was back on hard liquor again.)

Fumbled.

I don't know why I waited 'til then to ask. "What's your situation? You know, do you have a woman, or are you otherwise occupied?"

He had a girl. And I had a moment of clarity. In my drunkest state of mind, my sisterhood solidarity kicked in.

I'm sure I slurred my words when I told this man, who was the epitome of physical perfection, something like "I respect relationships. If you ever find yourself unattached, find me."

I stuck my index finger into his chest and reeled back on my stilettos from the impact and those two shots of tequila. He took my arm to stabilize me.

On my drunkest of drunk nights, I was still a lady.

Or maybe I was a fool.

Or maybe both.

HENNY. MIXED.

I was at my work desk, editing a particularly racy romance novel by Niobia Bryant, when my e-mail in-box went *ding*! It was an invite announcing that my favorite hip-hop magazine just got itself a new editor in chief. Hennessey, in a celebration/ marketing move, was honoring his ascent to the top of the masthead with a party at the very sexy Rivington Hotel. I RSVP'd immediately.

I'm usually not a dark-drink girl. My drink of choice when I'm not swilling champagne is always rum- or vodka-based. But the mini-bar is serving up cognac mojitos that taste like juice. Despite not eating since lunch, I drink one as I head to the rooftop deck over-looking Manhattan.

It's a gorgeous view, a perfect night with a slight breeze, and everyone I love in the city is up here, too. I talk, I laugh, I flirt with a young friend, too tall, too thin for my taste but just as cute and as interested in me as he can be. I'm flattered and amused that I can still pull guys barely out of college. (I promised him that I'd give him a shot at dating me when he turns thirty.) I see old friends, and I make new ones. At some point, my young friend says he's headed back to the bar and asks if I'd like another drink.

"Oh, no. I'm not even done with this one," I say gleefully.

"You will be by the time I'm back," he says with a wink.

While he's gone, I end up talking to Dean, a short, fat, unattractive man with a great personality. Even that is great. Everything is great. Yes, I am giddy. Yes, I am silly. But I am very far from drunk.

At least, I think so until I'm in a cab with friends on the way to Brooklyn around midnight, and suddenly, the motion of the car doesn't seem to agree with me. I make it home without hurling. Make it inside my apartment just fine. I plop onto the bed facedown and wonder. *How much did I drink?* I run through the number of drinks in my mind. I've done much worse and been much better. *What the hell is wrong with me?*

My phone vibrates next to my head. It's a text from Penelope telling me to drink water and stay off my phone. No texting. "Was I that bad?" I type back.

She tells me I wasn't. I'm not convinced.

I wake up the next morning with a hangover. I'm so disappointed with myself. I'm racking my brain about what I did last night that would make P think I was done, which clearly I was if I have a hangover.

I don't think I said or did anything crazy . . . did I? I was silly, simple perhaps, ditzy maybe. But that could be me on any given Monday with the right amount of sunshine in the sky. That's nothing to tell me to put my phone down about.

There's a message from Dean waiting in my in-box when I arrive at work twenty minutes late. Less because of my hangover and more so because it's raining heavy and the trains are delayed. I remember giving him my card because he was so funny and nice. In the e-mail, he says it was great to meet me, and he gives me a run-down of the services offered by the luxury-car company he owns. I respond with a polite thank you and say it was nice to meet him as well.

Later that morning, he calls to say hello. He doesn't have a fat man's voice. It's very smooth, hint of a Queens accent, but professionally polished. Lots of rumbling bass, and he laughs from the gut—a sign of genuine humor. If only he looked as good as he sounded.

He asks me what I'm doing later, if I'd like to accompany him to a private party at Gustavino's, hands down the most beautiful event space in New York City, with its floor-to-ceiling windows and beautiful gardens. I decline without explanation.

Dean asks if maybe we can get up later in the week. Maybe, emphasis on *maybe*, next week I can be free. Again, I don't want to mislead the man into thinking I am remotely interested in him as anything beyond a business associate or a friend. I tell him to call next week and we'll see.

The following week, Dean calls bright and early on a Monday to ask if I read the e-mail about his company that he sent the night after we met. I tell him I have not. He jokes with me about being so busy, says I must have a boyfriend or something. I answer that I do not; I'm just that busy working (and partying).

"No boyfriend?" He sounds surprised.

"No boyfriend."

He tells me that he is coming my way around noon to drop off an informational packet about his luxury-car services. I have no idea why he is so eager to get me interested in this. He's too nice for me to tell him no. I agree to meet him downstairs at the appointed time, but add I can't stay long as I'm reading on a deadline.

He calls thirty minutes before he is supposed to arrive to ask my cross streets. I'm a long walk from where he is, but he'll trek over anyway. Good exercise, he says. It only occurs to me then that perhaps his journey has less to do with his company and is more about seeing me. *Aw. That's sweet.* But the short, fat, unattractive man doesn't stand a chance. I feel bad that he is going so far out of his way. Did I mislead him?

Ten minutes later, he calls to say he's close. I should meet him in the lobby. I lollygag getting down there. I don't want to go. I'm thinking he might hit on me, and I will have to shut him down face-to-face. I should have told him I had a boyfriend.

I don't even bother to check and freshen my makeup or hair. I don't care if Dean finds me attractive. I will get the packet, and then I will send the short, fat, unattractive man on his way quickly.

I get to the lobby, and there is no sign of him. I look past the revolving doors and see a man with his back to me. He's tall, wide in the shoulders, and narrow in the waist. He is not even moving, but he is swaggering where he stands and wearing the stone-cold hell out of a black suit. Now, *that* is fine. And I can't even see his face. I forget about Dean and go outside to get a closer look at Mr. Swagger, to see if his front is as lovely as his back. I sneak up behind him and stand over to the side checking him out. He looks focused, has his game face on. He's waiting on a woman, no doubt. *Lucky chick.*

I look past him and down the block for Dean.

"Demetria?"

I turn. Mr. Tall, Dark, and Handsome is speaking to me, calling me by my government name. *Do I know you?* I want to blurt.

"I was scared I wouldn't recognize you if you had a hat on or something," he jokes, then spreads his arms wide and wraps them around me.

Who is this fine man hugging me?

"Here." He holds out a bag. "This is for you."

I look inside. It's a bunch of press materials and a hat with Dean's company logo. I look up. Dean is gorgeous.

"It's good to see you," he says.

He's smiling at me. I don't think I've said one word to him yet. "Yeahhhh," I slur out, trying to get a hold of myself. It's not really a direct response to his statement, but it's the best I can do. I'm staring at a fine grown man. The old-school type who pays the mortgage and sends me off to gather the groceries. The type who would meet me at the truck and carry them inside.

How in the hell did I miss this? I must have been drunk. Liquor usually makes people think folks look better than they do. Henny Mixed has made a fine man seem ugly?

"Too bad you're working though lunch. It's a beautiful day. I'd love to take you out." He looks out at the street.

I stop staring at him long enough to look out, too, and realize there are sunbeams everywhere.

"Yeahhhh," I slur again. I want to slap myself. I am not on any deadlines upstairs. My coast is clear. Basic dignity and an aversion to looking desperate keep me from telling him that I lied and I can go wherever he wants to take me.

"It's supposed to be nice tomorrow as well. But you're busy then, too." He sounds regretful.

I nod. I'm staring at him again. "Yeahhh."

God is a comedian. Only Dave Chappelle, Chris Rock, or Larry David could think up a scenario like this. Give a woman what she asks for. Make her so drunk she can't even realize it, and when it dawns on her that she has gotten it, she will have screwed it up so that she cannot keep it. *Wowzers*. This is like some Shakespearian comedy. Maybe this ends with a wedding, too?

"So next week you'll be free?" he asks, turning his attention from the sun and back to me.

I smile. "Yeahhh." I think I sound a little less slow this time.

He beams. I mean, bright beam, headlight-sees-deer-in-the-bright-light beam. "Then maybe we should get together for lunch or, better, dinner? I'd love to take you out." He takes my hand. Holds it. He looks so sincere.

"Yeahhh." My cheeks hurt from smiling so wide for so long.

"Well, I'll let you get back to work. I know you're busy." He gives my hand a little squeeze, then turns to swagger down the block into the high noon sun where he came from.

I watch him go until I realize I'm watching him go. Then I go back inside. *How did I miss all that fine?* I ask myself as I get on the elevator to my floor. *Was I that drunk?* But I couldn't have been that far gone, because I had sense enough to make sure that dude got my number. I shake my head in wonder at my own self.

Henny. Mixed.

I got to stop drinking that ish.

NSFW

I met a guy, Noah, at my friend's birthday party at Hudson River Café in Harlem. I rarely travel above Fifty-seventh Street—blame my Brooklyn snobbery toward Harlem—but the latin cuisine venue is a diamond in an otherwise rough area.

I'd heard amazing things about Noah leading up to this impromptu encounter. We had lots of mutual friends, and everyone spoke highly of him. When we finally encountered each other, he lived up to his hype. He was deep without trying to be and gentlemanlike. We exchanged numbers, and I was looking forward to hearing from him . . . but not like this.

I looked down at my phone, rereading his text. I was on the four train to Brooklyn, headed home from another night out, this time a magazine launch at the Studio Museum in Harlem. The text came through at the Nevins subway station, one of the few places you can get a signal underground. It read: "Kiss. You pick which lips."

Ugh. I'm more of a "Hey, just thinking about you" or "Have a wonderful day" kinda girl. I was a little offended that Noah would come at me like that, especially since our first conversation was about the marketing power of social networking, not anything sexual.

That text was the third one Noah had sent, and each one was increasingly worse.

I remember talking to a bunch of guys once about what women need to know most about men, and many said that men don't know it all. They act as if they do, of course. But generally, when a man effs up, it's not with the intent to do so. Sometimes you've just got to tell him what he did or is doing wrong. So I wrote back to Noah, letting him know that his texts were habitually stepping on the line circling my comfort zone.

He wrote back, apologizing profusely. The next time I saw him, he apologized again. He seemed genuinely sorry. And from then on, anytime he texted me, it was along the lines of "Hey, D, what's good?"

I was glad I'd said something. Otherwise, I could have lost a potential friend over an error in his judgment. He was a good dude who did a bad thing. I often say you have to learn the difference between a good man who effs up and an effed-up man given to occasional moments of grandeur.

A MONTH LATER

I threw a "house party" Saturday night with Bonnie, who lives across the hall. Three hundred people in the backyard of our building partying till four A.M. My BlackBerry was dead most of the night, so no e-mails came through. I realized this when the party ended and charged my phone.

I was sorting through a ton of messages while sitting on my

kitchen counter drinking water from a gallon jug, when I noticed one e-mail came from a guest at the party. It was from Noah, a.k.a. Good Guy Who Does Bad Things. *Er?* The subject read *"NSFW"* (not safe for work).

My curiosity got the best of me. I clicked. In summary, he said he's insecure about his looks, but is great at sex as his penis is very large. He talks to women about sex all the time because he's confident in his ability to please. He wants to know if I think he has a problem.

There were five attachments to his e-mail. As I waited for them to download, I felt a bit bad for him. He had such a low opinion of himself, and despite the negative traits he pointed out, I still thought he was really cute.

When the pictures arrived, I saw that they were, *all of them*, shots of his very hard penis from different angles. I wondered if he took them in the bathroom at my party[1] or if he actually kept pictures of his penis on his phone.

I sat on the e-mail for two days. I was completely blown but I didn't know how to respond or even if I should. Like a big reaction was what he wanted, right? I mean, that's why a guy shows a woman his penis on her phone, right? Then I was, like, dude was a perv, certifiably nuts, and I didn't want to flip and have him excited by the attention and continue doing pervish things. I mean, was this the beginning of some stalker ish?[2]

I told Penelope about the e-mail, and she called me a prude. "How big was it?" she asked. "Forward me the pics."

---

1 Viewing them on my computer later, I verified that he did not. I would give you my opinion of the width, length, and girth, but you have to figure that if someone keeps a series of pictures of his penis on his camera phone, he must feel that it's something to write home about.

2 In retrospect, I'm not sure writing about it is the best idea, either, if all he wanted was attention. But it's a tale worth telling, so here it is.

Bonnie was equally confused. "I'm sorry, what?" she began. "You're mad that a man with a big dick is interested in having sex with you? Am I missing something here?"

I questioned my outrage until I read the e-mail again. *Nope. Uh-uh. Still offended. I have to say something.*

I finally wrote to him: "I'm extremely uncomfortable with your last e-mail. Please don't contact me again."

He wrote back ten minutes later explaining he was "drunk and high." He understands my reaction and is very sorry.

I've been drunk. I've been high. (I was at a coffee shop in Amsterdam. It was legal.) I've done some amazingly dumb ish. I've never gotten the urge to send pics of my va-jay-jay or even my breasts from my camera phone or my computer. I don't even have pics of my va-jay-jay. Do most people? Am I rare?

The following morning, I was at my desk, typing away. My boss was on vacation, and I was still swamped. One of the guys from the mailroom called my name, pulling my attention away from my computer screen.

I turned around and found him carrying a gigantic orchid. He set the cellophane-wrapped flower on my desk.

I looked at him. I looked at the orchid. I looked back at him. "What is that?"

He looked at me. He looked at the orchid. He looked back at me. "It's for you."

"No, it's not."

He nodded. "It is."

I spotted the card and tore into the plastic to get it. Did Dean send me flowers? Did that amazing, wonderful, gorgeous man send me this gigantic thing? I hadn't had a man send me flowers since Evan. I ripped open the envelope excitedly and pulled out the card.

It was from Good Guy Who Does Bad Things, whom I'd since come to think of as Bad Guy Given to Occasional Moments of

Grandeur. I was deflated and immediately plopped into my chair to read it: "Blah, blah, blah. Sorry. Blah, blah, blah. Forgive me."

I looked up at the gigantic orchid towering over me. It reminded me of a huge, curved penis. Just like the pictures on my BlackBerry.

This was not irony. I should have sent it back. But then, it wasn't as if he'd ever know. Was the florist going to call and tell him? They'd either trash it—a shame, because it really was beautiful— or resell it.

I told the mailroom guy the backstory about the orchid. He agreed with my assessment that there was phallic imagery going on. He was disgusted, too.

"You keeping it?" he asked.

"I dunno."

Keeping the orchid wasn't about the orchid. It was about whether I'd forgive the dude. I couldn't figure out if he had made an honest mistake . . . again and I was being prudish, hypersensitive, or unusually conservative about the whole thing. Or if he was an effing pervert and I was having problems accepting that because he had such good word-of-mouth.

I thought about Dakar. I had the same problem judging him, too. Since that incident, I read a book by Gordon Livingston, *Too Soon Old, Too Late Smart: Thirty True Things You Need to Know Now.* Livingston is a psychiatrist with thirty years in the game. The first rule on his list is "If the map doesn't agree with the ground, the map is wrong."

I kept the orchid. I forgave but refused to speak to Noah again.

THE MORNING COMMUTE

I walked down the steps to the train one Friday when I was headed to work, and I thought, *How hilarious would it be if I ran into Cecil?* I didn't want to see him. Just thought it was funny that he was there so often, we'd stopped speaking, and I'd never seen him again.

Cecil was this guy I used to bump into on the train all the time. One week, we saw each other five times going to or coming from work. And we began seeing each other at industry events, staring at each other across the room.

I hadn't thought about him in a few weeks by then. After we first stopped speaking, I was nervous daily about running into him. I wondered how I would react when I saw him, if he would say or do anything crazy. He seemed like a nice guy, but then I found out he wasn't.

I reached the bottom of the steps, and whom did I see waiting for the train?

I go momentarily blank. Instead of walking to where I usually wait (his direction), I turn and go the opposite way. I've let my guard down too long to remember how I planned to react.

I stare blankly ahead, waiting for the train, and I can't help but laugh out loud at the way life works. And then? Well, then I realize this mofo is headed my way.

I don't look at him when he says hello.

"Go back to where you were sitting," I say in my adult voice. That's the one with the bass in it.

"Huh?" Cecil asks. "I can't say hi?"

I want to give him the are-you-kidding-me? look, but I will not give him the attention he clearly wants. "No."

"Oh." Pause. "Well, your hair looks nice, by the way."

"Uh-huh."

He walks a bit away but stands with his back to me while he waits for the train. I envision kicking him in the ass so he falls on the tracks.

The train finally comes. He walks forward to get on one car. I walk back to take another one.

I get off the subway forty minutes later, stop by Starbucks for my morning caramel apple cider and banana nut muffin. At my desk, I eat and check my Outlook, then a gossip site I'm addicted to, then my personal e-mail.

Well, I'll be . . .

There's a message from Cecil.

Months earlier, there is a fabo Fashion Week party at the Bentley dealership. I am standing at the bar with Penelope, twirling a piece of my fluff around my index finger and waiting for my drink. That's when the very lovely, bearded specimen I keep seeing on the train to and from work appears beside me. He elbows for room at the bar, bumping me.

"Mister," I say, glaring at him and pushing back into my space. "I know you see me standing here."

He assesses me for a few moments without saying anything. Then finally blurts, "You need a perm."

What?

I fix my mouth to curse him, and he cuts me off. "You're trying too hard for attention. I like it, though. But I still think you should perm it."

What?

I cannot find my voice for some reason. Then he pulls my hair. Smiles. Is he flirting with me?

"What's your name, cutie?" he asks.

He is.

God help me, but I find his surliness attractive. We chat about everything except the usual things people chat about when they first meet. He's talking about glass-bottom boats, the percentage of men in the United States who stand six feet or taller (14.5 percent), and perms, of course. He orders our drinks when the bartender returns. "You'll have what I'm having," he says. He hands me my glass of whatever, and, with a wink, he departs.

The rest of the night, he makes a point to speak every time he passes me. He stops by once, taking my near-empty glass and replacing it with a fresh drink. Another time, he pulls my hair. Again. And yet another time, he sidles up to Penelope and introduces himself as my "future ex-husband." He catches me on the dance floor doing my slightly tipsy two-step—normal for D.C., odd for NYC—and he grabs my hand and we dance. No bumping and grinding and backing it up—actual, real dancing. We are totally in sync. He knows my next move before I do. I'm totally feeling his energy.

"Mister, who are you?" I squeal.

He introduces himself with facts this time. Turns out he lives a block away from me and he works with my friend Zee. We chat for a bit until his ride, who's been getting backed up on by Penelope, heads our way. Mister's boy has sealed the deal and gotten P's info, and the friend is ready to bounce.

Before he departs, I suggest to Mister, "We should all hang out sometime." I never ask for a man's number, just let him know I am interested and available for pursuit. He agrees. Tells me to get his info through my girl, who will get it from his friend.

Oh, damn. Mister is cool but evidently uninterested. Men are never too busy to exchange contact info with a woman they are feeling.

The next day, Zion, Mister's coworker and my friend, hits me to ask how I enjoyed the party since his events team put it together. I tell him the truth: it was dope. He asks what was up with me and Cecil. He saw us kicking it.

"Nothing," I say. "He wasn't interested."

"Hmm. Well, that's good," Zee says.

"Huh?"

"I *think* he's married."

I knot my brows together. Oh. Well, I guess that is good indeed.

Two days later, I get an e-mail from Cecil saying something along the lines of hello, it was nice to meet you, I think you're beautiful, what your interests are, who you be with, things that make you smile, what numbers to dial, etc.

Huh?

I hit him back to ask, "How'd you get my e-mail?"

He got it from his boy, who got it from Penelope. *This effort from an allegedly married man?* I think back, trying to remember if he wore a ring. I don't know that I looked for one. Zion only thinks he's married. Is he really?

I guess I should have just asked Mister point-blank, but in my naïveté, I assume he can't be. Married whores take what's thrown their way, but they don't still *hunt* women . . . right?

Along with his explanation of how he found me, Cecil's listed a run-down of himself in his reply. It's impressive, admittedly. But how old is he? He's way too accomplished to be four years or less older than me. I ask. He's got me by eight. This again? The older-guy thing, as before, has its perks, but extraordinary drawbacks too. Cecil asks if his age is a problem for me.

"Why would it be? I converse with people of any age. That's all we're doing," I write back.

"So what if we were to be more?" he asks.

· "More . . . than friends?"

"Friends don't let friends run their hands through all that pretty hair. I ain't trying to be your friend, D."

I get off e-mail and hit Zion.

"Zee, it's Demi. Are you sure Cecil is married? Like, is he divorced or separated or something? I don't do married dudes of any fashion," I ramble. "He's pushing up forreal, forreal."

"Uh, D, lemme call you back." *Click.*

Later that night, I get a call from Zion. Seems when I called him, he hit the speaker button to answer, and when I blurted out my question, Cecil, *his boss,* was standing at his desk. Zee gives me the run-down. Mister is married. Three kids. The youngest isn't even a year.

What?

Cecil doesn't call or e-mail after that, but I do bump into him at a party two weeks later. He comes by, says hello, snatches my glass, and takes a long gulp. I see the wedding band on his finger as he tilts my white wine to his lips. How did I miss that?

"You don't want my germs?" he asks when I look at him crazy and refuse my glass. He flashes those teeth I once thought so pretty.

"I don't know where your mouth has been."

He screws up his face. "You still mad at me, D?"

I shake my head. "You're a married man," I say, cutting to the chase. "Act like one."

Instead of wasting my time trying to explain what he should already know. I walk away. I don't care if he's there for the kids, if he and the wife sleep in separate rooms, or if they're actually separated (i.e., still married). I'm nobody's mistress.

The e-mail from Cecil reads:

> *Are you really that mean and cold?*
> *Did I really hurt your feelings that much? I made an effort to move forward and you keep shutting me down. I guess what has me most upset is that you are treating me like I'm this evil pariah when we both know I'm not. I think you're a decent person despite how you treat me and I hope we can be friends one day.*

My immediate reaction: *Hurt? He thinks I won't talk to him because I'm hurt?*

In my angst, I pound out a response reminding him that he didn't tell me he was married before he e-mailed me telling me he wasn't trying to be my friend. I write that I don't speak to him not because I'm hurt but because if he took vows before God and everyone he knows to be faithful to his wife and he attempts to step out on her with a woman who lives around the corner from his family, then what kind of friend could his no-morals-and-no-character-having self be to me? I ask him again not to call or text or speak to or e-mail me anymore. And then I tell him he's a married whore. And I add a P.S. telling him to step his game up. He's over thirty. He shouldn't still be pretending to be the victim when *he* messed up.

I look at the screen and reread it. Edit it for typos and clarity. (I'm a writer, I can't help it.) But then I can't push send. I realize that what he wants more than anything is a response. Any response, even an angry one, is communication and starts a dialogue. The opposite of like is indifference. To send it would be to play his game. I push delete instead.

I try to do something relatively work-related, but I can't focus. I can't believe the audacity of this so-called man. How could he not get why I won't speak to him?

I focus long enough to do what I always do in times of social distress: find Tariq. I forward him Cecil's original e-mail. Tariq gives it a read and hits me back with his evaluation:

> It appears you are upset on behalf of all married women who have had their husbands cheat on them. So he is, like, "What the hell? I have moved on, and you haven't. Why are you mad at me?"
>
> Because you're not willing to help him cheat, he still respects you and wants to be a friend. It's a spin on the "keep your friends close and your enemies closer" outlook. Instead, he is wanting to keep the attractive girl close just in case one day something can happen. And if it can't? Well, it's okay, I still have her as a friend and her friends may do something. A man can never have too many attractive female friends . . . :-)

THE ATLANTA FIASCO

New York City is covered in snow. The heat in my apartment sucks. I've taken to sleeping on the couch in the living room under a pile of blankets and my comforter to keep warm. I pay a mint in rent, work a full-time job and keep a side hustle, and I have nothing to show for it other than a New York zip code and an apartment that I love . . . three seasons out of four. What happened to the high life I was supposed to be living when I got those two degrees by twenty-two?

I need a vacation. Somewhere warm. Anything over sixty degrees will do. And I need to crash with a friend because I have no money for a hotel *and* shopping.

I ask the universe for amusement; it responds with something I never expect. The next morning, Eddie calls from Atlanta. Eddie is a friend from the Old Country, i.e., Maryland, and I love him dearly. We met through friends back when I was on my way to becoming a freshman in college. We were both sixteen, and he would come over to my house after football practice, and we'd eat ice cream on my parents' front porch. He's also the source of one of my top-five dates, sitting on the steps of the Jefferson Memorial at midnight and talking for hours. When a guy has a personality and something to say, he doesn't need to spend money to be memorable.

We've shared adventures over the years—me almost drowning in the shallow end of the heated pool at his mother's house, him defending me from oversized attacking raccoons in the suburbs, him introducing me to Lil' Kim's *Hardcore* while driving 100 mph on the Beltway when he decided our lives should be best lived as a blur.

Eddie: (Pedal to the metal.) "These are the times of our life, D."

Me: (Buckling my seatbelt.) "It's always the overachieving students who die in car accidents, you know."

Eddie: "We should drop out of school, then . . . Oh, and a seatbelt is pretty useless if we crash at this speed."

I almost killed him once when he passed out after a party at his house. He fell out of the shower onto the bathroom rug, and in an attempt to get in to save him, I banged the door against his head.

His cousin was in town from Atlanta when the shower incident happened, assumed incorrectly that I was dating Eddie, and told me to put underwear on the drunk, naked boy.

Me: "Uh . . . he's not my boyfriend. I've never touched his penis."

The cousin: "He's family, but I'm not touching his dick."

There's a standoff over the drunk, naked boy until one of my friends, Brittany, declares, "I don't know what y'all have against big dicks, but I have no problem touching them. What drawer are the draws in?"

That's life with Eddie around.

He went to school in Atlanta when he graduated a year or two after me. We've been friends from a distance, except for the summers he returned to Maryland when I was still living there. Whenever we're around each other, we pick up where things left off.

I tell Eddie, whom I haven't seen in years, my current woes about needing a vacation. He tells me to come on down. I can crash with him.

The last time I saw Eddie, he was relatively clean-cut and wore pressed Polos daily. He drove a Q45 (twenty-first birthday present) and was an athlete, which means he drank but never smoked because of wind sprints. When he shows up at the airport (late), he pulls up in what he describes as a "vintage" something or other. It's an old hooptie with a decent paint job and a booming system. And when he opens the door to greet me and put my stuff in the trunk, it's like a Snoop video when a puff of smoke exits along with him. My clean-cut boy has a grill now. And dreds. Not cute, perfectly coiled locs; this is half-tamed and raggedy. Oh, and big black glasses. *Lil Wayne*, I think. *He moved south and turned into Lil Wayne.* What the hell happened to Eddie?

Eddie's townhouse is immaculate. A mini-version of his mom's home in Maryland. And that would make sense, since she decorated it, and Eddie, despite his appearance, is a neat freak. He tells me about his roommate, a rapper who had a moderate hit a few years earlier. Eddie takes my bags up to his room, where I'll be crashing with him. It's no problem. It's Eddie. We can sleep next to each other in harmony.

Friday is pretty tame. After we eat, we pick up two of his friends, also from D.C., at the airport. I've partied with one of them, Ty, a bunch of times at the Ritz or V.I.P. with Eddie in D.C.

Most of the afternoon, the guys sit downstairs smoking and playing video games and going crazy over some leaked Wayne mix tape. I go upstairs and read a book, a dog-eared copy of *Their Eyes Are Watching God* to let them have man time. Everyone's content.

Around eleven, Eddie wakes me from a nap to send me to the

shower to get ready first. I get all dolled up as I have no clue where the fun will take us. Eddie carefully picks out an "outfit" from his massive closet that will leave him looking sloppy and thrown together. I don't get it. I just don't get it. I see the Polos in there.

I put on my makeup while he presses his boxers and undershirt and jeans but not his shirt. He's telling me about one of the chicks he's dating, Anne from Ohio.

"She's crazy but has an amazing body," Eddie says. He breaks out the naked pictures as if I will get a kick out of them.

"Cute girl," I say. She's kneeling on his bed in a lace bra and panties in one; she's bent over touching her toes in a thong in the other. By the blur on the second picture, I assume she was in mid-booty-clap when the camera snapped. (Note to women: I have tons of guy friends. All they ever do with the naked pictures is show them to their boys to admire and their female friends to get a reaction.)

"Cute? That's it?"

"I'm a chick. I want to look at booties and boobies, I look in the mirror."

"Speaking of which, your ass is bigger."

I make a face at him in the mirror. "You think I'm getting fat?" I ask in horror.

He rolls his eyes. "Have you ever heard a Black man complain about a big ass?"

We head to Compound, a massive see and be seen nightclub, which features a pond as its centerpiece. Atlanta's traffic is always a pain, but it's even worse tonight. When we finally arrive at one A.M., the line is banoodles, and it's a hundred dollars for men to get in. We all agree: no way.

I'm the most annoyed, likely because I'm the only completely sober one in the car. Eddie, the driver, is high but not drunk. He told me that we'd stop by the liquor store for a bottle for me, as all he had in the house was Hennessey. Lots and lots of Hennessey. And no chaser. Um . . . (We already know what happens with me and Henny. Mixed.)

Eddie decides that our best option for the night is the strip club down the block. It shouldn't be more than twenty to get in. I have never been to a strip club. He promises me that Atlanta strip clubs are almost like regular clubs, but you know, like, with butt-naked chicks. I will not be the only fully dressed woman present.

I'm game . . . as long as I can go to the liquor store first. There's no way I can sit sober in a strip club for the thirty minutes it will take to get a buzz and not annoy everyone around me with feminist rhetoric about how degrading the environment is to women.

Eddie says the liquor store is inconvenient and the strip club is *right there.* Ty announces from the backseat that I will have to man up and take the Hennessey.

"I'm a woman," I remind him. "Can we at least get chaser?"

Eddie intervenes. "D, you're rolling with the Fellas this weekend. Be one of the boys."

"Henny? Straight?"

"It's not gin," he counters.[1] "You can do it. I got you. What's gonna happen?" He squeezes my thigh.

I've trusted him with my life before, and I'm still here. Nothing bad has ever happened to me with Eddie around. "Fine," I say. "Henny. Straight."

We park in the lot, and the guys go in while I drink in the car with Eddie. When I'm good, Eddie pays. "Something doesn't feel right about you paying to watch ass shake," he observes.

---

1 I'm deathly allergic to gin. Eddie was with me on the night I figured this out. Hives. Projectile hurling. Bad, bad night.

We find the Fellas at a table next to the stage. There's only one seat left, so I take it while Eddie goes to look for a chair.

While he's in search, his boy decides on a lap dance. Respectfully, he leans back and asks me if it's okay with me.

"Sure."

I can't watch though. I'm drunk, but I'm afraid that if I look the dancer in the face, I will see some sign of oppression or self-hate, and I won't be able to stay in the room. I look at the stage instead. I don't have on my glasses, so the girls' faces are pretty much a blur.

There's a woman on the pole inching herself up it with no hands, all thigh muscle. The chick gets to the top, leans back, and twirls herself down—still no hands—and finally makes use of her hands to do a slow-motion back flip off, land in a split, then pop her coochie on the floor like she's in an old-school Luke video. This chick belongs in Cirque du Soleil—but she'll probably make more money here.

There's another woman on the side of the stage, closer to me, who is doing a booty clap with each cheek going an opposite direction. And she's doing it in slow motion. My tush doesn't do that. If I try all this decade and next, my tush will not do that. I'm hypnotized by her booty. I think the same thing I did when I stared at the ceiling of the Sistine Chapel with Dude: It does nothing for me, but I can appreciate great art.

Eddie returns with a chair . . . and a naked woman he introduces as Cicely. I awkwardly stick out my hand. She leans in for a hug instead. She's uncommonly friendly, amazingly soft, and she's heard about me. Apparently, Eddie wasn't sure I would be comfortable at his house with all the boys, so he wanted a backup plan in case I wasn't. Cicely says she's working all weekend, but if I need girl time, I can hang out with some of her friends.

She asks for my phone and punches in her number, noting that she checks her phone in between dances and she's up anytime after two P.M. for me to call. Maybe we can go shopping tomorrow? She's rambling . . . naked. No draws. Just naked. All I can think is, *She's carrying on like we're standing outside the Louis Vuitton store in Lennox.* I thank her for the offer and promise I'll call if I need anything.

"You all right?" Eddie asks when she walks away—naked. I must have a stunned look on my face.

I forget about all of that looking at him. This dude is fine, and his arm is the size of my thigh. Suddenly, I cannot remember why we didn't date each other. He looks crazy, nothing like I remember, but he's still Eddie. And, well, bad hair and clothes can't hide fine.

Eddie takes a seat next to me and commences to playing in my hair as he talks to me about nothing right up in my ear. I am mellowed out. For once, my brain isn't on overdrive. I lean over and nuzzle into his neck. I am feeling him. Ty orders another dance, and that's when I realize the boys are on their second dance each. Eddie hasn't even had one.

"You want a dance?" I ask Eddie.

He laughs. "I don't suggest you dance in here, D."

"No, do you want me to buy you a dance?"

He smiles. "Sure. Pick a chick."

I decide on the one who can roll her tush in opposite directions. Eddie gets her attention and calls her over.

She's sweet as red velvet cake. Chats me up before she even looks at Eddie, then asks me if it's okay if he has a dance. This is like the best customer service ever. I've been in New York too long. I forgot about Southern hospitality.

I nod my approval.

"A double?" she asks.

I lean in to Eddie to ask what exactly that is.

"Two songs instead of one," he explains.

Oh. "Okay," I tell her.

Eddie's watching passively as a beautiful woman with bee-sting boobies and a booty bigger than Serena's wiggles, swerves, and gyrates for us. There's no hint of excitement in his eyes. I would think this is for my benefit, but Ty and the other guy do the same thing. They're all chilling as these naked women seductively take it all off and move it around. I expected strip clubs to be these wild dens of sin, with men pawing away at broke-down women who have seen better days and look disgusted with themselves. The women look happy and friendly as they dance. Oh, and they are beautiful. Detached, yes, but not like pitiful. It's no different from the look I have staring at my computer on the days I'm just going through the motions of work and waiting for six o'clock so I can go home and work on a freelance assignment.

Song one goes off, and the DJ plays a love song. All is well until the dancer leans back on the table, legs spread, bald va-jay-jay all in my face, and beckons me to her. I've broken out a mirror enough times to see my own; I don't need to see anyone else's.

I look at Eddie. He shrugs. I look at her. I shake my head. She literally pops her vagina less than an arm's reach from my face, way too close. I don't think mine does that. "No," I say definitively. She gets up and bends over in Eddie's face, clapping again. She's close enough that I can smell her. Apple spritz from Victoria's Secret. I wore the same scent in college.

When the second song is over, I pay, and she thanks me humbly. If she were a server at Houston's, I would have written in a thirty-percent tip. I give her an extra ten.

At four A.M., we leave. Eddie takes us to some hole in the wall with the best soul food I'd ever tasted. Back at the house, I shower, then change into one of his T-shirts and climb into the bed.

He cuts the light and gets in, facing me.

"You were drunk tonight," he begins.

"No, really?" I say sarcastically. Truth be told, I'm still not sober.

"I've seen you drunk before. You've never been all up on me."

"Henny. Straight," I remind him.

"Really? That's what it was?"

I know where this is going. "Uh-huh."

He kisses me.

Damn good but no chemistry. He's fine, but we've been friends too long. He's just my boy. He must think the same thing, 'cause he says, "I'm tired."

I nod into the pillow. "Me, too."

I roll over, scoot back toward him, and he throws an arm around me.

"Good night," we say to each other.

SATURDAY

I wake up sometime around one to the sound of Eddie's phone buzzing against the dresser over and over and over. Someone—a chick, no doubt—is blowing up his phone.

"Eddie," I say with a nudge to his ribs. "Answer your phone."

He moans in response.

The phone eventually stops buzzing . . . then starts right up again. I roll over and push him again. This time, that doesn't even get a response. He must be hungover, too. I pull the covers over my head to block out the sunlight and the noise.

It's three o'clock by the time I feel human, four-thirty by the time I'm dressed, and at five, we head back to the hole in the wall in the hood to grab something to eat. By the time we all reach the restaurant, Eddie's put his phone on silent. I lost count of how many times it had buzzed on the ride over.

"You know the chick who keeps calling is crazy, right?" I finally ask over fried fish, macaroni and cheese, and sweet tea (diabetes and a heart attack waiting to happen). I don't need him to tell me it's the same chick. I know.

He shakes his head and sucks at the BBQ sauce on his fingers at the same time. "She's young," he offers, taking another bite of a spare rib.

"She's crazy," I shoot back.

We all venture back to the house with the itis. The four of us lounge downstairs—the boys playing Madden and blazing, me sipping and half-asleep on Eddie's lap while he waits to play the winner.

By midnight, we're out again. Eddie has tracked down a go-go band playing in Buckhead, which I'm all for. I haven't been to a go-go since high school, but I listen to it almost every day.[1] There's a huge crowd—almost all D.C. heads—outside the venue door by the time we walk up a wide alley of clubs and find the one we're looking for. Eddie knows some guy working the party, which gets us to the front relatively quick. But that doesn't stop a female security guard from feeling *under* my bra for extra wire, then making me cross my legs at the ankle and bend over at the waist to make sure I'm not carrying any weapons *inside* my person. This is *after* I go through the metal detector.

Inside, I realize the place reminds me of the Taj Mahal back home in Maryland.[2] I'm a little shook. Despite the thorough security check at the door, I'm not all that assured that there are no weapons inside this club.

I have nothing to worry about. Eddie immediately spots some guys he knows and leads me to the front of the dance floor near

---

1 For the uninitiated, go-go music is a D.C.-based art form that's heavy on congos and cowbells and is best heard live.

2 It was a gutted warehouse off Benning Road that didn't at all live up to the glamour of its name. The first and last time I went there, the band kept shouting, "One fight, good night," but someone got shot (and killed) outside, and the band played on like the orchestra on the *Titanic*. I guess if you want to get technical, shooting isn't fighting. And the technicality is why I stopped going to go-go clubs.

the stage. I have no clue where the Fellas are, but I figure they'll be fine. They're boys in a club. They will amuse themselves.

Eddie hands off his phone to me to put in my purse so he won't lose it dancing. We spend the night working up a sweat. On the way to the car at four, I go barefoot, riding piggyback on Eddie with my heels in my hands.

We swing by McDonald's on the way to the house, and then we sit downstairs in sweaty club clothes eating and sobering up. At some point before we go up to bed, Eddie asks me to hand him his phone from my purse. I go to the couch to fish it out of my bag, and I flip it over.

Twelve missed calls?

I toss him the phone with a question. "E, that girl been over here before?"

"Nope." He finishes chewing. "Why?"

I shake my head. "Just asking."

"Uh-uh," Eddie says. "Speak, D."

"If she knew where you lived, she'd show up on your steps. Chick is crazy."

"You worry too much, D. Anne ain't coming over here," he says, brushing me off.

"She know I'm staying here?"

"I told her you were in town."

I repeat the question.

"Yeah, I told her."

"Have you talked to her this weekend?"

To my knowledge, he hasn't answered a call from her since I arrived.

"D, I got this," he insists.

I roll my eyes and drop it, wondering if he's lying.

*   *   *

By the time we go to bed an hour later, I'm borderline delirious from lack of sleep, too much liquor, and heavy food. Tomorrow's gonna be hell, because I have an eleven A.M. flight back to New York. I might get three hours of sleep. But it's all worth it. This was a desperately needed getaway from the city. As much as I love New York, sometimes I need a break from it to fully appreciate it.

I snuggle under the covers. Eddie, who's hot, is shirtless in boxers on top of the comforter. I've been asleep for maybe an hour when I stir to. The light is coming through the window.

I drift off back to sleep until there's a flurry of footsteps on the stairs. Maybe Eddie's roommate, whom we haven't seen all weekend, has returned. Then there's a loud *whoosh* and a sudden *bang*. I bolt upright in the bed, scared, and pumped full of adrenaline.

In the doorway is the shapely silhouette of a woman. She runs her hand along the wall, flips on the light.

I look at her with wide eyes.

She looks at me the same way.

Eddie lied to me. And he didn't tell Anne shit.

I smack Eddie's back with my open palm for maximum sting and so he wakes up immediately.

"You need to handle this," I tell him when he's halfway come to.

I get up, politely excuse myself past the shocked woman in the doorway, and head down the steps with my heart racing.

The Fellas are still tucked under blankets on the floor and the couch. Even in the dark, I can tell they're wide-eyed like kids at a day-care awakened at naptime, but forced to remain on their cots. They, like me, are waiting for the inevitable argument upstairs, but I'm waiting for the explanation first: How did Crazy get by them?

I sit on the couch at Ty's feet and grab some of his cover. He guesses whoever was last to come in last night must not have locked the door. Could be any of us. We were all pretty done. They both heard a sound (the door opening), but they never guessed who it was.

"How was I supposed to know it was her," Ty asks. "I thought it was Eddie's roommate. Where is that dude, anyway?"

We wait downstairs for the sounds of some screaming, some crashing from a thrown object, maybe a tussle when ol' girl most certainly tries to attack Eddie. But none of that happens. It's dead quiet. We're all sending quizzical looks back and forth when the silence is finally broken.

"D?"

Eddie is calling my name. I'm trying to figure out why when he calls again.

"D?" He's louder this time.

I look from one Fella to the other. They don't have a clue, either.

"Yes?" I holler back curiously.

"Come here."

Huh? I look at the Fellas again. They are just as confused as I am.

"D, come now, please," Eddie pleads.

I'm in an oversized T-shirt and Eddie's boxers. Not the best clothes to throw down in if this chick comes at me. I decide on step three that if she lunges at me, I'll jump on her and pin her down. I am not a fighter. By step eight, I decide to pick up the heaviest thing I can get my hands on and bash her with it if she makes any sudden moves. Maybe I am a fighter.

At the top of the stairs, I turn into the doorway of his room. Anne's sitting on the edge of the bed near the middle. Eddie is lying where I left him, but on his back with his hands behind his head as if he's chilling on a cushioned beach chair in the Caribbean.

Anne is gorgeous, as pretty in person as she was in the half-nekkid pictures Eddie showed me yesterday. Long black hair, smooth caramel skin, and a heart-shaped face with dimples that show even when she isn't smiling. She's young, too. Maybe twenty-two?

"Tell her," Eddie pushes.

Anne rises from the bed, her head practically bowed. She apologizes for interrupting my sleep, because she knows how early I have to be at the airport and she wasn't thinking properly when she disturbed me.

She goes on to say she was rude and disrespectful. And she hopes I can forgive her.

I'm sorry, what?

I don't know what to say. If this were an overacted sitcom, I'd break the fourth wall and start talking to the audience like Ferris Bueller did on his day off. Dead wrong or not, B&E or not, I would not apologize to any woman I find in "my" man's bed.

"That was nice. D," Eddie prods, filling the awkward silence, "do you forgive Anne?"

I look at him like he's crazy. He nods at me with a fatherlike expression that reads: *You know what you're supposed to do.* I look from him to her, back to him. They're both nuts.

"Sure. Whatever." I shake my head and am turning to go back downstairs when Eddie calls out to me.

"Where are you going? You can't sleep down there. Come," he says, scooching closer to Anne's side of the bed. He pats the empty space he's made. "Go to sleep. You have to get up in a few hours for your flight."

I look at him blankly. He looks at me as if his suggestion makes perfect sense. I look at her. I think about lying on the floor and sharing a blanket or splitting the couch with Ty and the other guy. They're cool dudes, but I don't know-know them like that. I ain't trying to be up under either one of them.

I accept Eddie's offer and get into the bed, turning my back to them. And yes, so we're clear, I know this is insane in the moment. But my only other option is snuggling up with strangers.

Of course, I can't go to sleep. I have my eyes closed listening to Anne and Eddie talk.

Anne's asking for money to take a cab home. Eddie refuses to pay because he didn't ask her to come by. He makes a compromise of sorts, saying he'll drive her to the MARTA in the morning when he takes me to the airport.

She rises off the edge of the bed. I know because I can feel the weight shift.

"Well, what am I supposed to do until then?" she asks pitifully.

I feel Eddie scoot closer to me. "There's room. You can fit here." I feel and hear him patting the bed on the opposite side of him.

I feel her weight on the bed. Eddie scooches toward me again to make more room.

Now it's the three of us—me, Eddie, in the middle, and Anne— lying in the bed.

Somehow, I'm not having the knee-jerk, appalled reaction I would expect from myself. Eddie ain't my man, and as long as he doesn't have sex with Anne while I'm in the bed, this doesn't register on my *oh hell no!* scale even though it probably should. I'm tired. All I want to do is go to sleep so I can catch my flight in the morning, to get back to New York where people are normal. This? This isn't normal. I am well aware.

I'm halfway to REM when I'm awakened by another sudden shift in the bed. I don't know how long I've been asleep this time, but Eddie's facing me, and his arm is over my body, but we're not spooning. My eyes burn when I open them, and I can hear Anne trying to sound authoritative without speaking from her diaphragm.

"My mother raised me better than this!" she's whining. I twist around to see her standing beside the bed. She's shouting at Eddie, who I'm not sure is even awake by the dead weight on my body. "She would be ashamed," Anne squeals. "I cannot sleep in the bed with you and another woman!"

"Well, where are you going to sleep, then, Anne? On the floor?" Eddie mumbles. He doesn't bother to turn and face her.

She hesitates, then defiantly snatches the comforter off of us and gathers up the fabric in a fury, marching to my side of the bed. I watch, fascinated, as she folds it into a neat rectangle and shakes it out like a beach towel so that it lands smooth and flat on the carpet. She leans over, unfolds a flap, snuggles herself inside the pallet, and pulls the covers over her pillowless head with an indignant *humph* as if she's upstaged us.

I stare at the lump of fabric on the floor. "Eddie?" I whisper. I nudge him for emphasis. I'm still looking at the Lump.

"Hmmm?" He is already sleeping.

"Are you a pimp?"

He snuggles me closer and into my neck asks, "Did I ever do that to you? Would I?"

Well, no. I wouldn't allow it.

"She's on the floor," I complain, turning toward him. I don't know why I care, but I do. Anne's nuts, she's insecure, she has horribly low self-esteem despite what I mistook as a moment of clarity before she decided to sleep on the floor. And I feel sorry for her.

"Well, you go sleep downstairs and let her have the bed," he suggests.

Ooh. I'm not *that* concerned.

When I awake to the sound of my BlackBerry alarm the next morning, the Lump is gone. The comforter is a heap on the floor. Eddie is knocked out next to me.

Where did she go? I wake Eddie to ask him. He peers over me as if I've imagined the Lump is gone. He doesn't even shrug before he rolls over, uninterested.

An hour later, we head downstairs with my packed bag. The Fellas are up. Ty tells us he got up to use the bathroom and saw the front door wide open. We assume Anne walked home.

Eddie doesn't call to see if she is okay; he takes me to breakfast. And two hours later, I board a plane back to New York.

HOLLYWOOD SHUFFLE

The lobby of the Mondrian hotel is something to write home about. I'm in Los Angeles. The flight was relatively cheap, and my suite at one of the city's chicest boutique hotels is free since I'm crashing with Bonnie. She's out here working the ESPY Awards, ESPN's annual red-carpet ceremony. I'm tagging along to attend the parties. She's warned me that she'll be busy all weekend and I'll be left to my own devices most of the time. This is fine, as I am an only child, and she's left the keys to her rental car, an envelope with VIP tickets and, when necessary, backstage passes to every event ESPN will be sponsoring over the next four days.

Usually, I avoid athletes at all costs. Eddie's okay, of course. But I had a bad experience with one in college. There was also my mother's last warning before she hugged me good-bye the first time I moved into the dorms. "No numbers, no letters," she said. "Just do it, and don't ask why." But that was years ago, and I'm an adult, not a wide-eyed seventeen-year-old. I don't expect any drama this weekend.

I step off the elevator and am immediately surrounded by a sea of tall, wide tan and brown men, most of whom I don't recognize, but I'd bet the bank they throw or catch a ball for a living. I recognize a few household names. I raise my eyebrows, covered by my gigantic sunglasses, and take it all in slyly.

As I walk through the lobby in my uncommonly short dress and unusually high heels, I can feel eyes on me. I spent forty-five minutes putting on my makeup to look naturally beautiful. There's a different beauty standard out West, one that requires a lot of work and enhancement to look effortlessly and authentically pretty. So now my cheeks are rosy, my eyes are bright, and although my lashes are fake, they are long enough to be dramatic and short enough to fool some of the people some of the time.

Yet no one speaks. Odd. In New York, men say something when they see something—better, someone—they like, especially if she's in a short skirt. Women barely have to do anything but exist to have a man chase them down the block to spit game.

I'm standing outside the hotel, waiting for a ride to the Playboy Mansion, when my internal compare/contrast of the coasts is interrupted.

"I like your hair."

I look over to find a pretty brown girl my height and a size smaller looking at me. She's got a frizzy 'fro, too, but hers is blown out, then recurled with heat the way Tracee Ellis Ross tends to wear hers.

I raise my glasses over my forehead. "Thanks," I say. "I like yours, too."

We strike up a conversation about hair, Black women's equivalent to the way men bond over sports, and by the time the shuttle bus arrives, I've learned she's a sports publicist from LA, and we've planned to hang out together at the party.

The ride is quick. I continue to talk to Tiffany as we travel down Sunset, and she laughs at me for losing focus once the bus turns

into a neighborhood with houses the size of hotels. The bus takes
us up the steep driveway and drops us off in front of the estate.
We're directed to the backyard, which appears to be the size of a
football field. I notice the women, Black and White alike, all look
like models. I suck in my stomach reflexively and curse myself
for not wearing my Spanx. The second thing I notice is how tame
everything is. If not for the women with leotards and bunny ears
greeting everyone, this could be your standard country-club outing.

I ask Tiffany about the missing den of iniquity, the one I was
expecting, and she giggles at my naïveté about LA. "All that wild
stuff is like from the seventies or for movie sets," she reveals.

Tiffany spends most of the night aggressively chatting up athletes about their representation. Let it be noted that publicists and
pimps are not so far apart when it comes to stealing clients from
the competition.

Despite my best efforts to flirt and chat up the men present, I feel
invisible. Just like in the hotel lobby. I'm all dressed up, at the place
I'm supposed to go, and nary a man is paying any sort of attention
to me beyond a courtesy hello. I immediately go into self-loathing
mode and deduce this to mean I am too fat for LA. I drown my sor-
rows at the bar with champagne.

I'm posted up watching the crowd with my back to the bar, supposedly signaling openness and hoping a friendly and attractive
stranger will stop and say hello, when one strolls over and strikes
up a convo. He says he plays ball for Oakland; he's engaged. And
he's trying to stay out of trouble this weekend. I finish my glass and
order another.

He babbles on about his would-be wife, and I scan the crowd
through the living obelisks for Tiffany. My eye catches a guy and a
woman canoodling on a bench nearby. They're oblivious to the rest
of the world until another guy, too short for basketball, too narrow
for football, walks up to the couple and leans in to whisper some-

thing in the woman's ear. She smiles. Her date looks sheepish. The guy says something else to her, ignoring the man she's sitting with. The man slumps; it's slight but noticeable. The guy walks off. The woman leans over to the man she was with, says something quick, then pops off to follow the nonbasketball player, nonfootball player guy. The man she left behind tips his head back and finishes his glass.

I search for Tiffany again and spot her on her phone by the entrance. I excuse myself from the engaged Raider and trot over. I hope she's ready to go.

I'm giving Tiffany a recap of the woman who just walked off from her date, and I notice that where I expect her to share my outrage, she doesn't. "That's how athletes operate," she says, as if it's all par for the course.

I cock my head, and she switches the subject to a few potential clients she's met. As we're talking, a guy walks up and starts conversing with Tiffany without so much an "excuse me" for interrupting. By his size and do-rag-covered cornrows, I assume he's a football player. And yes, I'm stereotyping.

"What's your name?" he asks Tiffany without an introduction or even a compliment.

I'm sure how appalled I am is written all over my face. I wait for Tiffany to say something about his rudeness, but she doesn't. She eagerly sticks out her hand to introduce herself. Maybe this is business. I get it. Money by any means necessary. She's new in the game and has to be humble.

"I'm Tiffany," she says to the player. I note she doesn't give a last name or bother to introduce me as per business decorum.

"What're you doing later?" he asks.

She smiles. "I don't know."

"Put your number in my phone," he demands. He doesn't smirk, doesn't even try to raise his swagger. He doesn't even say his name.

Tiffany takes his phone and punches in her ten digits, then hands it back. He slips it into his pocket, says "Cool," and walks off.

This is all it takes to get a woman's number out West? No wonder L.L. and Biggie were so eager to go back. "So that's it?" I say to Tiffany when I've recovered from shock.

"Hmm? What's it?" she asks cluelessly.

I shake my head. I'm not in Brooklyn; I'm in Rome, I remind myself. I'm supposed to be Roman.

On the ride back to the hotel, Tiffany invites me to hang out with her for the rest of the weekend since I'm by myself. She doesn't understand how I could possibly have fun on my own. Tonight she's hitting up a party hosted by Shaq where she promises a ton of athletes will be. I can't tell if she's excited for business or for pleasure. Tomorrow they're going clubbing. I pass on tonight; my jet lag is catching up with me. Friday? I'm all hers.

At the Mondrian, I head upstairs to check on Bonnie. She's been working since seven A.M. It's almost midnight now. I've yet to see her.

The room is empty, but there's a note on the desk. I kick off my heels and trek across the carpet.

"At dinner with the bosses. Borrowed your green Gucci. Will guard with my life. XOXO."

I pull out the desk chair and slump onto it. I think about my five-hour cross-country flight and how I should be living it up out here in LA—at least till two, when the night is done unless you know about a private party up in the Hills. But what's the point? The guys out here are hella cute, but they either ignore me or they're wack.

Is it me? Or them?

I sigh dramatically, all woe is me, and trod to the mirror to clean off my makeup before bed.

FRIDAY

I wake up at two. I guess I was more tired than I thought. Bonnie came back to the room, if the messy sheets on her bed are an accurate indication, but she is gone by the time I come to. I spend most of the day shopping, hitting up the Beverly Center, Melrose Avenue, Rodeo Drive, and the Grove, an outdoor mall, equally known for celebrity sightings and chain restaurants.

Around ten, I head out to a club with a name I didn't catch with Tiffany and her girl Sarah. There I discover that what I thought was an athlete-to-civilian holler, the one where the guy just hands over his phone and tells a woman to put her number in, is actually what constitutes spitting game in LA. I want to have fun out here—flirt a little, giggle some, have an adventure—but I won't be handing out my number to men without enough consideration to introduce themselves. I embarrass the first man who tries this with me with a loud "Are you kidding me?" The subsequent attempts are met with blank stares.

Now we're parked on some side street off La Cienega in Sarah's truck. We'd dropped by a diner that seems to be the unofficial after party for every club in LA, as we're out here with hundreds of other people. It reminds me of that scene in *Boyz n the Hood* where Ice Cube and Regina King are hanging out on the Strip, except we're in Hollywood, not Compton, and everyone as far as the eye can see is bourgeois.

I'm bored. We're killing time waiting for the athlete Tiffany met yesterday to call or text her back. He hit her around one A.M. and mentioned he was headed to a party in the Hills. She's been blowing up his phone for the last hour trying to meet up. He hasn't bothered to respond. My guess is he found a woman who hit him back faster.

Tiffany is sharing her frustrations with Sarah in the front seat while I text Penelope to ask if the wack holler in LA is common or situational. I hate when people come to New York, have a bad time, then think the whole city must suck because their tour guide did. I don't want to stereotype a whole town based on two days of underwhelming experiences.

Penelope types back: "LA is wack, that's why I left. It's not you."

I'm staring out the window, taking in the scene, ignoring the trite conversation in the front seat, and wondering if we're going to get food anytime soon, when I spot a bright red car cruising down the street like we're in a residential neighborhood. Red anything out here makes me nervous. Despite the foo-foo chi-chi environment, I'm thinking Bloods, not Kappas.

"What's with the red Bentley?" I ask the LA natives holding down the front seats.

Sarah doesn't bother to turn around. "Suge Knight," she says, as if this should be obvious. "He's always out here."

He drives by our truck, peering into our vehicle as he passes. He smirks at Tiffany and Sarah. I doubt he can see me with the dark tint on Sarah's back windows. My first thought is that he looks a lot less intimidating in person, like a really large cherub. It's the cheeks.

"Now I really feel like I've seen LA," I quip. "We should follow him."

I'm joking, but Sarah puts the truck in drive and pulls out behind Suge's Bentley.

"Ohmigod! What're you doing?" Tiffany blurts at Sarah. "We can't follow Suge Knight!"

We're breaking the Second Law of Celebrity-Industry-Civilian Interaction, an unwritten rule that says anyone living in a major city and remotely associated with the entertainment industry (i.e., the Industry, as if it is the only one that ever existed or mattered) cannot get excited about, approach, or acknowledge a celebrity in any manner inconsistent with how they would acknowledge a civilian or industry colleague. To do so is to reveal yourself as a groupie, a newcomer, and someone who does not belong on the inside. There are few things you can do that will get you blacklisted, or clowned, faster.

I would never contemplate this in New York, but on vacation? Who cares? My brooding mood is replaced by the anticipation of an LA adventure.

"We're already following Suge Knight! Let's ask him to breakfast!" I suggest.

Sarah looks at me through the rearview mirror. I can tell by the look on her face that she's intrigued.

I don't know what I'm doing. I just know for the first time in thirty-six hours, I'm not bored. "Honk the horn," I demand, only because it sounds like a good idea.

"At Suge Knight?" Tiffany screeches.

I realize they might know something I don't. "Is this dangerous?" I ask. "We're women. You think he's going to fight women?"

Nobody says anything. "We're fine," I say convincingly, although I have no idea. "Honk."

Sarah does, and I tell them to wave from the front seat. They do, and the Bentley's hazard lights go on. The car pulls over.

Tiffany and Sarah are giggling wildly in the front seat.

"Now what do we do?" Sarah asks.

"Um, pull over," I instruct from the backseat.

She does, maneuvering the truck in front of Suge's car. She pulls to a stop, and she and Tiffany immediately pop open their doors.

"Noo!" I shout.

They slam the doors back, trapping themselves inside. They turn around to look at me, baffled.

"Wait for him to come to us," I demand.

Tiffany puts her proverbial foot down at this point. "Suge Knight is not going to come to us. He's Suge Knight!"

"He's a man. We're women. Wait," I tell her. "Just wait. And if he leaves? He does."

We sit. We wait. And wait. The car doesn't move.

"He's not coming," Tiffany says pessimistically. "We should have gone to him."

The driver's-side door of the Bentley opens, and Suge Knight gets out, dressed in a red shirt, a red hat, and black jeans.

Sarah practically hyperventilates. "What do we say? What do we do?"

"Say hi," I instruct.

Tiffany flips back around. "You can't just say hi to Suge Knight."

"Say hi, *Sugar Bear*. See what he does." I laugh at the lunacy of it.

Suge approaches the window, and Sarah powers it down quickly. Tiffany leans across the console and says as chipper as ever, "Hi, Sugar Bear!"

Suge doesn't say anything. He stares at us blankly. I wonder if in my whimsy I've gone too far. I remember that this is a man who is notorious for whupping grown men's behinds. Maybe, like Mos Def said, I shouldn't be high-posting this far from home. I think of the worst-case scenario: Suge flips, Sarah floors the accelerator, and maybe, maybe, we run over Suge Knight's foot. We should be able to escape.

Suge smiles, chuckles. He laughs. Hard. He introduces himself as "Suge," as if we don't know who he is, and asks us our names, extending his gigantic hand for a shake. Finally, a man in LA who knows how to speak to women.

Suge says he's hungry and asks if we'd like to join him and some of his boys at a diner on Sunset. I pipe in and tell him sure and that we'll follow him there. He nods, smiles, and walks back to his car, still chuckling.

Sarah rolls up the window. She and Tiffany watch Suge in the rearview and side mirrors. I turn around in my seat and watch through the back window. We wait until he's in the car and shuts the door. Then we all squeal at the top of our lungs.

I sit next to Suge at the diner. He doesn't say much, just mostly talks to his boys, tells us we can order anything we like. The average meal is almost ten dollars. *Um . . . okay.* It's the thought that counts.

When the waitress comes to take orders—there are eight of us, including Suge's friends, all male—Suge gives his order, then sends the waitress to the kitchen to put his meal in first before the rest of us can say what we want.

I talk to Tiffany and Sarah because the men are only talking to one another, as if we're at a junior-high dance. I'm baffled, which is a consistent feeling for me in this town. Back East, when women agree to go to a diner with men postclub, it's the time when men lay down their best mack lines. A guy becomes a politician selling a pretty constituent a passionate stump speech on why sex with him in the next hour is the best choice she can make for her future. I don't get LA game. At all.

When everyone else's food comes, Suge gets up from where we are all sitting in the back of the restaurant and plops down in a front section by the window. One by one, his entourage finishes their meals and follows him, leaving us, the three women, alone.

If Tiffany and Sarah at least reacted, I would think this was a unique circumstance, but they don't even acknowledge how odd this is. Perhaps because it's not to them.

Tiffany goes on about the athlete who still didn't hit her back and how we would have had more fun at the party in the Hills. She's probably right. We finish eating in twenty minutes, and I declare I'm ready to go. It's four A.M. I'm tired. Plus, the guys are on the other side of the room.

"Y'all got enough to cover this?" I ask Sarah and Tiffany, railroading them to accommodate me.

They reluctantly reach into their designer purses, and we throw enough money on the table to cover our food, tax, and tip. Then we walk out the diner, *clacking* our heels hard on the floor and waving to the guys as we leave. They, including Suge, look confused. I look at them, shaking my head in wonder, and purse my lips in classic Black girl disappointment.

Sarah's just started the engine to her truck when there's a knock on the window that startles all of us. It's one of Suge's boys. Tiffany rolls down the passenger-side window hesitantly. I would, too.

The guy hands her a fifty-dollar bill. More than double what we left on the table. "Suge is a gentleman. He wouldn't invite women anywhere and not pay for them," he says. "Suge doesn't do that." He pulls a knot from his pocket and peels off a hundred.

"For valet," he adds, then walks back in the restaurant. That was all for show. He knows as well as I do the valet was closed when we arrived. I turn to look inside the diner and see the whole table of guys, Suge included, are watching this play out.

Tiffany calls out a "thank you" after him, and Sarah pulls out of the parking lot. I lean my head against the window and chuckle to myself. Out of all the men I've met in LA, Suge Knight and his entourage are the closest I've come to finding gentlemen.

SATURDAY

Bonnie is passed out on her back, snoring, when I get back to the hotel. I hear her as I walk down the dimly lit hallway. I want to tell her my Suge story because even though it was a totally underwhelm-

ing evening, it was still an evening that included Suge Knight. As
a woman who grew up on Death Row music, I am highly amused.

When I wake up around noon, Bonnie's gone, of course.
Tonight—or, better, this afternoon—is the ESPY Awards. She'll be
working nonstop all day.

I get dolled up for brunch downstairs and use the fifty dollars
from Suge that Tiffany passed back—we split the money three
ways—to buy myself an overpriced breakfast at the hotel restaurant.

I sit at a table where I can get some sun, despite the umbrellas
on the patio. The restaurant is sparsely populated. I imagine that
everyone—as in the athletes and their handlers—is prepping for
the awards show already. I've sat in on enough photo shoots for
Vibe and *XXL* to know how long it takes to get camera-ready, even
for the guys.

Across from me is a table of three men. They watched me strut
by, and they are clearly talking about me as they keep looking over.
I feel like Stella the first time she met Winston when she was on
vacation that time getting her groove back. Except Winston actually spoke.

"Hello," I shout over to them to get to the point. I even smile to
emphasize that I'm available to be approached, properly, which I'm
learning is relative.

They smile sheepishly. I can't. I reach into my purse for my
glasses and put them on to block any eye contact.

After I wolf down an expensive salmon omelet, I return to the
room to prep for the awards show. It takes more than three hours
to rewash my hair, dry it, beat my face to perfection, and slip on a
strapless, too-short yellow dress with a gigantic bow and a sweetheart neckline. I put on heels that hurt but look good enough to
make me not care, then head downstairs to catch one of the seemingly trillion limos that are taking everyone from the Mondrian to
the Kodak Theatre.

I meet Bonnie backstage and realize this is the first time I've
seen her awake since I arrived in LA two days ago. She's too busy
to chat, with directions and questions constantly flying at her
through her headset, but she suggests I hang out in the VIP lounge
backstage. For all of the strings Bonnie was able to pull, she wasn't
able to get me a decent seat to the show. I would have had to sit
in an upper tier, so I told her not to worry. Half the celebrities and
their handlers are in VIP, anyway.

It's another sponsored event with more liquor and food—now
an LA thing and one of the traits I love about the city, since I
can't remember the last time a party was catered in New York.
I stop by the seafood station and, of course, the bar for a glass
of champagne, then watch as a who's who of guests trot by. It's
every athlete worth his or her star power—Terrell Owens, LeBron
James, Carmelo Anthony, Serena Williams, Lisa Leslie—and some
folks whose star power hasn't peaked yet, like a chocolate cutie in
a brown-and-white pinstripe suit with as many buttons as it has
stripes. Oh, and he's wearing a matching hat. With a feather. I can't
identify him, but I overhear someone refer to him as the next big
thing in basketball.

I stay in VIP when the show starts. It goes well, the highlight
being a Destiny's Child performance and watching all the male
athletes literally run out of VIP to catch the live and up-close view
of Beyoncé wiggling it around onstage.

I am supposed to meet up with Tiffany for the after party at the
Sky Bar even though I don't really feel like going. So far, LA has
been like one long, bad night at a club where you get approached
by either old men, ugly men, bad-breath men, or corny men, and
even though you're all dressed up, not one guy you'd actually consider asks for your number.

Tiffany is nowhere to be found in the crowd when I arrive, so
I sit on a perch by the Mondrian's pool and gaze out at the par-

tiers getting it in on the makeshift dance floor. I'm looking at all the pretty women in the room—tall, modelesque, impossibly thin with short spandex dresses that reveal flat stomachs and impossible curves. I wonder if my experience in LA would be different if I was two sizes smaller in the waist, two sizes bigger in the chest, if my shoes had another two inches and my dress lost another two. Would that change my odds of being approached?

"Party's too good to be looking like that," says a bass-filled voice.

I look over to see if it's directed toward me and see the chocolate drop from VIP approaching in his country suit. I smile. I can't help it. He's cute despite the suit.

"Someone sitting here?" he asks, pointing to an empty stool next to me. I catch the glimmer of his wedding band when he gestures. *What's with all the taken men approaching me?* I shrug. "It's yours."

"You're not having a good time?" he asks. He's got the biggest, prettiest, whitest teeth ever. Just as quickly as I notice, I remind myself that he is a married man.

"Can I be honest?"

He nods.

"I'm not a big fan of LA," I say.

The cutie laughs. "It's okay. I prefer Miami."

"That's where you're from?"

"I work there. From Chicago."

Aah. That could explain the suit. I tell him about D.C. and where I live now, too. We end up comparing the best and worst of America's five most major cities. When there's a lull in conversation, he asks the question that was on his mind when he approached, I imagine: "What's a pretty lady doing over in a corner by herself?"

Maybe it's all the rosé champagne that makes me so honest. Or maybe it's because he's a stranger and I'll never see him again. Or maybe because he's taken and I have no shot.

"The guys here ignore me. Like, I came out to LA with my girl to have this amazing weekend partying and flirting and acting a fool, and it's like I'm invisible."

He laughs, a deep, hearty, from-the-belly guffaw. "I promise you're not invisible. Every man in here noticed when you walked in." He flashes that smile, and my eye darts to his ring.

Off limits. Off limits. Off limits, I repeat to myself.

"And no one spoke? Not one single person?" I query.

He shakes his head, chuckles to himself. "Guys are here for the weekend," he begins. "They're not looking for wives and girlfriends. They're looking for . . . the night. Nothing about you seems temporary."

Somehow I don't take this as a compliment. I screw up my face at this backhanded, suspect flattery. "I feel like I've just been described as 'nice,'" I tell him. That's how kind people describe those with good hearts and unfortunate faces.

"You look like you require more than what most men are looking to work for this weekend," he clarifies. "It's a good thing. It'll take you far. Just wait for the men to catch up."

I smirk. *So it's not me.*

We sit in silence, me finishing my bubbly, him nursing whatever's in his glass. Seems like it's time for this night to come to an end. I tell him it was nice to meet him, stick my palm out for a shake. I realize I didn't catch his name.

"You are?" I ask.

"Dwayne," he says.

I tell him my name, we say "Nice to meet you" in unison, and I head upstairs to pack. What's the use in staying at the party? I've given LA my best shot and come up short.

I fold.

NO LETTERS. NO NUMBERS.

I don't usually do clubs in New York, especially not on weekends, for a number of reasons:

1. I can party (and drink) for free during the week.
2. Industry parties don't require a specific dress code other than coming fly.
3. Weekends are for chilling with friends who are like family.
4. Like most Brooklyn dwellers, whenever possible, I prefer not to leave the borough.

One Saturday night, I make an exception. A friend is having a housewarming to celebrate the purchase of his second condo. His shindig is winding down, but the festive mood isn't. Me and my girls decide to keep the party going like Jesus with the wine and head to the city to Crash Mansion, a club I've attended many times, but only really enjoyed the night Usher had his *Confessions* album release party there. It's not the ideal place to party, but some friends are working the door.

The cab pulls up in front of the venue, and we exit into sheer pandemonium. People everywhere. Despite the craziness, my boy at the door keeps his word and whisks my girls and me to the front of the line and past the cashier.

Inside, it's crowded. *Check.* More men than women ("I'm in a sausage factory," Penelope observes gleefully). *A surprising, unexpected check.* And they're all tall—really tall! And well constructed— really well constructed! *Check. Check. Check.* And glittering? It's the ropes of diamonds (or CZs) hanging from their necks . . .

That's when it hits me. "Oh, no! They are all athletes!" I whine to my friends.

Some women would have thought they'd found the platinum at the end of the rainbow with all these well-built, well-paid ballers (literally) in one not-so-big room. But for me, this is somewhere within the last circle of Dante's *Inferno*.

1997

I had the Amber Rose cut before Amber Rose. Well, maybe not. My hair was just as platinum blond but a little longer. I'd just gone natural and I wanted to see my waves and curls.

I am eighteen, living in LaPlata Hall, an all-female dorm on the north side of University of Maryland College Park. It's where all the freshman and sophomores (and some juniors who didn't have enough sense to move to the better dorms on the south side) are housed. My dorm is sometimes called Playa Hata Hall or the Chicken Coop. Had I known that when I selected to live there the year before, I still would have picked it. It was one of the few dorms on that side of campus with AC, and it was all girls. I didn't want to live with boys (I had my reasons).

It's the first week of school sophomore year, and I'm newly single. The guy I was dating all through freshman year unceremoniously dumped me over the summer for another woman. My best friend from high school, a dude, met the new woman at the beginning of July and proclaimed her more curvy, with *real*, long hair. I was mortified that he'd compared me with her and found me lacking. I quickly got out of that lane and got into another. I'd already been thinking about getting rid of my perm, so the next day, I took out my jet-black, bone-straight weave that passed my bra strap and shaved my head. Two months later and two days before school started, I bleached it platinum blond, much to my parents' chagrin.

I am blond, bright blond, and walking to the cafeteria behind my dorm to get a croissant, because I can eat one, even two, a day, every day, and never gain a pound. And that's when I hear a . . .

"You gonna dye my hair blond, too?" he calls out.

I think about ignoring him, whoever he is. But I turn around to see who is speaking as if he knows me but clearly doesn't, as I don't recognize his voice.

He's a football player. I can tell by the build. Probably a running back. Big, but not massive. He's cut in a V—wide shoulders, narrow waist. And since he's wearing a cutoff T-shirt with "Football" typed beneath the university's logo, I know I'm not stereotyping. His guns are wide, firm, and bulbous and have the stretch marks of a man who got real big real fast.

I shield my eyes from the sun with a hand in the salute position and look up at him. Six feet, easy. Curly hair, dark eyes, broad nose. Finer than fine and totally my type.

My face must give away that I like what I'm seeing, because he smiles—real big, real white. Perfect.

Jesus.

I clench my teeth together in the back to keep from smiling. I give him the blankest, dullest, least-impressed look I can manage. And then I turn away dismissively.

Just a year earlier, my mother gave me a warning: *No letters, no numbers.* I'm not supposed to deal with any man who throws a ball or anyone who crosses burning sands.

"Blondie!" He hustles up beside me and matches my pace.

I clench those back teeth again. He smells good. Polo Sport? *Sniff.* I dunno. But damn . . . *D, keep walking.*

"You're not gonna talk to me?" He laughs, half at my audacity, I'm sure. He looks like a man who's not used to hearing no.

I keep walking. He's still right beside me.

"You're not that mean. They told me you were mean, but no one so cute can be so—"

I stop abruptly, turn, and look up at him. "Who told you I was mean?" I snap.

He's smiling down at me as if he's won this battle. And maybe he has. But he *will* lose the war.

He squishes his mouth around, trying to get rid of his smile. The result is a cocky smirk. "My boys."

"Your teammates?" I ask pointedly.

"Does it make a difference?" He's *so* cocky.

"I don't know any football players."

"I know."

I look at him blankly, waiting for him to continue. His eyes are jet black. Kinda narrow as if he's got some Asian in his bloodline. And that skin? Not a bump or a blemish, not even a bruise. Either he never leaves the bench, or he runs his ass off and doesn't get hit. I wonder if he exfoliates.

I'm not playing his game. I turn and start marching toward the dining hall again.

"No, no, no, no, no!" he cries. He grabs after my arm to stop me. I yank away. I'm about to yell at him for touching me when he blurts, "I asked about you. I saw you in the dining hall on the south side, and I asked who you were. You haven't dated anyone on my team."

I look at him blankly, waiting for him to go on.

"So I want to get to know you," he says, all cocky again, smiling hard enough that I can see his dimples. You could pack up my whole dorm room and store the contents in them.

I want to gush, but I just keep looking at him with my least impressed look. His shoulders slump just a little; the smile drops. It's like watching a balloon deflate. I feel awful, but it's necessary. No numbers, no letters.

"A lot of cute girls," he begins. "I mean, women . . ." He pauses to get himself back together. "My team has run through a lot of women. I like that everyone knows who you are, but you haven't hollered at any of them. I was just wondering if—"

I cut him off. "I don't date athletes."

The corner of his mouth snarls up. "I didn't introduce myself to you as an athlete," he spits out.

"I'm late meeting someone for lunch," I say, excusing myself and dismissing him. I'm so not meeting anyone, and I'm intentionally vague about the pronouns so he assumes it's a guy.

He's frustrated. I can tell by the look on his face "You're tough, Blondie."

I assure him that I am already aware of this.

"So, I guess I won't be seeing you around?" he says with a laugh. "Guess not."

I turn, walk toward the caf, and notice he's not walking behind me. I turn to look for him, and he's walking away. He looks back just in time to catch me looking.

I smirk now because I've been caught red-handed taking in the view. "I made you lose your appetite?" I call out by way of apology.

He shakes his head and looks at me pointedly. "I ate on my side. I only came over here to find you."

He turns, walks off, dismissing me this time. I watch, mouth hanging slightly open as he saunters off without looking back.

MONDAY

My phone is ringing off the hook. My roommate, Nessa, walks in, looks at the phone, looks at me on the bed watching TV with the volume turned up too loud.

"I know you hear the phone ringing," she says dryly. She's from the West. They have an odd sense of humor over there.

I nod.

The phone stops, then starts up again.

"You want me to answer it?" she asks.

I know who it is. I shake my head.

Nessa picks up the phone anyway. "Demi's phone," she answers. Pause. "Uh-uh." Pause. "Hold on." She covers the receiver, holding it to her chest. "It's Jason," she says to me.

"I know."

She looks off to the side, as if there's a candid camera hidden in the corner. "Who's Jason?"

"I don't know," I lie.

"Then, er, why is he calling?"

Now I look off to the side. "I don't know."

She gets back on the phone. "Young man?" Nessa is twenty-two. She took some time off before she came to college, but she's the same year as me. She's four years older than most of her friends, which makes a world of difference at this age. "You're looking for Demi?"

I don't know why she's wasting her time. I already answered the phone the first time it rang. When I discovered who it was, I hung up.

At the Student Union party on Saturday, I saw Jason, the football player who said he traveled cross-campus to find me last week, pushed up on a girl who lives down the hall. I didn't even know the boy's name till he called and tried to explain himself over the outdoor intercom to my building. But if he didn't do anything wrong, why is he apologizing?

"D," my roommate calls, snapping me from the memory. "He wants to know if you'll come downstairs to talk."

"No." I know I sound like a child.

"Jason, Demi is unavailable right now," Nessa says into the receiver. "You should, um . . . reach her later." Pause. "Okay, bye-bye."

She hangs up, then sits on the chair across from my bed. She doesn't say anything, just waits. She's gonna drive her kids crazy with this mess when she has some.

I cut off the TV. "Yes?" I take the bass out my voice. I'm respectful, as if I'm talking to my mother.

"What in the heck was that?" Anybody else ever notice folks from Cali talk straight up Southern?

I shrug like the teenager I still am. She waits. I blurt out everything. My story is interrupted when the phone rings again. We both look at it. Then there's a knock on the door. We look at each other. Did someone let Jason in and then tell him where I live?

Nessa shushes me, thinks for a moment, then calls out, "Who is it?"

"Sabrina!" she calls through the door. Sabby is my ace. We met the very first time I ever got drunk. I'd literally crawled to the shared hall bathroom and thought I was dying. She came in to tinkle, found me and my roommate thinking the end was near, and brought us water. We've been inseparable ever since.

I rush to open the door.

"What in the hell is going on downstairs?" she says before I can get a word out. "Jason Randolph is at the front door and won't let anyone use the intercom to call upstairs!" Sabby doesn't talk. She exclaims. "And he's asking everyone who comes by if they know *you!* And to tell you to come downstairs!"

"Are you kidding me?" I blurt.

The phone had stopped ringing, but now it starts up again. I go back to my desk and snatch it off the receiver. "Hello?" I bellow.

"Can you come downstairs, please?" It's Jason. Again.

"Oh, my God! What are you doing? No, I'm not coming downstairs. Go home!"

"I will stay here all night." He sounds calm, as insane as he is.

I look at Sabby and Nessa. Nessa mouths that they will go down with me.

I glare at her like she's lost her mind. She nods.

"I'll be down in a sec," I say into the phone.

"Okay. I'm on the side by the di—" he says.

I hang up.

I bust open the doors as if I'm about to fight this big Black man. It's just me. I told Nessa and Sabby to stay inside. I can handle this. I will tell Jason in no uncertain terms to leave, and I will call campus security and complain that he is harassing me if he doesn't.

He's the first thing I see when I get outside. There is a line of angry students behind him, waiting to use the intercom that he hasn't stepped away from yet. None of them is bold enough to say get out of the way. Not that he would have listened anyway.

I'm furious. But Jason seems not to notice.

"Hey," he says with a big, doofy smile while leaning up against the railing comfortably.

I glare at him, ignoring the way his gray shirt falls over those defined shoulders, and move over to the side and out of the doorway where we are blocking people's path to the entrance.

"Are you kidding me?" I yell again when he is near. "You've been ringing my phone for the last twenty minutes, and all you have to say is hey? What are you doing here?"

He looks baffled. "I came by to see you. You look nice." He smiles. There go those dimples. Is he slow? Maybe he's received one too many hits? I just look at him blankly.

"You think it's acceptable to blow up my phone? To tie up the intercom so no one can get into the building?" I'm still yelling.

He's unfazed. "You came down, didn't you? I wanted to see you." He shrugs. "How was class today?"

I suck my teeth. "Ask the girl you were cuddled up on at the party how her classes were," I spit out.

He laughs. "Oh, you're mad about that?" He sounds surprised.

I cross my arms over my chest. Lean back and stick my hip out for emphasis.

"You go out with me, she's gone," he says, waving a hand to demonstrate that she's an afterthought. "I'll never talk to her again. Promise."

I narrow my eyes at him and lean in like I misheard him. "What?"

"I'm serious. If that's what it takes for you to go out with me, that's what I'll do. You want anything else?"

"Just like that, huh?"

"Yup." He stares down at me, testing, teasing, waiting for what I'll say next.

I go to my default. "I don't date athletes."

"You want me to quit my team? I will from this moment on. I renounce my throne. I'm no longer Prince of Zamunda. Does this make you happy?"

I laugh at his Eddie Murphy impression from *Coming to America*. I didn't mean to, but I did.

He smiles down at me, and what a beautiful sight it is to behold. My reflexes betray me. I smile back up at him.

"You eat?"

I look at my watch. "Nope." I was avoiding coming downstairs to go to the dining hall because I didn't know which door he was waiting at.

"Dining hall on my side is still open," he suggests.

I think about it. Really think about it. "I'll be fine." I'll starve it out till morning or wait till the cafeteria opens again for late-night snacks at nine. Worst-case scenario, I'll get on the campus bus to Route One and go to Danny's, the Chinese carry-out, for greasy lo mein.

"You want to go upstairs?"

"I don't know you!" I blurt. "I'm not inviting you to my room!"

He chuckles. "I wasn't asking to come up. Only asking if you were going up or staying here with me."

"Oh." I should go back. Nessa and Sabby were instructed to come out after me if I wasn't back in five. They should be here any minute.

He bites his bottom lip, and his dimples come out. "I want you to stay," he says, looking me in the eyes.

Lord, he is fine. Crazy. But fine.

I shake my head, sigh . . . and take a seat on the top step.

Jason has a million study halls and practices. But over the next two weeks, he finds his way to LaPlata Hall often enough that I never go more than two days without seeing him when he's not at an away game.

I think my roommate scared the bejesus out of him the first time they met. Nessa and Sabby, as promised, came downstairs to check on me after I'd gone to curse him out for causing a scene. They found me, well, us, sitting on the top of the stairs getting to know each other.

Sabby waited at the front door to observe from afar. Nessa

marched over to us. She's a powerhouse at four-foot-eleven. Although the drama had passed, Nessa still had some ish to get off her mind.

"Young man, you won't call Demi's phone repeatedly again," she began firmly, speaking to Jason. Note how she was telling, not asking. "I live in that room as well, and it's a nuisance." She waited like someone's mother for his acknowledgment of wrongdoing. "Young man, have I made myself clear?"

"Yes, ma'a—hold up, what's your name?" Jason said, looking up at her from his seat.

She gave him the mama eye, waited until he rose and stuck out his hand for a formal introduction. He gave his first and last name as if he was meeting someone's parents.

"Nessa," she informed him. "And you won't call late, either. We go to bed early," she lied.

He looked back at me to see if she was serious. I nodded. She was. I didn't even bother to object, because I wouldn't win. She only went into mama mode when something wasn't right. She knew my mother's warning, too (my parents had practically adopted her at this point): No letters, no numbers.

Jason agreed, and she left without a good-bye and with a pair of cut eyes at me that said, *I'm watching you.*

Jason and I sit outside when he comes by to visit. His idea, not mine. When it rains or gets too windy, we move inside to the lobby. When he's free during the day, he'll pop up outside one of my classes to walk me wherever I'm going next. He avoids my room at all costs.

The public display bothers me. Not that we're doing PDA, but because we're always in public, everyone always sees us. I don't like the attention, and it seems the whole campus knows he's putting in time. The chick down the hall and her friends whisper whenever I pass them on campus. His teammates make grand invites for me to sit at the ballers' table when I stop by the south-side dining hall for lunch. The known groupie chicks look me up and down, clearly wondering what Jason sees in me. And the dudes? They don't even holler anymore. It's as if "Off-limits" is carved in my head like a Jason plus Demi heart in a tree trunk.

By Homecoming, Jason's still coming by *at least* three times a week, despite practice, despite study hall, despite away games. I finally suggest we go upstairs . . . to the lounge on my floor. I'm tired of the people who stroll by over and over and over to see what we're up to. You'd think with all that's happening on this campus, interest in us would have died down by now. It's not as if he's the star of the team. Besides, we're just talking. In public. I haven't even kissed him. And as much as I want to hop all over him, I'm not going to. Especially not with people watching. No one ever comes into the lounge, so we have it all to ourselves. Still, I sit with my back to the door so I don't see the girls on my floor, and other floors, strolling by.

In early November, six weeks after we've met, Jason stops by with his boy, actually a man in his mid-twenties, Bobby. We hang out in my room for the first time. My roommate is there, and the door is open (Jason wanted it open). Nessa knows the work Jason's been putting in and has softened her stance toward him.

We talk, play video games on my Nintendo 64, and listen to Erykah Badu's *Live* album ("Tyrone" on repeat, Bobby's choice) for a couple of hours. I'm sitting on the bed next to Jason, watching him play some game, when his character dies and he decides it's time to go. It's eleven fifty-five. He always leaves before twelve.

Jason rises off the bed, leans close in front of me so I'm assaulted with delicious man scent, and places the palm of his hand on my inner thigh just above my knee . . . and possessively squeezes.

Then he lightly kisses me good-bye on my cheek, holding his soft lips there for just a moment.

This is the most contact we've ever had, other than a lingering hug hello and a longer one good-bye. I almost pass out from equal parts sexual frustration and excitement.

Literally, my knees are too weak to stand. Nessa, bless her heart, sees Jason and his friend to the door. When they're in the hall, she turns the lock behind them and slumps against the door.

We're in the corner room closest to the elevator bank, so we wait. Wait, wait, wait . . . for the *ding* of the elevator.

Ding!

We wait . . . wait . . . wait . . . long enough for Jason and his boy to get on and the doors to shut. Wait . . . just to be sure.

Okay.

We scream into our pillows like junior-high girls. Nessa? She's hopping around bent over till she lands on the bed on the other side of the room, kicking her legs in the air like a bug that's been flipped on its back. Me? I fall over on the bed in a fit of giggles and laugh until I have to hold my stomach.

"He. Is. Fine!" Nessa declares, sitting up. She's yelled it loud enough for the neighbors to hear through the cement walls. This is all fact, no opinion. "He touched your knee, and I got hot! Damn, damn, damn!" she says, mimicking Florida Evans.

I still can't stand. I close my eyes and remember Jason's scent and picture those lips on my cheek and that hand squeezing my inner thigh . . . possessively . . . just above the knee.

I shudder.

I am officially a goner for Jason Randolph.

When My Jason comes by now and I know he's on his way, I stand outside and wait. There's no sitting in the main lobby or even the floor lobby. When he comes up, I sit on my bed, try to get him to sit next to me, but he insists on the chair across from me at my desk. We talk for hours all the time, never on the phone, always in person, and I am practically dying for this man to make a move. Now I'd just jump on him. At eighteen, I just waited.

There is no tough Blondie anymore—as a matter of fact, I'm not even blond. The day before Homecoming, I went to the barber for a shape-up, and he cut the blond out because *he* thought I'd look better without it. I was pissed because I loved my blond hair, but I didn't bother to dye it back. Too much maintenance to keep the roots light.

Since I'm now a ball of mush for Jason Randolph, I've dropped my guard. There's no playing hard to get. He calls, I answer. I call him to say hi and even just sit on the phone and breathe when I have nothing to say. I even volunteer to travel to his side of campus to hang out. I don't want him to be the only one putting in effort, and I want him to know I don't take-take-take, but I will—I want to, even—give-give-give.

He repeatedly declines when I offer to walk over to his side of campus during the day or take the bus over after dark. He insists he doesn't mind coming to me and/or he doesn't want me out at night by myself. At first, I think that's sweet. Then I think it's . . . odd.

One evening, I go down the hall—past the homemade posters advertising a full sew-in weave, plus hair, for sixty dollars, past the sign notifying all that a professional piercer will be visiting next week—to Natalie's room. She's been dating the star of the football team for a year. I don't know her super-well, but she's a friend of Sabrina's, and I figure since we're in the same boat, dating athletes and all, she might have some good insight.

I tell her my dilemma with Jason.

Natalie thinks it's sweet that he's willing to put in the effort

for me. "You don't wanna go over there, I promise," says Nat.
"It's a bunch of dudes in one suite. They're always messy and
musty."

Her roommate, Brittany, who's lying on her bed, snatches off
her headphones—I can hear Jay-Z's "Where I'm From" blasting
across the room—and sits up on her elbows, looking at me pointedly. We've never formally met.

"Eh . . . you're probably his south-side girl," Brit says. She has a
thick "area" accent, is stacked like IHOP, and has a hard swagger
and the mentality of a man. I didn't know she was even listening to
Nat and me, but clearly she was.

Huh? That's impossible. "I see him almost every night," I say defensively.

"He stay over?"

"Um, no."

"Didn't think so. You fucking him?"

Wow. She's really blunt. "Uhhh . . . no."

She laughs. "Oh, you're a good girl?" she asks incredulously.
"Well, you might be the official, but he's fucking on the south side.
You can believe that."

I'm standing there with a stupid look on my face. I don't know
what to say.

"You seriously think Jason Randolph is practicing celibacy?" Brit
cracks up and puts her headphones back on. "Bitch, please."

Brittany immediately becomes my ride-or-die. She's got Nessa's
bluntness but without the mama-bear protectiveness. She'll tell
me I'm wrong but won't harp on me when I do wrong. And she
doesn't give a damn about the numbers-and-letters rule.

But for the love of Hova, she can't understand why I have not
jumped on Jason.

"Any man coming to my room every day for months on end is humping me," says Brittany as we're walking from Intro to African-American Studies in LeFrak Hall. We've known each other for a week and change now.

See why I love her?

We get to South Campus Dining Hall, where I order my daily lunch of lettuce, tomato, and tofu with tons of ketchup and a bit of light mayo on a croissant. I buy a tub of water to wash it down and meet her at the back tables behind the athletes. I will not sit at their tables, the ones where you first walk into the dining hall through the main doors. I will not look like a groupie.

I see my boy Sean in the checkout line, holding his tray and looking for a seat. He's cute, chocolate, and off-limits, as he has a girlfriend. I wave him over to join Brit and me.

When my phone rings, Sean is telling me about this band he's in love with that he knows I will love, too, and I should come over sometime so he can play the CD for me. The only person who calls me on my phone during the day is Mum. Everybody else knows not to run up my precious daytime minutes.

"Hello?"

"Hey." It's Jason.

"Hey."

"Hey."

We're so simple.

"What're you doing?" he asks.

"In the dining hall."

He sounds excited. "On my side?"

"Yeah."

"Can you come over at two-thirty? I should be back in my room by then."

This is a surprise. I check my watch. It's one-fifteen. I was planning to go back to my dorm and knock out, maybe see who's fighting on Springer. I was up until two A.M. with Jason last night. Ever since Brit pointed out there might be a woman on the south side, I've been keeping him by me after midnight to see if he puts up a fight to get back to his dorm. So far, nothing serious . . . other than us driving Nessa crazy with him being in the room at all hours of the night. He'll lie on the bed with me now, still doesn't stay over.

I'll sleep later. This is what I've been bugging him about, and he's finally giving in.

"Um, yeah."

"Is that too late?" he asks. "I can skip."

"No, no, no," I insist. "I'm done for the day, but I'll stay on this side."

I look over at Brit, who couldn't care less. Nessa would be all in this conversation.

"Cool. I'll hit you when I'm back in the room," Jason says.

I hang up, and Brit, who I thought wasn't listening, asks, "So you're finally going over there?"

I laugh.

"Still think you're number one, which means you ain't the *only* one," she says, taking a huge bite of her cheeseburger.

"I'm just going over there. Nothing's gonna happen. Nothing ever happens."

She takes another bite, chews as slowly as possible to keep me waiting. "Just throwing it out there so you remember when he tries to put it on you."

"If," I correct.

"When," she restates.

I look over at Sean for backup. He's pretending to ignore us.

Whatever. I look back at Brit. "Why are you trying to discourage me? I thought you wanted me to hump him?"

"I said any man coming to *my* room all the time should be humping *me*. You?" She laughs. "You wouldn't know what to do even if he was lying there butt-naked. Do you even know how to seduce a man?" She starts laughing at the thought of me trying.

I don't, but I'm too embarrassed to ask, so I blank-face her.

"Try this," she offers when she's composed herself. "Rub his dick three times. Once is accidental, twice is coincidence, three times is intentional. He'll take it from there."

"You want me to rub his penis?"

Sean nearly spits out his juice. Now he's laughing and nodding at Brit's advice.

"Call it a dick, baby," Brit says. "And rub that thing like you're trying to get a genie out a bottle! Trust me, it'll work. Right, Sean?" She can't even hold in her laughter and starts howling at her own joke.

Sean can barely breathe from laughing so hard.

I roll my eyes and slump back in my chair, watching them fall all over the table.

"Don't look at me like that, D," Brit howls. "I'm serious, I'm dead serious."

I don't care if it works or not. I'm not grabbing Jason's . . . Jason's . . . penis!

I wait until they've composed themselves to ask Sean if I can crash at his spot until two-thirty, since he lives on the south side, too.

"Yeah, I'm done for the day," he responds dryly, like he can't believe I asked when I know the answer is yes. "I'll let you hear Dave Matthews."

At two-twenty, Jason calls to tell me he's back in his suite. I take directions to his room from the dining hall—I only come to the south side for class and have no clue where the dorms are—'cause no dude is gonna understand that I'm just kicking it in another man's room whether he's "just" a friend or not.

Jason's waiting outside for me when I get to Charles Hall.

"Hey," I say, walking up and zeroing in on his juicy lips. I have yet to kiss this man, and it's killing me not to.

"Hey," he says. "How are you? I'm exhausted." He covers a yawn with his hand.

"Oh, um, well, I can come back later," I say. I don't wanna go, but I think he's trying to brush me off. Maybe Brit was right. Maybe I am the north-side girl and he's had a change of heart about having me over here. Maybe his south-side woman, who does things I don't, called instead.

"Uh-uh." He pulls me into a tight hug right out in public on the south side.

I grin and bury my head in his chest. *Another woman, my ass.*

"You can take a nap with me, right?" He leans in and kisses my forehead for emphasis. I can feel the mass of muscles moving in his chest as he leans down.

I'm weak in the knees like SWV. "Sleep only," I say firmly, stepping out of his embrace.

He looks insulted that I would suggest anything more. "I wouldn't ever try anything *unless you asked me to.*"

Ask! Ask! My brain is shouting to my mouth. *Ask!* But, as Brit predicted, I do nothing but grab his outstretched hand and follow him inside the building.

His dorm room—better yet, suite—is like an apartment. Basic furniture but a gigantic living room that has offshoots to four different bedrooms. It's ginormous. I didn't even know this was a housing option. I assume, incorrectly, that this living arrangement is just for football players.

Jason turns the knob on the unlocked door to his room. It's a double, but he doesn't have a roommate. The twin beds are pushed together to make a queen-size, and he's moved one of the couches from the living room into his room.

I take a seat on the couch and lay my jacket across my lap before I slide off my low-heeled boots. They're a rarity. I usually won't walk in anything less than a three-inch heel.

I'm nervous. I've never been to the room of a *may-an* I'm dating before. My ex? He lived off-campus with his parents, his sister, her husband, and their son. There was always someone home. We usually hung out in my dorm room, my turf, where I was always comfy. And most of the guys I've dated were boys. Jason Randolph, who's stripping off his sweatshirt and is almost down to a wife-B that practically glows against his smooth, chiseled skin, is a bona fide, certified *may-an*.

And it's as if he's pulling off that shirt in slow motion. I unglue my eyes from him when his A-shirt rides up, revealing perfectly cut abs.

Damn. If I knew what to do, I'd do it. And no, Brit's advice is still not an option.

"You want a shirt?" he asks from behind me at his closet.

"A shirt? For what?" I squeak without looking at him.

"What're you nervous for?" he asks.

I turn to look at him. He's shirtless. *The cross. Jesus, keep me near it.* All sorts of thoughts go through my mind. Then I catch myself and look up at his face. He's holding back a smile.

"I'm not nervous," I lie, trying to sound sophisticated and as if I see bodies like his every day. "What do I need a shirt for?"

He looks me up and down. "To sleep in. I don't like street clothes in my bed."

I fold my arms over my chest as I summon up some of my gone-missing feistiness. "If I'm getting in your bed, I'll keep on what I got on," I challenge. "You can change your sheets after I leave."

He smirks, biting that bottom lip. Out come those dimples. "You ain't blond, but you're still tough. Get in the bed," he demands the way Teddy Pendergrass did about his lights.

I roll my eyes, and he walks over and pulls me up toward him, spinning me so my back is against his chest. He's got one arm across my midsection, holding me there against his wall of great-smelling man. He reaches down to intertwine our hands. "Don't be nervous," he says into my neck, kissing the nape quickly. "Okay?"

I exhale. "Okay."

I pull out of his embrace, glance back with my best version of a sly look, take my time unfastening my watch, and throw it onto his dresser. And then I get into the bed . . . with every intention of taking Brittany's advice.

I lose my nerve.

He walks around the bed and climbs in wearing his boxers. White. Silk.

My back is to him, and he immediately pulls me close to him before we fall asleep so that we are spooning. I know what I was supposed to do. But when I pictured myself doing it, I was just so awkward and fidgety and messing everything up. Jason Randolph is a *may-an*, and I don't want him to know how inexperienced I am. A *may-an* needs a woman. And me? I'll be one soon. But I ain't yet.

Sigh.

I fall asleep long after Jason. I lie here awake, nervous, smelling his man scent and listening to him snoring lightly until my lack of sleep finally catches up with me. Now I'm awake again. Jason's still asleep. He's got a firm grip on my waist. I couldn't go anywhere if I wanted to, which is just fine, because I certainly don't want to. He's nestled into my neck, and every time he exhales, I feel his lips on my skin.

It's driving me crazy . . . in a good way.

I lie there for only God knows how long, letting him breathe on me and liking it way too much. I try to sync my breathing with his, but he inhales too slowly. I need more air.

Eventually, I wonder what time it is. I don't have anything all that pressing to do on the other side of campus, but I don't want to overstay my welcome. Better for him to think I left too soon than stayed too long. I try to move away from Jason without waking him to get my watch off the dresser. As soon as I move an inch, he grabs my arm back, mumbles, "Stay," and kisses the back of my neck. He settles his big hand with a grip on my thigh, and I lie in this new position with my arm tucked beneath me . . . until it starts to fall asleep.

"Jason?" I whisper loudly, trying to wake him but not startle him.

He answers me groggily, and I roll counterclockwise to face him. He pulls me in till we're smashed against each other and puts his arm behind my back to keep me there.

Jason's lying perfectly still, but he is not asleep. I can tell by the way he's breathing. And I can *feel* that he's attracted to me since we're pushed up all close. Pressed against him, facing him, knowing I have an effect on him gives me some confidence.

I look and find his mouth is right above my nose. I *scooch* up till we're almost lip-to-lip.

"Jason?" I whisper.

He opens his eyes slowly, breaks out into a huge smile when he sees my face right in front of him. "Hey."

"Hey," I say, and lean in for a kiss—just a peck, I promise myself—before I lose my nerve again.

That peck quickly turns into, well, more than a peck. We're making out in just less than a minute before Jason flips me on top so I'm straddling him. As a habit, I don't French kiss. Frankly, I think it is gross. Yet I have my tongue suspiciously shoved down Jason Randolph's throat.

I have a moment of clarity and pull back, sit up, look at him as if he's a stranger, because I'm a *woman* I don't know anymore. I soak up the view of that body, that expansive mass of rippled, brown, broad flesh, and run my hands over it, across it, up it, until

I firmly cup his chin in my hand, holding him still so I can lean in and thrust my tongue into his mouth for another must-have, much-needed kiss.

Who am I?

Seconds later, he's grabbing at my jeans, but there's no way these stretch Parasucos are coming off in this position. He realizes this and holds me to him as he effortlessly flips me over and releases me gently on the bed, as if I'm some precious jewel being laid out on black velvet for show. I reach up with both hands to fondle that wonderful display of man breast above me, waxing on and waxing off like Daniel-san. Finally, he lies on top of me, giving me the full pressure and pleasure of his man weight. He grabs the back of my head, pulling me to him urgently, and kisses me deeply the same way I did when I was over him.

I'm about to do numbers. Oh, yes, I am. I am doing numbers! And if Jason Randolph's jersey was in Roman numerals, I'd do letters, too.

I splay both of my hands on his shoulders and push him up. He immediately backs up, looking confused. I hold his gaze and run my hands down his chest, over his solid abs, and keep going till I'm below his waist and have found what I'm looking for.

He drops back down before I get to the third stroke, covering me and wrapping a broad forearm beneath my back as he kisses me again.

"You sure?" he eventually mumbles against my lips.

I nod. "I'm sure," I say.

We envelop each other a little longer. I'm running my hands across his wide back, letting my lips taste, bite, nibble, and kiss every place they can reach—chest, shoulders, cheeks, lips, ears, neck, biceps, hands, forearms, fingers. Jason's doing the same to me, and just when I think I'm about to explode from need, he gets off the bed, heading to his dresser for a condom.

I'm still on the bed, attempting to wiggle out of my Parasucos . . . when there's a knock at the door.

"Come back later," Jason hollers out. He looks over at me knowingly and smiles real wide until his dimples come out.

I'm so corny. I blow him a kiss, and he catches it.

Correction: we're corny.

There's another knock.

"I'm busy," he calls out again.

"Motherfucker!" a woman yells. "You better open this door!"

I assume it's her who starts banging on the door. I don't think with her fist, because the object sounds too solid and too big—unless she's a huge chick.

"Motherfucker!" she yells again. "I want my money . . . bitch!"

I cover my open mouth with my hand and stare at the door. When I finally look at Jason, he looks terrified. I don't know what face I made, but he starts moving toward the door. Everything's in slow motion and super loud.

Bang! Bang! Bang! Bang!

I can hear at least two more female voices screaming in the living room, but they're not as loud as the main chick, who's still calling Jason all kinds of names and demanding her "motherfucking money . . . bitch."

He's almost at the door when I see the knob turn.

I'm shaking my head. "Jason!" I yell, pointing. I want him to move faster. He can't let them get in. Women never go after the guy. They always attack the girl. I see visions of myself getting stomped out by some Timbs-wearing New York girls and my face slashed by the razors all of them keep under their tongues.[1]

---

1 That was the prevailing perception of NYC girls on my campus, who, until you got to know them, seemed standoffish to anyone not from "up top" and incredibly unladylike in their Timbs and hip-hop/sports apparel compared with the extraordinarily prissy girls like me from Prince George's County.

Suddenly, everything speeds up.

"He's got a bitch in there!" the main chick yells frantically.

The door opens.

Oh, shit! Oh, shit! Oh, shit! I'm sure the chick is still yelling, but all I can hear is my own thoughts. I'm shaking as I scramble back on the bed to get as far away from the door as possible. I couldn't care less that Brit was right about the south-side chick. I'm more concerned that I'm about to get jumped.

Jason stiff-arms a short, light-skinned chick wielding a fat book-bag until she's back in the living room, then slams the door in her face. He locks it and leans his back against it. I can practically see the wheels turning in his brain.

Boom! Pause. *Boom!* Pause. *Boom!*

"Motherfucker! You don't know who you're messing with!"

Boom!

I'm guessing light, bright, and crazy is using her backpack full of books to slam against the door. She must be getting tired, because the hits are not coming in rapid succession anymore. But they're louder, which means harder. Combine that with her unrelenting holler, and I assume she's trying to break the door down.

Slam!

What is that?

Boom! Pause. *Slam!*

"Broke ass! I'm fucking you up and I'm beating that busted bitch, too!"

I can hear another girl in the background shouting something I can't make out. Something about a bar?

Boom! Slam!

Crack.

It's the wood door. Someone's kicking the door. They're about to break the door down.

Shit. Damn. Motherfucker.

Jason seems as stunned as I am. His eyes are wide, and he's still leaning against that damn door in his white silk boxers.

The cracked door seems to encourage them. There's a flurry of kicks now, followed by the sound of more wood splitting. There's not even yelling. They're fully concentrating on the door.

Jason must have finally realized what I could have told him the first time she called him a motherfucker. These chicks are not giving up until they get what they came for. Definitely some money, and maybe me, too.

"Jason, do something!" I finally yell. He's just standing there. "Give her the money!"

Boom!

That door is coming off the hinges any second. It ain't a reinforced door found in the PJs, it's a regular wood door made for civilized college students.

Jason finally snaps out of whatever trance he's in and goes to the closet, throwing on the clothes he had on earlier. He's taking his sweet time, and those girls are still pounding on that door. I keep thinking about having a cut-up face, of trying to fight three chicks who are wild and crazy enough to try, and accomplish any second now, the beating down of some man's door. I just hope they don't stomp me. I've seen that happen to someone before. He was in the hospital for a week and had almost a hundred stitches.

I close my eyes and pray—what else can I do?—and wonder what I got myself into.

Crack!

I open my eyes. Jason's sitting, putting on his shoes. I'm disgusted. I'm 'bout to get my behind beat up in here, and he wants to move in slo-mo?

"What the fuck?" I start yelling at him. "What the fuck?"

He ignores me.

"What the fuck?" I yell hard enough that I see the spit fly out of my mouth.

That gets his attention. He turns around, too calmly for me, and looks at me as if I'm crazy. "I'm going out there to handle this," he says evenly.

But he just sits there.

Boom!

I flip out, diving from the corner of the bed, across it, and just far enough to start pummeling him with my fists. I'm about to get attacked, and this man doesn't give a damn. I should open the door and let those crazy chicks in, and we can all beat his ass, or at least try. If I'm taking a whooping for messing with someone else's man or even for just being in the wrong place at the wrong time with the wrong man, he's getting his ass kicked, too, and first. If I go down, he goes down too.

I land as many blows as I can in a fighting fury before he turns, snatches my wrists together with a force I couldn't predict, yanks me up, and swiftly flings me—by my wrists—back onto the bed. I'm so stunned, I lie there motionless even after he lets go.

"I'll be right back," he says firmly, glancing back at me sprawled on the bed. "Don't come out here."

I watch, speechless, as he walks to the door, bracing himself for battle. He quietly unlocks it, quickly pulls it open, then slams the door behind him.

I ain't that stunned. I immediately jump up and scurry across the room and lock it.

I can hear the chicks yelling. Something breaks. There's the same girl screaming about her money and the bar. Jason yells that if she touches him again, he's kicking her ass whether she's "a bitch" or not. She hollers again that she'll beat him and the chick in the room unless she gets her "motherfucking money . . . bitch."

With her most recent threat, I get on the good foot and throw on my boots in case I have to run. I grab my watch from the dresser and go into Jason's closet, looking for something I can use as a weapon.

"You think I'm playing with you?" the chick yells.

There's a *boom* on the bedroom door, followed by a creaking sound.

I rack my brain thinking of whom I can call to help me. I'm pulling a blank. All my girls are prissy suburban chicks like me who ain't brawling to defend themselves, let alone me. Nessa's too grown for this, Natalie's on scholarship, and Sabby? She's like a cuddly house cat. I need someone who will hold me down.

Brit.

I grab my cell from my bag and dial her room. She answers on the second ring. "What up, bitch?" Mind you, there is no caller ID on the campus phone.

Boom!

I drop down to the floor on the side of the bed. I don't know what that was, but it's louder and more massive than all the other noises that came before it.

"Oh, my God, Brit, you gotta come get me. I'm in Charles Hall. In Jason's room," I ramble frantically. I'm yelling into the phone over all the noise. "These girls." I stop to catch my breath. "They came to his room. I'm still in here. They're in the living room. I'm gonna get jumped. I don't know what's going on. Brit, oh, my God, you gotta help me."

"Shit. I don't know where Charles is. Fuck, fuck, fuck. Can you get out the window?"

See why I love her?

I run to the window hopefully and look out. "I'll break something if I jump."

"There's no one there to cover you? His roommates can't get you out?"

"I don't know—"

"What in the hell is going on in here?" It's a dude's voice yelling over the fray.

"Oh, my God. Oh, my God, B!"

Everything goes quiet for a moment. Then the girls start yelling something about T.G.I. Friday's.

"Hold tight, D. Calm down. We're on our way," Brit promises.

"We?" I ask, but she's already hung up.

There's more yelling, a dude threatening to beat everyone's ass for "fucking up this shit" and that same girl demanding her money. If I had money, I'd slip it under the door to make her go away. Her primary concern is that money, not me. I'm just indirect collateral to make sure she gets it. I have no doubt she and her girls will uphold their promise to beat me if they are not paid.

Suddenly, I hear the girls screaming, and there's a tussle in the living room. I run back to the closet, searching through everything in a frenzy. I'm hopping up and down to see what's on the top shelf.

There's nothing. *Damn.* I turn around in the closet, looking for anything I can use as a weapon. If he was a hockey player, I could use a stick. A tennis player, I could use a racket . . . sort of. A soccer player, I could . . .

I drop to the floor, tearing apart Jason's shoeboxes until I find the cleats with the spikes. I slip the shoes over my hands. If anyone comes near me, I'm smacking them with these spiked cleats. What other option do I have?

I sit on the couch with the shoes on my hands, wondering how long I'll be stuck here. I'm guessing it's been ten minutes already. Maybe there's hope, though. The girls' shrieking is moving farther away.

There's a knock at the door, softer than a bang but still hard.

I don't say anything. I don't even move.

The knock comes again. "Demi?" the man says. It's not Jason. "It's Bobby. Open up."

I rack my brain. *Bobby? Oh, the old guy.*

"Who's with you?" I ask.

"It's just me. Everybody's in the stairwell. Let me in."

I ponder the dangers of letting a man I don't know into a bedroom with me. I think about Brittany's suggestion of a cover. There are at least two full-sized men involved in this now. They should be able to hold the women off so I can run away.

"Can you get me out of here?" I ask through the door.

"I'm gonna try."

I slip off a cleat and unlock the door to let Bobby in. I get a glimpse of the door as I open it. It's busted up with scratches, dents, and some holes. A couple more kicks, and it would have been down.

Bobby closes and relocks the door, then turns to take a long look at me. He busts out laughing. "Bourgie, you got some hood in you, huh?"

I realize I must look a fright. A cleat on one hand, makeup smeared from sleeping . . . and other things. I don't care. I'm not going down without a fight.

In the presence of a male stranger who seems to be part of the solution, I lose it. "What the hell is going on?" I plead with a cracking voice. I'm trying to choke back tears. "I just want to get back to my room."

He thinks for a moment, takes a seat on the couch. "You can't leave just yet. Soon. The situation is being taken care of. You're safe. No one's gonna hurt you."

I keep the cleat on. I'm not that trusting. "How do you know?" I challenge. I sound hard, but I don't look it. I've got tears running down my face.

"It's not about you. The guys . . ." He seems to be calculating the risk of telling me.

I wipe my face with the back of my uncovered hand. "I want to know."

"It's stupid. Jason and some other guys went to Friday's a couple nights ago, and they left without paying. The bartender is a chick he used to . . . date. They're not . . . involved anymore, so she's not giving up free food and drinks. Maybe she got in trouble with her manager or something."

I calculate the tab for three to four guys. Two hundred? Yeah, I see why she was pissed. Not sure he's giving me the whole story though.

"You're telling me he's not seeing her anymore? Then who else is he going out with?"

Bobby sighs. "It doesn't matter." He pauses, choosing his words carefully. "Look, when you get out of here . . . don't come back. This ain't for you."

No shit.

We sit in silence for a bit, waiting for the noise to die down completely. Bobby finally excuses himself and goes out into the living room to check everything out. I can hear him talking to Jason.

I can't hear the girls, and I feel safe again. I throw the cleat onto the floor and wait for Bobby to come back. I wipe my face with my hands, trying to get the running mascara from under my lids. I remain standing, wishing Bobby would hurry up.

Jason calls my name. I don't answer till Bobby calls and tells me to come out.

I snatch my bag from the floor and walk into the living room. There's a mess. The couch is flipped over, the halogen lamp pole is cracked on the floor, and there are papers and ripped up books everywhere. I march to the window without acknowledging either Jason or Bobby and look for the girls. I don't see them. I walk to the main door, snatch it open, run down the steps, and go as fast as I can to get out into the courtyard.

"Demi!" Jason calls after me.

I keep going. I hear Bobby call Jason back, but he's still behind me when I get outside.

"Demi!"

"Leave me alone!" I roar at him. I'm loud enough for anyone with a window facing us to hear. Then I run down the sidewalk, my bag flopping at my side. I'm taking Bobby's advice. When a guy's own friends tell you to leave him alone, you leave him alone.

I don't stop running until I'm in the middle of McKeldin Mall and hear my phone ringing from my bag. I park my butt on a bench by the sundial and fish it out. It's Brit.

"Where are you? I got a ride! We're leaving now!" she yells when I put the phone to my ear. She's super-amped.

"Brit, Brit," I say over her exclamations. "I got out. I'm on the mall. I'm out."

"Aww, man. You cool? You all right? We need to come over there still?" I can hear in her voice that she's itching for a fight.

I shake my head, even though she can't see me, and talk her down. "No, I'm fine. I'm on my way back to the dorm. I'll stop by when I get back and tell you everything."

"Come straight here," she demands.

I promise her I will. But before she gets off the phone, I have a question: "Brit, who's 'we'?"

"Oooh. Me and Sabrina. That bitch is 'bout it."

PRESENT

Athletes love hip-hop, but they don't get to make music videos. So instead, some of them turn every club outing into an impromptu live video shoot sans the cameras. (For reference, see football player Pacman Jones making it rain to the tune of eighty thousand in a Vegas strip club during NBA All-Star Weekend 2007.)

My tunnel vision on all of these beautiful male bodies widens, and I finally see the forest for the trees. (I'm not distracted by shiny things, but chiseled arms do get my attention.) The men—all athletes . . . and Damon Wayans?—are on the stage, vibing to "Throw Your Hands Up" which I last partied hard to in undergrad. They are facing the crowd/audience—us—down on the main floor as if they are performers. Most are standing around posturing, and some are partying way too hard, like it's a fresh Kanye track instead of an ancient tune.

I look around at the women. They look as if they've gathered for a Black porn-star convention. Spandex bodysuits with belts circa JJ Fad and Oaktown 357, scraps of cloth posing as skirts and tops, and cheap glitter dresses. Big, big hair and loads of makeup.

"Someone just wipe her down—forehead, nose, cheeks, chin," Penelope quips as one particularly sparkly woman switches by.

And then I notice no one in the audience is even dancing, not that the music would inspire such. The ballers are looking down at us. We are staring back at them. It's like a zoo. But who are the animals?

"Hey, guys," I say to my friends when we've been there not even ten minutes. "I'm gonna head back to Brooklyn . . . now."

SHE DON'T BELIEVE
IN SHOOTING STARS . . .

This guy and I have been trying to arrange a date for two months. It hasn't happened, not due to lack of interest but because we both have the worst schedules ever. Lately, it seems I am perpetually editing a manuscript on deadline. And he, a lawyer, is working triple-time representing a politician whose legal woes are splashed across the covers of the *New York Post* and the *Daily News*, well . . . daily.

On his rare days off, he actually leaves Brooklyn headed to Miami, where he went to undergrad, or Houston, where he went to law school, or visits his brother in D.C. where he's from. Me? I turn off my BlackBerry for a day and call that a getaway. Between freelancing and working, I can afford a vacation, but I don't have time to plan one, much less actually take one.

I should add for complete disclosure that this guy and I have sort of never met. I am in D.C. visiting my parents for Thanksgiving and escaped postdinner to meet Tariq at the Park at Fourteenth, one of D.C.'s premier social venues. I arrive before Tee, so

I wander around until I find Spencer, a D.C. socialite-marketing-guru-party promoter-lawyer sitting at a table he bought. He is there with a gentleman who has his back to me, a gentleman who has a gigantic 3-D star etched into his hair. It is, in a word, fabulous. I've been searching for a barber with the skills of an artist ever since I'd started thinking about shaving my head. I stare until Spencer breaks my temporary fixation with an offer of a beverage from his champagne bottle.

I am chatting up Spencer, swirling my drink in my flute, and thinking of a witty compliment for Stars, when I see Tariq and a friend near the bar. I make my way to meet him and the tall choco-late man he is speaking to. When Tariq doesn't introduce me to his friend fast enough, I interrupt their conversation and stick my hand out to the stranger.

"Excuse my best friend's rudeness," I say boldly. "I'm Demetria. You are?"

The stranger and I become engrossed in a conversation that doesn't include Tariq, who eventually walks off. My attention is to-tally swept up until the beautiful specimen mentions he has a . . . girlfriend. Sort of.

"We broke up, but she hasn't moved out yet," he explains.

I shake my head, thank him for a lovely chat, take his number to be polite when he insists, and go in search of Tariq and my original interest (not in that order), the guy with the stars. When I return to Spencer's booth, Stars is gone.

"Where's your boy?" I demand of Spencer.

He raises his brow as if to say *who?* He throws parties for a living, which means he schmoozes professionally and knows of a lot of people but actually only knows-knows a few. And he went to Howard University, which means the entire city knows him. Practically every male with a degree falls under the definition of Spencer's "boy."

"With the star in his head," I clarify.

"Who, Reggie?" He shakes his head. "Bounced."

He's barely paying attention, instead watching a woman with a big tush in a little dress wind her waist to reggae music. You'd think since he works in a club that sight would lose its novelty, but apparently not.

"So how do I find him?" I ask, bringing his focus back to more important matters. My quest is less about finding the man and more about finding his barber. I want stars, *those stars*, etched in the side of my head, too. All the better if I can get it done on this trip home and just have a barber in Brooklyn trace over the design so it stays. Who knew D.C. has such dope barbers?

It doesn't.

Spencer can't find Stars's number, but he has his e-mail and his government name. I track down Stars on Facebook, more personal than a random e-mail, and hit him with the God's honest truth: "The stars are sick. I need them in my life. I live Up Top and go back Monday. Think I can get your barber's number?"

Turns out Stars lives in Brooklyn and is only in D.C. for the weekend to visit relatives. And his barber? He's a family friend based in Brooklyn. His shop, Skills, is conveniently located on Flatbush Avenue, a fifteen-minute train ride from my house. Stars offers to escort me personally to meet his barber to make sure I get A-list treatment.

"It's a date," I write back. "I'm looking forward to it."

A last minute freelance assignment where I'm being flown to Miami to interview a female rapper for the cover of *The Source* forces me to cancel our outing. This, I'll discover later, is for the best, since the barber said he doesn't cut women's hair.

Stars informs me of the discrimination the following afternoon and promises to avenge my creative honor. Within the week, he convinces the barber that an exception has to be made for the sake of superior style and e-mails me to declare that as an advocate for the fashion-forward, he has been successful. I can now have all the stars I want.

Cute. Very. But we still can't manage to meet up.

I try to hook up with Stars once when Spencer is coming to the city for a mutual friend's birthday party. I e-mail Stars to ask if he'd like to meet me there. He can't. He is headed to Miami that weekend for a wedding.

We e-mail a few more times (I'm not a phone person; I don't think he is, either), but he sort of fades into the background, caught up with his own obligations. I pack my schedule to the hilt with parties, work, and sleep (in that order).

One random Monday, when he's no longer in my mind's forefront, Stars hits me again. "I've had enough," he says. "I'll see you this week."

"I'm busy," I tell him. And it's the truth. I would love to hang out with him, but the city has exploded with A-list parties I can't bring myself to miss. I can go out every night to the hottest venues in the city, listen to the best DJs in the world, and drink top-shelf champagne *free* for several days straight.

"Cancel," he says flippantly. "This is *the* week. Make it happen."

I respect the *cojones* on this dude. Me, cancel my party life to accommodate him just because he half-asked, half-demanded that I do? My inner alpha female objects. But she's also pretty intrigued with a man who has manned up on her. Most don't try, much less get away with it.

I cancel Thursday's events—much to the displeasure of my friend Kenneth, who is looking for a roadie to join him on a rooftop soiree at the Shelburne hotel. Apparently, there is a Rémy party, for the liquor, not the incarcerated rapper. I argue to Kenneth that he's only going for the women anyway and would likely leave me to my own socializing devices as soon as we made it past whoever's holding the guest list at the door. He doesn't offer a counterargument, because he knows I'm right.

I meet up with Stars at Tillman's, a quaint soul-food restaurant with great music and expensive drinks. My first question after we exchange pleasantries is about the stars. "How do you get away with that as a lawyer?" I want to know.

He doesn't. "I have them cut in Friday before I leave town," he explains. "When I get back to the city Sunday night, I shave my head."

Stars is a lawyer who throws parties, like Spencer, in Houston, Miami, and occasionally D.C. The plan is to turn that hustle into a marketing goldmine for young Black professionals and the corporations trying to capture their disposable income. His day job funds his weekend lifestyle.

I get it. I edit titillating tales of characters being speared and disrobed in ten-page love scenes, but my current office is pretty conservative. (I moved to another publishing company—better title, better pay.) For work, I snatch my fluff back into a low bun. At six P.M. and on weekends, I release it into a carefully pinned faux-hawk or a gigantic corkscrew-curly afro. I fit in fine running around the city, bouncing from one industry event to the next, or even when doing interviews for *XXL, The Source,* or *Vibe.* But my day job? Not so much.

"Sometimes you have to be who you need to be in order to get to who you want to be," Stars says.

I nod. Stars reminds me of my dad, my favorite roadie. Each time I fantasize about quitting my just-to-pay-the-bills day job and freelancing full-time as a writer until I can land on somebody's masthead, my dad gives me the same line.

"We'll get there," Stars says, with a confidence I'm not always sure I have. Then he signals the waiter for another round of drinks.

Two cocktails and a couple shared appetizers later, our date is coming to a close. I excuse myself to the ladies' room to apply a fresh coat of lippie and blush. When I return, Stars is fiddling with his BlackBerry. He looks a little guilty when he sees me approaching the table and puts it back in his pocket. I assume it's work, then wonder if he was texting another woman. I shrug at either option but make a mental note of it. I've been on enough great first dates not to expect anything but a good time. That's what dating is, no?

He walks me to the train like the gentleman he is, and I promise to text him when I am home safe.

On the train, I pull out my phone to check my missed texts and BBMs. Instead, I find this message:

> *I will take the opportunity while you are in the ladies' room to tell you that I had a great time tonight!!! The best part about first dates is the hope that is in the air . . . and I hope this is the first of many . . .*

Stars and I kick it twice a week for a while, even decide to do Valentine's Day together, although we've only been dating a little more than a month. It's a spontaneous decision, and doing the obvious, such as going to see a good Broadway show or getting a reservation at a semidecent restaurant (all booked) is impossible.

Two days before the big day, both of us are pulling a blank about what to do. I want things to go well, so I decide that instead of pushing for Stars to pull a magic rabbit out of his NY Yankees fitted, I'll make a masterpiece out of minimalism. I call Stars from the grocery store on February 13 and announce that I will cook our Valentine's Day dinner.

Him: "Okay."

Me: "Okay?"

He has this habit of never saying or doing what I expect. I can predict most people. Perhaps this is why I am so fond of him.

Me: "I don't cook. You don't even want to know what I'm cooking?"

Stars and I have a conversation one day while sitting in a diner sharing banana nut waffles, Greg's favorite breakfast dish. We'd just walked along the waterfront in Battery Park City. I took him there to show him the Statue of Liberty, since he'd never seen it. He took me for breakfast at dinnertime after.

He starts our talk with "I like you. I really do." I keep waiting at the pause for the "but." And finally, I realize there isn't a pause. It's a definitive statement that needs no negating. I cut a corner of the waffle, dab it in syrup, and lift the fork toward his mouth.

We've started seeing each other more on weekends now since Stars hasn't been traveling as much. He's been talking about focusing on law, giving up the party life. Splitting his energy between two fields means he's not excelling at either one, and he's deciding to focus on the one with more longevity and more stability. I have to actively talk myself out of reading into this change of heart that he is starting to settle down.

One day at work, I'm toiling away at my desk like a good editor . . . Let me stop. I'm at my desk revamping my résumé, because while Stars has decided that "good enough" is good, it's inspired me to go gung-ho after my dream of becoming a magazine editor.

My BlackBerry interrupts my search for the right action verb to describe dealing with a growing roster of authors that includes *some* who require significant hand-holding. I want to call it managing, but it's really more like coddling. But you can't put that on a résumé. I hope it's Stars hitting me to confirm our plans for tonight. Last week, I'd invited him to join me at a friend's birthday celebration in SoHo.

I flip over my BlackBerry to find a message from a young woman who reads my blog, asking me if I'd do an interview for her site, which she listed. My blog is less than a year old, and it's the first time anyone's asked me for an interview.

Him: "Nope."

Me: "Um . . . well, then, I'll call you when I get home."

Him: "Okay."

So I cook—better, bake—the only real dish I know how to make: vegetable lasagna.

The next evening, I meet Stars downtown after work. He appears in my lobby with roses, a card, and an expensive-looking bottle of white wine. I wasn't expecting anything, so I'm positively giddy as soon as I spot him holding my gifts.

We head to Brooklyn. While I fuss around in the kitchen, pretending to know what I'm doing, he stands at the kitchen table, watching me and chatting about nothing and everything. And by the time we cuddle up on the couch to watch *Love Jones,* we've done nothing but spend what I guess for most is a chill, typical date night on what is supposed to be some over-the-top day.

It was one of the best V Days ever. I realize that its more about who you're with than what you do. I look over at Stars and smile, bite my inside cheeks to keep it from getting too big. I haven't met a guy who's made me do that since Mr. Ex.

By April, things are still going well with Stars. I'm dating only him now, not because we're exclusive but because I lack the time or energy to date anyone else. Being Nola Darling is more complicated in life than it is on-screen. My senior editor added a few new authors to my roster, and I'm working on a big project to create the outlines of a multiauthor miniseries of books. It's taking up more of my time than I expected, but I'm gunning for a promotion, so I'll do what it takes. Between that and freelancing and the blog I've started writing for HoneyMag.com about dating and relationships, I don't have much free time, but I make time for Stars. I've accepted that I really like him.

Her site is a compilation of party listings for professional Blacks in major cities throughout out the U.S. Nice. Penelope and I had a similar idea years ago. We decided we should review events and chronicle our lives one party at a time. We were too exhausted from going out ever to make the time to get that idea off the ground.

While searching through the site, I click on a link to the venue where I met Stars, at the party Spencer threw. It leads to another link, where there are nothing but pictures of Stars, called by his government name, of course. I scroll down. He's grabbing a woman to him and planting a kiss on her cheek.

I scroll back up to check the date of the post. December. Eh . . . I didn't want to see that, but what can I say? I hadn't so much as been on a date with him by then.

I e-mail the girl, A'lana, back, confirming that I'll do the interview. I can't help myself. I know I should mind my business, but I can't.

"Your site has a picture of my friend Reggie," I write. "Great guy."

She writes back a minute later. "I'll send you the questions in a sec. Reggie's my best friend's boo. Personally I can't stand him."

Her "boo"? What does that mean? Is he her date, her boy-toy? Her man? Her "boo"?

My stomach is in knots. The sixth-sense kind. The intuition kind. The kind that Oprah says are the signs of God speaking.

Damn.

I immediately look up the picture again, searching for a photo caption that IDs the woman. Her name is Erin. I dial Stars at work.

"Hi. Who's Erin?" I ask, cutting straight to the point.

There's a long silence. "Erin? She's a good friend."

"Is she your girlfriend?"

Another lengthy pause. "We're good friends."

"I asked you a yes-or-no question."

"Let's discuss this later. Are we still on for tonight?"

"Don't dismiss me."

"D, later," he says firmly. "I'm at work."

I only agree to abide by the unwritten rule of Blackness No. 4081: Never cause another Black professional drama on his or her job. The job is holy ground, like Mecca. Act a fool in the street, act a fool at home, in the club, but by no means act a fool at your work or someone else's and confirm to White people that the stereotypes most Black people think they hold in the backs of their minds about us are true.

"Fine. I'll see you later."

Click.

I stare at the résumé on my computer screen, but I don't see it. I am fuming. I want to shoot Stars.

A'lana hits me back with interview questions as I'm prepping to leave work to meet Stars.

I scroll through her e-mail. In the body of the letter, she asks, "Can I ask how you know Reggie?"

I write back with the truth. "I've been dating him for a few months."

When I get off the elevator and my phone restores the signal it lost in the shaft, there's another message from her. "Can you call me?" it reads.

So I do. She mentioned to her girl Erin that I inquired about him. Her girl is really upset and wonders, if I don't mind telling, what exactly is the nature of my relationship with Stars. And when I say dating, could I be more specific?

I tell her I'll call her back and hang up as I rush down the subway steps to meet Stars. I want to be on time for this.

When I walk into the party, Stars is waiting for me at the bar closest to the entrance. He's leaning on the counter ordering a drink. When he spots me, he calls the bartender back and orders a white wine. I approach, and he kisses my cheek, offers me my glass, then introduces me to his boy.

Odd. This was supposed to be a date. What's his boy doing here? I can't ask without being rude, so I'm rude.

"What's your boy doing here?" I ask Stars in front of his guest.

He looks startled. I'm usually the epitome of Miss Manners.

"We work together. He wasn't doing anything, so I invited him. Is that not okay?"

He's his bodyguard. Insurance that I won't make a scene if there's an audience. That's fine. He wants his coworker to bear witness to this, I'm totally okay with that.

I plant the wine on the bar without taking a first sip. "Who's Erin?" I ask.

He sighs. "Can't we have a good time and do this later?"

I look at him, baffled. "Her girl told her we were dating and said she's pretty upset. Why would she be upset? Is she your girlfriend?"

He hems and haws, nothing of relevance said, no clear answer revealed. Three minutes of rambling boils down to "You and I are you and I."

My stomach tightens. I know what that means. I shake my head and sigh. Everything is always good until it isn't. "No, we're not. We're done."

He was in mid-drink when I said it. He slams the glass on the bar after the words come out. His boy, who's long since turned to watch the room, looks back over his shoulder. I stare at Stars blankly.

"What does that mean?" he demands.

"It means don't call me anymore." When I replay this story to friends, the women say I'm being hasty. The men say some version of "When it's over, it's over. No sense in dragging it out." The latter is my logic.

"We can't be friends?" he asks.

"Fuck friends. I want an answer."

His response? He lifts his glass from the bar, swirls the cubes around in the brown liquid, and takes the last swig to the head. He taps his boy on the shoulder and circles his index finger in the air, the universal signal for *wrap it up*. And then he strolls out of the bar. His boy offers a polite but confused good-bye and follows him. I laugh. Because what else can I do? Go after them?

I ignore the slow ache building in the right side of my head and think of Mr. Ex. Nothing will ever be as painful as him leaving. If I can get over that, I can get over this.

I liberate my BlackBerry from my purse and text A'lana to say Stars is free and clear. We are no longer dating. Then I lift my untouched wine to my lips, plaster on the best smile I can manage, and sashay further into the room to give the birthday boy my wishes for wheels, wealth, and the gift of insight so he can always see for himself.

On Saturday, I'm sitting on the kitchen counter in pum-pum shorts, a wife-beater, and knee-high socks with the stripes at the top, eating crackers and reading British women's magazines. This is my Single Girl's Weekend afternoon ritual.

My BlackBerry rings. It's Stars. I answer out of curiosity, the cause of a lot of life's drama.

"I want to be totally honest," Stars begins. He convinces me that what he says will be worth the listen, and these are his confessions: There are a few women he's been dealing with. Me in New York, another woman on the East Coast, a couple more in two Southern states. He reasons that I know how often he used to travel when we met and that he hasn't left the state in the last few months. This should be an indication of where his interest lies, since he's been keeping himself in the city. He says nothing of whether his out-of-state friends have been coming to see him instead.

"So I was Miss New York in your pageant of women?" I say. Instead of asking, I should have hung up.

He digs himself deeper trying to explain. The woman I found out about? A "friend." Their relationship is "light." Now, one of the chicks in the South? Well, their relationship is "heavy." She's been around a long time, she's met his family, and she cries when she drops him off at the airport.

That's when I hang up. I don't need to hear about the fourth woman. When there are tears and family meetings going on, that's more than "just" dating. I don't know what exactly "light" means in relation to the other woman he's dating on the Eastern Seaboard, but if she's upset, she's probably more than just a "date," too.

I wonder what word he'll use to describe me when the woman I found about inevitably calls to ask, "Who's Demetria?" Am I "light," too, after four months of seeing each other a few times a week?

Probably so.

I say "eff it" to this whole affair and pick up my BlackBerry to vent to Tariq about how blown I am by Stars's revelations and how much I don't care. He listens for a while, ten minutes worth, before he interrupts.

"So, exactly why are you so angry, then?" he asks.

I rattle off some generic reasons about everybody wanting to be a pimp but not knowing pimping ain't easy. Didn't Stars grow up on Too Short, too?

Tariq knows me too well. "No. Tell me why you're mad, son," he jokes, quoting a Puffy skit.

I sigh, roll my eyes, and huff.

Tariq waits for my mini-tantrum to end. "You done?" he asks, not even sounding annoyed.

I am. So I spill. I like being single, as in not married and without a boyfriend. I do. And I have to say that these days, because otherwise, someone will remind me that I'm over twenty-five and assume I'm just dying not just to be in a relationship but to jump the broom.

Um . . . that's not always the case. There are extraordinary virtues and vices to being in a relationship or married, just as there are for being single. Everyone always talks about the horror of being single and the joy of being paired off. But I'm smart enough not to believe the fairy-tale hype I peddle in the books I edit for Harlequin. Every bed of roses has its thorns.

But Stars has made me rethink living just enough for the moment, or me, or the city. Maybe there's still something to this relationship and happily-as-possible-ever-after (if you work really hard at it) thing if you're with the right person. With Stars, I was starting to believe in something, want something bigger than all about me, me, me. That's why I'm so mad. My perspective shifted, and now I'm stuck thinking about a new way of living with no one to live it with. I want more than me, and now all I got is me.

"You're enough," Tariq reminds me.

"I know." I say it because it sounds good. But right now? I don't feel like I am.

MISERY LOVES COMPANY

"Miss Demetria Lucas."

He's pronounced each word so that my name takes three complete seconds to say. He sounds as if he's happy to see me.

I'm standing by an outdoor rooftop pool, taking in the view of the city. I'm at Sky Studios, a fabulous triplex penthouse with a rooftop pool and an all-encompassing view of New York City. It was featured in *Brown Sugar*, in the party where Sanaa Lathan bumps into Taye Diggs when she moves back to New York. I'm here for Common's pre-MTV Awards BBQ.

I don't have to turn around to know it's him. I haven't heard his voice in years, but I would recognize it anywhere. The last time I heard it, he was moaning in the middle of the street.

I turn to face Dakar Jameson and open my mouth to speak, but no words come out. I knew this moment would happen someday, just never thought it would be this soon or catch me so off-guard. In my mind, I would confront him about that night, tell him all the ways it ruined my life, and make him carry around the baggage of what he did the same way I did, the same way *I do.*

Instead, I just stare. I feel lightheaded, and I know it has nothing to do with the two glasses of rosé I drank. I look at Dakar wide-eyed, like I can't believe he's here in front of me, then shake my head and walk to other side of the pool, the farthest I can get from him. I head for the hallway leading to the venue's main room, a garden patio.

He shouts my name across the water as I scurry off. When he calls after me again, I start to run in my heels. My half-empty glass of champagne splashes all over my black button-up sweater. I think about the pool and how I can't swim if I trip and fall in. I'd rather drown than talk to him again.

I dab at my sweater with a napkin as I walk down the steep steps to the second floor and scan the crowd for my friends. I'm here with a bunch of people, including Penelope and my finance folk, who will stay till the party ends at eleven, then head back to the office to get in another two to three hours of work before going home and showing up at the office again long before nine-thirty A.M. when the markets reopen.

I spot Penelope by the bar and make my way over to her. As soon as I'm in hearing distance, I tell her I'm going home.

"Oh, my God. What's wrong? What happened?"

She's not being dramatic. She just knows me well. I never leave a party early. I don't stay till the lights come on, of course, but everyone who knows anything about me knows that I hate sitting in the house. My apartment is used to sleep and change clothes in. That's about it.

"I just . . . gotta go." Penelope knows the Dakar backstory, but I don't want to freak her out by telling her he's here.

"Oh."

She's offended, but I don't have the time or the energy to kiss her emotional boo boo. "You stay and have a great time," I encourage. It's the best I can do. "I'll be fine. Don't worry about me. And tell the girls I'll talk to them soon."

I'm getting ready to lean in for a double-cheek kiss good-bye when I spot Dakar in the crowd, too close for comfort. I don't mean to, but I tense up; my hand starts to shake so much that Nell notices. She looks from me to Dakar and back at me.

"Who's he?" she asks.

I shake my head. "I'm fine," I lie unconvincingly. All in one sentence and without stopping for a breath, I tell her again that I have to go and I hope I will see her soon and I'll text when I get in. I wave her off and make a beeline for the elevators, dropping my champagne flute on a passing waiter's empty tray.

A gaggle of people get off the lift. I see some familiar faces, quickly air-kiss a few folks I know, and lie about an oncoming migraine to explain why I am leaving what looks like the biggest party of the night.

On the walk to the train, I wonder what Dakar is doing back in the city. Last I heard, he'd moved to Atlanta, gotten married, was raising his wife's kid as his own. New York City, wide and long and overpopulated as it may be, is not big enough for the two of us to coexist. I just got to the point where I can go to a party again without a guy by my side, usually some over-six-foot security-guard-looking dude who doubles as my date. And I just stopped freaking out every time I see a man in the distance who shares Dakar's height and build. And there's so much more I had to get over. I was supposed to tell him all of that, but when the clichéd push came to shove, I pretended he was King Kong and I was a hysterical blonde.

I trek to the next corner and head down the steps to the F train at Broadway-Lafayette to Brooklyn. I stand on the platform waiting for the next train, which will show up in who knows how long. I spot a man who looks like Dakar across the tracks on the Uptown platform. I squint, look closer. It is Dakar.

He's casually reading a magazine with his headphones on, bobbing his head to the beat without a care in the world. This while I stand across from him thinking of all the ways that night turned my life upside down.

I stare at him, baffled. "The Incident," as I've come to call it, is replaying in my head. All of the terror, frustration, confusion, fear, and embarrassment rush back, and suddenly, I'm not afraid anymore. I'm pissed.

On autopilot, I seize the moment, marching back up the stairs, crossing over to the Uptown platform, and taking the steps down as quickly as possible. I walk up to Dakar with a confidence I never knew I had.

He looks up, startled.

"Hey," I say. "We need to talk."

He looks confused but says "Okay," and follows me up the stairs, where we can speak without so many people in earshot.

At the top of the steps, I whirl around. He's got a cocksure stance that conveys that he couldn't care less what I'm about to say, but I unleash on him anyway.

"You need to know what you did to me," I scold.

I look into his eyes for the first time in years and tell him about the morning after, when my dad told me that what Dakar did to me was my fault for getting drunk and going to a man's house.[1] How I still blame myself. How I scrubbed until I was raw trying to get the stench of him off me. How I finally got home the morning after on a ninety-degree day in August after a two-hour commute to Brooklyn[2] and curled under my comforter in my un-air-condi-

---

1 Every other man I've ever told this story to has said some version of "Do you know how many drunk women have been in my apartment? I've never . . . I would never . . ."

2 I insisted on taking the train. I wanted to be "alone."

tioned room. How I slept at a friend's house on her couch that next night because I no longer felt safe alone. How every time I fell asleep for that night and the next week, I awoke with a start, scared that he—or someone new—was there waiting to hurt me. How I lost my desire to touch Mr. Ex for months. And when I finally got up the nerve to have sex again, I felt used and ashamed and had to choke back tears to keep him from freaking out. And I wasn't always able to hide that, either. I tell him about being unable to trust myself to discern character and not trusting men in general. I tell him about going to the NYPD Special Victims Unit in Harlem to report him and leaving without pressing charges because I couldn't retell the story without feeling like a whore who brought it all on herself. I tell him about how I thought I was damaged goods and no longer good enough for any respectable man to want. And finally, I tell him how I wanted to quit New York and move back home and give up on my dream, and the only reason I didn't the day after it happened was that I was too broke and too ashamed to face my parents.

"You fucked me up," I finish bluntly. "And you need to carry that with you the same way I carry that night with me."

I've just spilled all the messy details of my life, and pitiful though they may be, I don't feel that way at all. I feel like I've accomplished something. I stare at him defiantly, stoically, after I've said all the words to him I've been dreaming of saying for years.

He seems small to me now. At six-foot-one, he towers over me, of course, but he looks frail, nonthreatening. Like if I blew at him like a dandelion, he'd scatter into a million little particles and cease to exist.

He says nothing. I walk off, summarily dismissing him. This wasn't a conversation, and I don't care if he has anything to say. I just needed him to know what he'd done, and I feel relieved to share the full burden of what happened that night with someone else.

I'm almost to the steps to catch my train home whenever it arrives when I hear Dakar's muffled words.

"I'm sorry," he says, making sure I hear. His head is down, but he yells it loudly enough for anyone passing to hear.

I didn't really expect him to say anything. I turn and look at him from a distance.

"I never meant to hurt you," he says. "I-I cared about you. A lot. I was drunk, too. I threw up after you left. I'm really, really sorry, Demetria."

He's yelling it over the sound of a train coming on the downtown track. It could be mine.

"That guy almost killed me!" he bellows.

I nod at him repeatedly, just taking it in, my mind flashing back to him lying in the street. Dakar's got tears in his eyes, and I believe his apology is sincere. I never wanted him to say "sorry," because I thought he never would. But it feels . . . validating, I guess, to have it. It's true. Misery does love company.

I yell "Thank you!" over the dull roar of the coming train and rush down the stairs to catch my ride home.

CAST A WIDE NET

Do Black women know how to date?

This is the question that crossed my mind as I was sorting through the tons of books that came across my work desk last week.

After Stars and I ended, I took my newfound free time to get what I came to New York for: a magazine job. A few months of focus later, my dream came true.

An editor from *Essence* had begun reading my blog on HoneyMag.com and asked me to send over my résumé. After a couple of vigorous interviews, I was offered a position. I'm now the relationships editor at *Essence* magazine. It's literally in my job description to know everything possible about men, sex, dating, and relationships. When I'm not interviewing experts, probing men to figure out what they want, asking women if they're willing to do it and what they expect in return, on photo shoots with hot men, searching the city for men (a.k.a. "cutie run"), or, you know, actually editing my pages in the magazine, I'm poring through the advice guides piled on my desk.

The current titles include *Stop Calling Him Honey . . . and Start Having Sex!; It's Not Him, It's You; Toxic Men*; and twenty more books that follow the same theme. I was reading (or, better, flipping through) all of these pages, and I wondered how much of it actually helps. In just two months and over a hundred men interviewed later, I've come to a startling conclusion: most women, including me sometimes, don't know how to date.

So many women spend all their time trying to find the One and hold on to him so tight that they forget how to just get to know someone and have fun. They think about marriage before the date.

I had this revelation when a woman, a single actress in her thirties, stopped by the office. She looked around at my office, which is decorated with pictures of shirtless brown men in varying hues flexing their muscles, and said I must be the woman she'd heard about.

"You know where the single men are, right?" She said it like we were coconspirators in an illegal sidewalk enterprise.

I nodded. It's also in my job description to find cute men who want to meet Black women and feature one of them on *Essence*'s Single Man of the Month page each issue. I'm required to find them for random other reasons, too, and provide them on demand. I keep files under my desk where men are sorted by age and geographic location to make sure I never come up empty.

"Can you hook me up?" she asked after a long pause.

That's another thing I've noticed a lot of Black women do. It's as if we're afraid to say that we want companionship.

"Sure. What do you want?" I asked.

She rattled off the basics—he should be kind, funny, honest, attentive, blah, blah, blah. (I think it's sad that isn't a given.) I interrupted her to ask what age range and physical traits she wanted. All of the guys in my files are prescreened and must meet my dating standard. If I won't date them, I won't offer them up to anybody else.

"Oh . . ." she said, then paused to think. "Late thirties, anybody attractive."

I liked her openness. Most women run down a list of traits they can't compromise on. A forty-one-year-old detective popped into my head. He looked thirty-five and had the body of a CGI character out of *300*. And he was also really nice. I'd been dying to link someone up with him. He came highly recommended from a co-worker who met him at her gym. She described him as "very sweet but not my type" and graciously passed him along for my files.

I threw him out there to the actress.

She scrunched up her face. "A cop? No, his profession is too dangerous. That would never work."

Blank stare. It's a date. Does it have to "work" beyond dinner?

That got me wondering what the point of a date is for most women. Is it to end with a white picket fence, two and half kids, and a dog? Or is it to have a good time, a meal, maybe a stroll and some nice conversation? I argue it's the latter. A relationship is the former, depending on whether you want to marry or not.

The actress wasn't the first person I've heard skip over today and hone in on forever. It happens whenever I suggest to women who complain of not going on a date in ages that they go out with the mechanic, the construction worker, a mailroom man, or whoever is nice, blue-collar, cute, and employed. The response is always a list seeking a number of degrees and awards and accomplishments, including home ownership and either a professional title with "vice," "executive," or "senior" in front of it or a name with a comma and some letters at the end. And there's always—always—a comment about the man suggested not being on "my level," as if his résumé determines his character.

I get it. You want someone with the same drive and ambition, who has the same outlook and lifestyle as yours. But you don't have to marry a guy because you break bread with him or sit next to him at the show. I'm not saying have sex with him or go on a second date, even. I'm saying *go out* with him. Once. It's two to three hours of your time, where you are having a new experience doing something new with someone new. Think of it like a movie. Three hours of entertainment, and then it's done. Even if it goes terribly wrong, you're bound to get something out of it—a new restaurant, a free meal, maybe even a good Facebook story. And if it goes wonderfully right but he's not for you, well, at least he was as good as a good movie. Maybe you can kick it and have fun another time. Maybe not. The end.

Is the potential for "just" a good time really a waste of time?

WOULD YOU DATE YOU?

I spend three-fourths of my work-life listening to and reading about single people in search of a great catch. Forty-three percent of Americans older than eighteen are single (96 million people). We're approaching the majority. Still, the marrieds (along with the *Washington Post*, the *Economist*, the *New York Times*, *Nightline*, and several other major media outlets) like to make us feel bad for our choice. And yes, single is a choice. Almost all of us could get married to some just-anybody dude within a year. We choose to stay single either because we like it or because we're looking for the best fit. That said, sometimes I wonder if we singles are really the great catches we're looking for.

I keep a daily e-mail chain going with a group of friends, East Coast professionals in their late twenties and early thirties. Each morning, one of us throws out a Question of the Day. One of those recent questions was "Would you seriously date or marry yourself at this point in your life if you were the opposite sex? Why or why not?"

The answers were mildly fascinating.

Man 1: "I'd date me. There's a lot of perks if you're into a good time. But marry? Hell nah! I'm in these streets by trade [note: it's for legitimate work]. That would be a lot of strain on a nascent relationship. But don't tell the ladies that. Lol!!!!"

Man 2: "No. I'm an asshole . . . but I got a big ego."

Woman 1: "No. I ain't shit."

Demetria: "Yeah, I'd marry me, but I'd negotiate some rules on the amount of time I require. I'm busy, pulled in a lot of different directions. I have a lot to offer but not a lot of time to showcase it. I'd have to see some demonstrated effort that I can come before partying, socializing, and work for the long haul. I like ambition, but I'd want to be sure I was at least near the top on the list of priorities."

Woman 2: "I'm a damn catch. Hell yeah, I'd marry myself. I'm not the baddest, but I'm Michelle in the making. But if I had to marry myself, that means I'd be a dude. And if I was a dude in [any East Coast city], settled down would not be on my mind for another seven years (mid-thirties). Ashamed to admit it, but truth talking."

Man 3: "Right now . . . nah I would neither date nor marry myself simply 'cause I don't have the patience. But I know in about a year I would be someone's ideal husband. I'm not where I think I should be mentally to remotely think about anything serious. But based on my track record of personal growth, I should be there shortly."

Man 4: "I would date and marry me. Period . . . end of story."

Woman 1: "After further consideration, I still wouldn't date myself right now. I'm still rough around the edges and very career driven. I know one thing; I'm an amazing fuck! I'd fuck myself any day."

I wonder if anyone is ever not rough around the edges. My parents have been married for thirty-four years. Dad? Still rough around the edges. Mom, too. We should all be looking to improve ourselves but, perhaps, accept that some edges can't be buffed softer. It might be easier to find someone who just accepts your flaws (and/or ambition).

I wonder how many of us think we must be perfect in order for another person to like us. And I wonder if this expectation could be one of the reasons so many singles prefer to be single, and for some, not even date.

I followed up with Man 4, asking for more insight to his response. I was quite curious about why he was so confident that he was a good catch.

He replied, "I would date and marry me because my heart is open to loving and caring for someone else. I want to share my life. I'm not perfect, and I don't expect my partner to be, either. In fact, I think the imperfections are what make for a great relationship. I also know how to be a friend, which is another dimension that is much needed. I'm pretty confident I know what it takes to keep a good relationship together, and it has nothing to do with how often I go out, where I am financially, my diet, where I live, etc. To put it plainly, all that is required is a willingness to do the work . . ."

Am I willing? Are you?

GIVING TO GET

With the exception of Stars, I haven't dated anyone halfway seriously since Evan. I've been caught up in work, partying, dating, me, and I make no apologies for it. But every once in a while, I wake up in the middle of the night, and my queen-size bed feels too big and my plus-size New York apartment outsized for just one person. *Sometimes* I want again what I thought I was building with Greg. I can find it when I combine people the way Nola Darling did.

I tell all of this to Sean, my friend from undergrad who married his college sweetheart. They're living in suburban bliss in Maryland with their newborn son.

"What do you want?" Sean asks.

I tell him I want a functional AB hybrid without realizing it's a trick question.

"Everyone wants something," Sean says. "But what is anybody doing to get those wants, desires, and expectations met?"

I think not much. In my conversations with men and women,

I hear the same things I say sometimes, complaints about what they're not getting, followed by "I want, I want, I want." But honestly, what are we giving to get what we want?

I had a conversation with a group of men recently who wanted their women to cook them food *and* fix the plate. My knee-jerk reaction was "Hell no! It reeks of servitude. Fix your own damn plate." Perhaps that attitude is why I'm so dissatisfied with dating sometimes.

I tell this to Sean, too, over brunch at Busboys and Poets in D.C. when I'm in town for the weekend. He listens carefully and then tells me a story.

He went to dinner with his father, his father's new girlfriend, and his own wife. It was a steakhouse where the flame-grilled meat was served sizzling on its platter. The group talked, and the food arrived. Dad continued to talk as his girlfriend reached over with her steak knife and cut up her man's food into the bite-size bits he preferred. When she was done cutting, he was done talking and proceeded to eat his food as if a grown man eating child-size portions of cut meat that someone else had divided up was the most natural thing in the world.

At the end of the meal, the bill came. His father whipped out the wallet as the girlfriend chatted with Sean's wife as if she didn't have a care in the world. And she didn't. She knew her man was taking care of his end of the deal *because she took care of hers.*

She gave and she got. She catered to him as a man and made him feel like a king (because who other than royalty, if then, is getting their food cut?), and he took care of his woman; she ain't got to worry about the cash flow. Their relationship worked well because they were *both* upholding their end of the agreement.

Sean tells me all this to say that the problem with so many relationships these days is that folks aren't holding up their end of the deal. Men want their plate fixed and the floor swept and head freely given, but they don't want to take the trash out, pick up the tab, and investigate bumps in the night. Women want roses and Maxwell concerts and to talk and talk and talk, but they don't want to get freaky with their own man in the bedroom or iron his shirt every now and again.

"You must give to get," Sean tells me, recounting how much he hates opening his wife's car door and what he could really do with all the time he spends attending yoga with her to make her happy. Then he tells my delicate ears the XXX version of what he gets from her when he gives to her.

"Learn to give to *your man*. You'll never be happy otherwise," Sean adds. "If you're waiting around for someone else to give, then you'll be waiting a long time to get what you want. It's on you to take the first step."

Is it really that simple?

He nods. "Try it."

I'm skeptical. "And what if I give and get nothing in return?"

Sean looks at me blankly like he can't believe I had to ask. "Then leave," he says with a shrug. "If you're not getting what you want, why would you stay? You think he's gonna change?"

He laughs at his own question as he flags down the waitress for another round of drinks. I don't find it funny, probably because I know or have heard from too many women who would answer "yes" to his question.

DATING CODE OF HONOR

For most of my dating life, I've operated by what I call the Golden Rule of Relationships. That is, under no circumstances do you date an associate's former flame. That broad definition of a man who was once important but is no longer includes anyone who paid for dates for a woman in my wide-reaching circle of friends, all of their exes (of course), jump-offs, one-night stands, and any person I was aware that a current associate was crushing on, whether he'd expressed mutual interest or not. Oh, and no man remotely close to an ex-boyfriend. And when asked by a woman not to pursue, take the loss. I figure this is a ladies' game, and all must show respect to keep the operation running smoothly.

I was steadfast about this, and it made sense because . . . well, why would I want to violate this rule? Associates don't need penis in common any more than friends do. It's just bad business.

But as the dating game continued, my social life kept expanding, and Facebook, Twitter, Foursquare, LinkedIn, and other social networking sites continued to unite the world in one common group associate-ship, it became increasingly difficult to meet anyone who hadn't already known someone I was just meeting in the biblical sense, much less paid for a few dinners or drinks. I also realized people held claims on people that were, frankly, ridiculous. Like, I'm sorry you dated a guy in college . . . ten years ago. Let it go. Or even that he was a jump-off for three months three years back, and you want to call him off-limits? Let it go.

Naturally, I thought the rules should adjust to accommodate the new social setting. So I wrote up . . . new rules. Yes, like Bill Maher. The Dating Code of Honor is less about a preference for having penis in common (not preferred) with your Facebook friends and more about opening up a wider dating pool, lest single ladies be forced to dabble with old men, mean men, broke men, and all other undesirables for the sake of meeting someone "new."

I set forth the following:

Article 1: Married folk must remove all exes from their personal basket and return items to the shelf for consumption by the general market. Said married people are not obligated to hook up, arrange blind dates, or introduce their single friends to said exes.

Article 2: Currently booed-up people can still claim exes off-limits, *if* the ex is within the last three years. Upon entering a monogamous relationship, they must release all exes with whom they parted ways more than three years back into the open market for general consumption.

Article 3: All college boos must be released back into the open market for general consumption at three years postgraduation.

Article 4: All great loves[1] remain off-limits to the circle of associates, regardless of marital/dating status.

Article 5: One-night stands are in play after ninety days.

---

1 Anyone of your friends would say fits the description of Big on *Sex and the City.*

Article 6: Jump-offs who have not been active for more than twelve months are fair game.

Article 7: Your ex's inner circle of friends remains off-limits unless the ex grants permission. His associates are fair game without asking permission.

Article 8: In the case of a man who has been "claimed," i.e., an interest has been expressed, but a return interest has not been expressed, said man is in play of friends and associates after a period of seven days.

GROWING PAINS: I GOT ISSUES

"Who's your White girl crush?"

I was sitting across the table at Houston's from Nathan, a guy I had started dating. I don't know why women ask men these dumb questions. It's a setup for an argument. Maybe I just didn't have anything else to talk about.

"Easy. Scarlett Johansson."

Okay. I get that. Beautiful face. Curvy body. I think she's gorgeous, too.

"Black girl?"

"Best all around?" He likes to answer questions with questions.

"No, break it down. Like if you were building the perfect woman."

Best face: Beyoncé.

Best arms: Jada Pinkett or Angela Bassett.

Best booty: Beyoncé or Tracee Ellis Ross.

Best boobies: Keyshia Cole.

232 DEMETRIA L. LUCAS

"Legs?" I ask, dipping a fry in honey mustard sauce.

"Oooh. I dunno." He takes a moment to ponder.

"Not Bey?" I offer. Chick's legs are amazing. Wide and firm. Mine are wider, but the general shape is the same.

He smushes up his face. "Uh-uh. She doesn't have legs. She has ham hocks."

Pause. *Ham hocks? Really?*

"Tina Turner."

I have no idea what he's talking about. "What?"

"Best legs. I'm going with Tina."

"Oh."

He looks at me curiously. "What's wrong?"

I'm fixating. *Ham hocks?* I don't know why this bothers me. I don't have a face like Bey, arms like Jada or Angela, and nothing close to a donk like Tracee. His liking what those ladies work with doesn't bother me a bit. Maybe it's because my legs have always been my physical "selling" point, and if he thinks Bey has "ham hocks," how can he be interested in my dark meat?

"What, D?" He sounds concerned.

"Nothing." I'm pouting. Pause. This is stupid. What am I upset over? *Really?* I perk up to keep the peace. "Best all around?"

"Kerry Washington. She's just sexy . . ."

I get that, too. Kerry's mouth does this unique thing when she talks. Some teeth-lip-mouth thing. There's a good-girl quality, but she might also be bad for a man. That, and her booty sat on twenty-twos in *The Last King of Scotland* and *I Think I Love My Wife*.

Now he's making a face. He's thinking.

"What?" I ask.

"No, no. Not Kerry," he says, all animated. "You know who's perfect? Like dream-woman perfect?" He doesn't wait for my response. "Joy Bryant," he blurts.

What? She's a beautiful woman, but she's a stick. A beautiful

"Really, D? Really?" He sighs like an overspent parent with a willful toddler.

I should have kept my mouth shut. He is *soooo* through with me right now. "Oh, just—" I begin, finally trying to keep this from escalating, but he cuts me off.

"I'm a man. I like women," he says plainly. "Skinny ones, thick ones, tall, short, dark, light, whatever . . . it's that simple."

I feel like an ass. Not an asshole. The whole ass.

But he's not done. "You need to deal with your issues about yourself. Don't take it out on me," Nathan says.

Touché.

I apologize for flipping out; he waves it off and accepts. We move on to another subject and pass the remainder of our outing in compatible conversation.

I go home, think on my crazy. Whenever I date the same person for more than ninety days, the interaction brings out all of my baggage. Some men are happy to carry it. Others not so much. Either way, I like my issues buried in the back of the closet where they belong. But if I don't start unpacking and unloading, I'm screwed.

So are you.

stick! What is he doing sitting across the table from me? I a
a stick. I'm more like a log—not a huge log, but—okay, n
that's a bad analogy. If she's an appetizer, I'm an entrée. I h
eat entrées, and I am what soul singer Bilal Oliver called "
thing to hold on to." And Nathan likes, like, an appetizer?
never be an appetizer. I don't want to be an appetizer! I like b
meal! Although, admittedly, I've been faithfully running four
a day for the last couple of weeks in hopes of becoming a hea
leaner meal.

I realize I'm thinking crazy, but I'm too far gone to stop m

"I am a thick chick!" I declare loudly and righteously on
of all sizes eight and up worldwide. If there was a soapbox pr
I would have stood on it purely for effect. "And I eat! And I'm
gonna be a two! Or a four! And my thigh is wide and stron
I like it that way! So if you want a stick with little stick legs
have to go find one, because I'm not starving for anyone!" I
pound my chest proudly if I didn't have breasts in the way.

He blinks at me. Once. Twice. Three times. "What the h
that?" he blurts back at me.

Not the answer I was expecting.

He waves a hand all over the place in front of his face lik
Yayo. "That! What was that?" he bellows, referring to my wi
burst. He goes in before I can answer. "I didn't ask you
weight or be a-a-*stick!*" His voice goes up on the noun. "I
you're not skinny. I can see! If I wanted a stick, I'd be sitting
from a stick. I'm sitting across from you, you know? And
the first time this week. If I didn't like what I see, I wouldn
seeing it!"

I feel like an idiot. But old habits die hard. I'm not taking
blame for this one. "So how can skinny women with skin
be your ideal?" I squeak. I'm so irrational I don't even have
bass in my voice.

WEIGHTY MATTERS?

I've been wondering for a while if the collective weight of Black women is affecting our ability to pair off. And by weight, I mean the numbers on the scale, not our emotional baggage, although for some of us, that is heavy, too.

I can't help but notice that in nearly every run-down of what it is that Black men are looking for in a Black woman, weight inevitably sneaks onto the list, usually in the form of "she works out" or "she stays fit" or "she is concerned about her health or personal appearance"—i.e., *she's not fat*.

Some men, like an Essence.com commenter on a story I wrote once, just make it plain:

> *There are very few successful, fit black women available. People talk about this high ratio of single black women to men, but it is a myth. If you exclude fat women, the ratio is 1 to 1.*

Hmmm. Based on the reigning statistics about Black women's size, "fit" Black women *might* be hard to come by:

- 69 percent of non-Hispanic Black women are over-weight or obese, according to the Office of the Surgeon General.
- 55 percent of Black women are physically inactive; they do no spare-time physical activity, according to an Aetna study on women's health.
- 82 percent of African-American women over the age of forty are overweight or obese, according to data gathered by the Centers for Disease Control.

Yikes!

Before you ignore the point and jump to defend Black women, this is me acknowledging that being overweight or obese is an *American* issue (just like being single):

- 61 percent of adults in the United States are over-weight or obese, according to the Office of the Surgeon General.[1]
- 40 percent of adults in the United States do not participate in any leisure-time physical activity.
- 58 percent of non-Hispanic Black men are overweight, also according to the Office of the Surgeon General.

But this isn't about the all-reigning "them," this here is about us. So back to my initial thought.

---

1 *Vogue* Editor-in-chief Anna Wintour observed this in a *60 Minutes* interview when she described "most" of the people she observed in Minnesota were the size of "little houses." I guarantee you she didn't encounter many Black people on that trip.

I once spoke on a panel about relationships for the New York Urban League. The following day, one of the women who shared the dais with me received an anonymous e-mail. He, whoever he was, wanted both her and me to know we are single because, in so many words, we are fat. She's a self-confessed ten.[1] I'm a size smaller, give or take my mood (like many, I'm an emotional eater). He wrote:

> *From your stomach down is where your problems comes [sic] in. Brothers are visual . . . I'm just trying to feed you the real deal of why you may be having a hard time finding so-called real love or marriage. ITS [sic] THE STOMACH: the mac & cheese, the spaghetti, the fried chicken and friend [sic] pork chops have become YOUR OWN WORST ENEMY, like a hater girlfriend, KEEPING BLACK MEN CLEAR OR [sic] WANTING TO MARRY YOU!*

Hmmm. Never mind that I haven't had pork or chicken in over a decade. It still stung. I figured that meant there must be some truth in it, so I rolled the idea around in my head for a week.

I thought back to an article I'd read in *Elle* while sitting in Barnes & Noble one rainy Sunday afternoon, reading a stack of magazines, as per one of my single-girl rituals. In "Big Love," writer Amy Maclin detailed her struggle with her weight and pointed out how being "fluffy" (she gained twenty-five pounds) had a disastrous effect on her relationship.

With the extra weight, sex with her boyfriend dwindled, and the rare times it did happen, he couldn't keep it up. He avoided

---

1 The average height of a woman twenty to seventy-four years old is five foot four; her average weight was 164.3 pounds in 2002, according to the CDC. Depending on her structure and whether she works out, that puts the average woman somewhere between size ten and size fourteen.

mentioning what the issue was until they were fighting about their sex life and he just laid it on the table: he wasn't as attracted to her since she had gained weight.

Ouch, right? If you're like me, the knee-jerk reaction is to tell her to throw deuces and bounce. I mean, a man who loves you is supposed to love all of you, right? And, like, if he's balking at weight, how will he ever handle something really mega like "for worse" (sickness, being laid off, parents dying) if you even ever get to the altar?

She didn't bounce, though. Actually, neither did I the evening a guy told me he'd never dated a woman my size or a woman who didn't have a flat stomach. I cried hysterically that night, then the next day in the middle of a restaurant. And again when I read the "Big Love" article months later. Yes, in the bookstore. Bad, bad Sunday.

In fact, I began to think the same way Maclin did. Like her, over the next couple of weeks, I told anyone who would listen what my date said. And as many times as I heard, from men and women alike, "If he likes you, it shouldn't matter what you look like," I couldn't help but think they were saying it to be nice.

Hmmm.

If weight can affect our relationships, wouldn't it follow that it can affect our ability to get into a relationship?

Maybe the anonymous, not so nice man was on to something. I just wish he'd been a lot nicer in saying it.

SICK AND TIRED OF
BEING SICK AND TIRED

This is an open letter to angry and bitter women. It doesn't come from a place of judgment or mocking or accusation. When I initially published a version of this essay on my blog, it was met with very angry replies. Many ladies said they couldn't relate personally, but they knew women it applied to. Some said I was perpetuating a stereotype of women. Other women, usually the ones I was talking to, became enraged and began to attack me personally. They argued that it was their right to be angry or bitter and whatever other labels I wanted to hurl, but who in the hell was I to tell them that wasn't a way to be?

I thought maybe I'd overstepped my bounds, exaggerated the depth of the issue, until I found this response on my blog post:

I've accepted life for all the garbage it is and I don't complain to people about it. I've accepted that men and love are a huge waste of time. I actually feel sad for everyone who believes in all this trash. It's easier to live with no hope than to live with high hopes that get knocked down. Wake the fuck up, ladies!

The personal attacks I brushed off. But I was deeply troubled by women who thought that angry and pessimistic were the ideal way to be. It's a defense mechanism to guard from hurt. Maybe you got that honestly, maybe it was passed from generation to generation with good intention. But mad at the world, or men, or even just me, is no way to live.

So, with that in mind . . .

Dear Angry and Bitter Women:

We must get over our anger and bitterness. We must get over our anger and bitterness in general, and we must get over our anger and bitterness when it comes to men.

Yes, I am aware we have many very valid reasons to be angry and bitter, from street harassment to slavery to Soulja Boys' entire musical catalogue. Add in our reigning stats on HIV, rape, marriage, and alleged missing-in-action "good" Black men, and there's no arguing that we have cause to spit hot fire like Lil' Kim going at Nicki Minaj.

But here's what I want to ask you: How's your anger and bitterness working for you? That no one does anything right, people were made to ruin your day, water isn't wet enough, and all Black men suck philosophy on life? Because as far as I can tell, it's not getting you anywhere. Not with Black men, not at work, and not within the world at large, not even with each other.

Confession: I'm a woman and don't want to hear from bitter women, those women who hardly ever have anything positive to say. A popular definition of insanity is doing the same thing and expecting a different result. Angry and bitter ladies, you're acting crazy! And it's driving me and every man you meet batty, too. I've downgraded friends to associates over it. I've blocked people on Twitter and deleted Facebook friends because of it.

If that's my woman-reaction to angry and bitter women, what do you think men, who are only so joyful to point out they have options in the form of mythical doting White women, passive Asians, and eager-to-please Latinas, are thinking? If you're already under the impression that life is so hard, why make it harder with a bad attitude?

It's time to drag out my favorite (paraphrased) quote from Katt Williams. (Yes, I know he's got issues. But when he's lucid, he drops bombs.) So here it goes:

> *If you are twenty-five, still talking about men ain't shit, ask yourself what's wrong with you that you keep attracting ain't shit men.*

Seriously, ladies, we have to start asking ourselves some tough questions.

I'm not calling you out for being bitter and angry to turn you into a docile Stepford wife who lets the will of men run rampant over your life. I don't want to silence you. Quite the opposite, actually. I'm calling you out to empower you, to let you know you don't have to be an angry or bitter woman to be a strong woman, to point out that complaining about the way of the world doesn't change the world.

And while we're talking about the world, it doesn't owe you, me, or anyone else anything. If you want the metaphoric spoon to bend to your will, you're going to have to do a little more than complain. You're actually going to have to act.

Right now, you're whining and pointing out why any solution to anything won't work, especially if it comes from a man and especially if it requires you to change anything. Black men got issues, no doubt. But we do, too, and we can't keep waiting for them to address theirs before we address ours. It's a ball of confusion. And we're all losing the game.

I want you to do better. I want you to be happy. I want you to mobilize and lead a one-woman revolution, even if it's from under the dryer while you're waiting for your roller set or acrylics to dry. It can be as small as saying "For everything I whine about, I will at least try to do something about it. Either that, or I won't complain." Even if it's as simple as saying "I will try a reasonable suggestion that does not offend my values and morals before I knock it." Even if it's as simple as not having a knee-jerk reaction to argue with people who are generally trying to help. Here's a little something I've noticed: when someone says something that stings, there's truth in it. Instead of attacking the truth, evaluate the sting.

That which you are not willing to act on, I beg you to stop complaining about. Because, like, really, if it's *soooo* bad and it's not inspiring you to act, why should anyone else?

With love, sincerity, and your best interest at heart,

Demetria

EXCEPTION TO THE RULE

Last summer, my then editor in chief Angela Burt-Murray scrapped the column I'd spent my entire weekend working on. She ran down to my desk in her stilettos, and although our offices are carpeted, I could tell by the quick-step flurry that it was her. I sat still, staring at my computer screen, hoping that if I didn't move, she wouldn't see me. Ineffective, I know. But I hoped it would work anyway. Every time she's ever run to my desk, it's resulted in me scrambling to complete a last-minute addition to the magazine.

I heard her stop at my cube. Then I heard her exclaim my name when I didn't turn around immediately.

I swiveled in my chair. "Yes, Angela?"

She clapped her hands together gleefully. "I have an idea. I know it scares you, but it's really good. Come."

The first time she ran to my desk, we ended up with the Single Man of the Month column. Good. The last time she ran up on me,

I ended up on three blind dates arranged by my mother, my best friend, and, of course, Angela. Interesting.

I reluctantly allowed Angela to drag me down the corridor to her corner office. I plopped into one of her comfy beige chairs like a petulant teen. She chuckled at my dramatics—this is our routine when she's in a great mood and my stories are in on time—and proceeded. The images for the October issue were in. Blair Underwood, Boris Kodjoe, and Lance Gross were gracing the cover. She reached for the contact sheet on her desk with hundreds of images from the photo shoot, individual and group shots of the men. There was a picture of Blair Underwood in the back of a limo, his legs set wide in a classic man sprawl, sipping from a cognac glass. Boris? He was being all caramel and fine in front of a late-model Jaguar. The pictures of Lance Gross had him disrobing next to a motorcycle, his impossibly solid abs being further kissed by the sun. His build reminded me of a guy I used to . . . let's say date, only because that's a convenient definition.

Years back, when I began working in publishing. I met a man. Harold worked for the same company—different division, different floor. When I took the job, I was so focused on impressing my new boss that I barely noticed Harold when he came by.

Months into the new gig, I was all dressed up with somewhere to go, likely drinks with the girls at Ideya, the coconut mojito spot in SoHo. I'd made it as far as the elevator bank when I heard a man with a Southern drawl say, "Wow, D, you look nice today."

I turned to offer a "thanks" to whoever had been so kind. My eyes met his, and I smiled. He smiled wider. Such teeth! Such lips! Such skin. Smooth, dark, rich. Right then, I fell a little bit in love. Blame it on every Light Bright Black Girl's unconscious yearning for a shot at brown babies.

It took forever for Harold to ask me out. Three months, to be exact. But in the meantime, he would come by my cube and chat with me regularly, sometimes pulling up a chair so he could stay awhile. When he was busy, he would make time to stop by my desk, lean on the top of my cubicle wall, and say, "Give me ten seconds." I would stop what I was doing to stare at him for that fraction of a minute. I'd look into his eyes and fantasize about all the things I wanted to do to all this broad-shouldered, bald-headed, chocolate-colored *may-an* if only I could allow myself the opportunity.

When our ten seconds were up, we'd give a big sigh—had to get some release—and cheese at each other for a few moments till he had to go back to his office.

I had it bad for Harold.

"Damn!" I muttered a little breathlessly. "He could still get it."

Angela smiled and peered over onto my lap to see which shots I was looking at. "That would be the reaction we were going for," she said. "So," she added. "Since this is the men's issue, we need to create another feature around them. A survey. Demetria's completely random and informal probe into what men think about almost everything when it comes to women, marriage, sex, and dating."

When Angela finished, I waited for the catch. There's always a catch. She said nothing to fill the void. "That's it? A survey?" I asked. I exhaled a breath I didn't know I was holding.

She nodded. "Yup. You ask men whatever you think readers want to know. Oh, I need it by Friday."

My head snapped up. That was in a week.

I spent the rest of the afternoon coming up with questions: *Dear men, do you care if your woman has more sexual experience than you? Would you be bothered if your woman used a vibrator during sex? Have you ever measured your penis? If you had to choose between a woman with a perfect face and one with a perfect body, which one trumps?*[1]

I worked through lunch to come up with a list of fifty questions to poll men about. I sent it to every man in my database and asked them to fill out the form and forward it along to another Black man between the ages of twenty-five and fifty. The goal was to reach as many Black men as I could as quickly as possible.

That is how I reconnected with Harold.

The morning after the call for men hit the tristate area, an unexpected e-mail reached my in-box. "Hello," it read. "How are you? I tried to contact you after you left, but the message was returned. Why didn't you keep in touch? Give me a reason I can't take you to dinner."

I stared at the screen and read the message again. Keep in touch? Dinner? I screwed up my face. For what?

PAST

I am watching *Love Jones* for the fifty-millionth time on the TV mounted above my work desk the day Harold calls and asks me to hang out with him. He suggests we plan to get up in Brooklyn after work, get something to eat, probably somewhere in Park Slope, then maybe catch a movie in Brooklyn Heights. Of course, I say yes. Plus, this is just dinner, right?

On the night we are supposed to rendezvous, the weather is awful. By the time Harold gets to my house, on time, it is raining

1 Results: 49 percent of Black men said they were uncomfortable dating a woman who was more sexually experienced, 70 percent said they would not be bothered if you used a vibrator during sex, 72 percent of Black men said they had measured their penis, 42 percent said they preferred an attractive body to an attractive face.

like a Mississippi field storm. He rings the bell, and when I open the door downstairs, he is dripping wet and bearing flowers, kinda like Eriq La Salle in *Coming to America*—minus the jheri curl.

"You're wet," I say.

"I had to stop to get flowers. I didn't want to come empty-handed," he says back.

I take the tulips, suggest we stay in and watch a movie since it's pouring. Our eyes lock, and a million words of longing pass between us, both of us knowing the weight of my seemingly convenient suggestion. Finally, I break his gaze and look away. I can't contain my smile, and I laugh at us trying to resist what's inevitable. Harold smirks and gestures for me to lead the way up the steps to my apartment.

We're halfway through *Gladiator* before Harold practically throws me from the couch where I am nestled between his legs.

"You're too close. I can't concentrate," he says frantically.

I laugh. "I didn't even touch you," I say. *But I thought about it. Oh, have I thought about it.* I'm trying to be a good girl, though.

"You don't have to," he confesses. "I'm thinking about touching you. That's enough."

I laugh again. That makes two of us.

"Get behind me," he demands, sitting up and scooting forward. He waits as I reposition myself on the couch, then pulls off his sweater, leaving him in just a white wife-B practically glowing against all his ebony-hued skin. If I were in a teen movie, this would be the moment where I take a loud gulp. I just try not to stare. Harold settles between my legs and goes back to watching the movie in seeming peace.

Now I cannot concentrate. His heavy man weight on my chest is driving me crazy. We're at the scene in the movie where Russell Crowe shouts to the crowd, "Are you not entertained?" *No, actually* I think, *I'm not, but I want to be.*

Harold seems oblivious to me and my raging hormones behind him. I realize this means he's a gentleman and not going to make a move anytime soon. I daydreamed about this moment for months. This is my chance. I at least have to squeeze a man breast. Something!

I slowly move my arm from where it is propped on the back of the sofa and run my hand in slow motion from his shoulder to the base of his neck, down the center of his chest, taking a long, lingering feel of firm muscle just before my fingers land on solid abs. I tremble. I knew he had a six-pack!

He still doesn't react, and my arm gets stuck in the most uncomfortable position ever. I have no choice, I tell myself, but to run my hand up vertically to graze his chest again. It's an excuse. I've always heard from my AKA girls they amount to monuments of nothingness. I need to let them know there's an exception to the rule.

I move my hand up, then over to get a feel of Harold's left man breast. My other hand joins in the fun and finds his abs. And the next thing you know, I am unabashedly feeling him up.

I. Am. Entertained!

Harold shifts and turns to face me. I pause, let my hands fall where they may, but don't take them off him. He is metal, and I am a magnet. I think he says, "D, do you know what you're doing?" I'm not really sure. All I can concentrate on is the plump lips that have been thrust in my face.

I'd like to be a good girl, but I am a good woman instead. I grab the back of his smooth, bald head and pull him toward me hurriedly.

Now he's grabbing at my waist frantically, catching the space where my shirt rides too high and my pants sit too low. I've practically ripped his shirt off in order to feel skin, glorious skin.

We tumble off the couch onto my cow-hair rug but never break contact, which is for the best, because I will die—stop breathing and just die—if he stops touching me with his hot hands. He drags his nails down my back without me even having to tell him that's my thing. I grab his head firmly and bite his lip in response. He moans.

He flips me onto my back, pinning me to the floor. His eyes are boring into me. In the tense silence, there is nothing he can request (within reason) that I will say no to. He leans in, raising my baby tee and crushing me with his man weight. I wrap my spread thighs around his waist as he unhooks my bra in one seamless motion. His mouth is headed for my right breast, and my hands are fumbling to pull up his shirt when he jerks away from me.

Huh?

He jerks again, collapsing into himself with the spasm.

Again. Is he epileptic?

"Um, Harold?" I squeak.

He's kneeling in front of me now, breathing way too hard. I scoot back and pull my shirt down, watching him as he buries his head in his hands. He's shaking. I'm staring. I don't know what else to do.

"Harold? Are you okay?" I ask timidly. I reach out to touch him, and he flinches away and leans over further as if he's in pain.

"Harold?"

He springs to his feet and begins to bounce like a heavyweight boxer in a ring, circling his neck around. "I'm hot!" he shouts. "Ooooh, I'm hot." He fans himself with both hands, then swings his arms to get limber. More fanning. "I'm hot! I'm hot!" he repeats.

"Do you want some water to cool down?" I ask when I finally find my words.

Harold doesn't answer. He keeps bouncing, swiveling his neck, wiping his forehead, which I realize then is dripping with sweat. Why is he so hot?

Suddenly, he just stops. He stands completely still, as if he's coming back from some out-of-body experience. He looks at me, grabs his sweater from the edge of the couch, and does a semidignified jet for my bathroom. I hear the door lock. He turns on the water. I'm still kneeling on the floor, wondering what the hell is going on.

I don't know what to do. Do I call the police? Call 911 and ask them to help? Does this qualify as an emergency? I straighten my clothes and take a seat on the edge of the couch while I stare at the closed bathroom door, trying to figure out what to do next.

I'm still debating—call a friend? call my mother?—when I hear the door unlock several minutes later. Harold returns to the living room with a dry brow. He's put on his sweater and he looks like his usual well-composed self. I look at him. He looks at me . . . as if nothing happened.

"I'm going to head out now," he says, all matter-of-fact as if he didn't just completely spaz out a few moments ago.

I'm baffled, but I nod. Whatever gets him out of the house the fastest. "Okay, then." I add a nod for emphasis.

"Good night," he says formally. "Thank you for having me over. You have a nice place."

"Thank you," I say.

"I'll see myself out."

I give him the chipper voice. "Okay. Good night."

As soon as he's out the door, I put on all of the locks, even the chain, which I hardly ever use, and stand with my back against the door. I wait there until I hear the downstairs doors open and close before I say out loud, "What. The. Hell. Just happened here?"

I don't see Harold again until Friday. He's made it his business to come upstairs every day for months, and then three days pass without sight of him. He hasn't called, either.

I'm watching *Boyz n the Hood* with my coworker on the TV above my desk when Harold strolls briskly through our space. "Demetria," he acknowledges curtly and with a nod. "Ali."

"Harold," I acknowledge in the same dry tone.

He never breaks stride as he heads to the offices of the senior editors.

Ali, who has witnessed my entire office love affair with Harold from a cubicle diagonal to mine, is quiet for a moment. "So," he says just when I think he's going to let that exchange pass without commenting. "What was that?"

I stare at the screen. "Nothing."

Ali gives a wicked laugh from behind me. "Nothing? Didn't sound like nothing. Didn't look like nothing."

"It was nothing," I snap.

He laughs. "I'll bet."

Harold exits the higher-ups' offices and leaves our space without any acknowledgment of me. I keep watching the TV. It's the scene where Ricky gets shot. He made himself an easy target, running in a straight line instead of zigzagging.

"Nothing, my ass," Ali says.

Another week passes with no sign of Harold. I call him—work and cell—he sends me straight to voice mail. I call from Ali's phone; he answers, then tells me he's busy, he'll call me back. I go down to his floor to chat with him in his office. His door is closed. I don't know if it's the journalist in me or the woman in me who has got to hear from him what exactly happened that night (I have my ideas. I want them confirmed.) And further, why he's put me on ignore when I did nothing wrong.

I try a few more times but still get dodged at every turn. Finally, I realize I'm just not going to get any answers. When Harold comes upstairs now, he doesn't even speak—not to me or to Ali. He barely says anything to the higher-ups, and he used to joke with them all the time, too. It's as if he's cut the entire division off. I don't get it. I mean, if we'd had sex and he'd changed, then there'd be a precedent for why he's behaving this way . . . but we didn't because I think he came on himself. What gives?

For the next year, Harold pretends I don't exist. I accept that it's for the best that things never went further with us. When I accept a new job at another publishing house, I throw a huge celebration (any excuse to party) and invite a bunch of my coworkers to attend. Everyone I invite shows up. Except Harold.

PRESENT

I stared at the computer screen. I couldn't believe the e-mail reached him and, further, that he responded. It's not as if he didn't remember our history.

I fired off a response. "You made it clear that you were not interested. Why would I stay in touch?"

Ninety seconds later, he hit me back again: "Not interested. Are you crazy? I could not have been more interested. What would give you the impression I wasn't interested?"

Me: "Um, you ran out of my house—literally. And then never spoke to me again. I don't know what you're calling that up North, but below the Mason Dixon, that's still called not interested."

I pushed send.

That was a year ago. He never responded.

A GOOD JUMP-OFF
IS HARD TO FIND

It was a rainy Saturday in Brooklyn, and after lying on the couch all day, I finally got enough motivation to do something other than watch chick-flicks like *Cabaret*, *Beaches*, and *Sweet Charity*. Around nine, I went to join my girls at a friend's brownstone to watch a *Real Housewives of Atlanta* marathon. For good measure, and because it's bad to show up empty-handed, I grabbed a gallon of sangria from the liquor store on the corner.

A couple of tipsy hours later, we were joined by an informative male guest. And because women and men—or, er, man—cannot gather for any amount of time without discussing relationships, that's eventually what the topic turned to. That's how I learned that a good jump-off is hard to find. Who knew?

I'm not a jump-off-type chick. I've tried sex for just physical attraction—Dude, Jason, Isaiah, Harold—and it's always gone haywire with no sex taking place. I figure God must be trying to tell me something, like Celie and Shug Avery. I'm told I don't know what I'm missing, but I'm okay with missing it now. Sex, for *me,* is a physical way to express what I already feel emotionally, and it's not a way to force shared emotion. It's way too intimate for just a thrill, and I prefer to reserve the act for someone I care about.

Anyway, for those who believe in sex with no strings, I'm told it's hard out there. Lots of people seem to be confused about what exactly a JO is. My girls and their guest asked me to put the word out about what the rules entail for current practioners.

1. JOs don't hang out together. If you're friends first and hung out before, then sure, keep at it. But if your arrangement is solely based on sex, don't expect a public appearance together. Ever.
2. Do your biz and go. No cuddling, definitely no spending the night, and no breakfast. But I'm told that it is "man duty" to remain a gentleman and make sure the lady gets home safely.
3. Kissing is supposedly optional. I don't know that I could do someone I couldn't kiss, but whatever. Some think it's too intimate (unlike sex?) and should be reserved for people they actually care about. Follow your partner's lead on this one.
4. No phone calls unless it's to set up an arrangement.
5. No standing appointments. Reliable access to sex is a perk of being in a committed relationship. If your JO wanted to be committed to someone, he'd be in a relationship.
6. JOs don't grow into more. So if you want more than sex upfront, don't think sex is the way to get to that "more" point.
7. Stop catching feelings. Yes, the sex is good, but always remember, this is just sex. If you do catch feel-

ings, avoid the "I'd like to upgrade" conversation, and cut your losses immediately.

7. Although it is arranged sex for nonprofit, etiquette still applies. It's good form for the host/hostess to offer the warm cloth postcoitus. However, said host/hostess is not required or expected to wipe down the guest.

8. Condoms. Always use them. Don't even think about going raw.

9. Discretion. It's crass to brag and put people's biz in the street. Oh, and your arrangement is pretty much over when/if word gets back to your partner. Real players move in silence.

10. It's not all about you. Not even now. You're still showing up to the bedroom—or wherever you like it—with another person. You are expected to make sure they enjoy the session and get off. If they are selfish, feel free to talk their biz far and wide as a warning to others.

11. Foreplay. You don't have to break out your bag of tricks or do all that you reserve for a significant other, but you are obligated to make sure your partner is ready to play. He must do the same.

12. Acknowledge your JO in public. It doesn't have to be a long and intimate conversation, but a "hello" and a cheek kiss are good form.

GREAT EXPECTATIONS

Penelope had just recounted a story of love and loss. I did my girl-friend sympathizing duty as we rode with GVG in a cab headed to Cafeteria, an after-hours restaurant with velvet ropes and a doorman, after 2 A.M. GVG took another approach to Penelope's dilemma. You know men can't stop themselves from solving a problem.

"Learn to swallow," GVG told Penelope. He was joking . . . I think. "It'll keep your man happy and at home. No man will leave his woman if she swallows," he added.

The phrase *learn to swallow* became a running joke that summer. Every time a woman complained about a boyfriend who was hanging with the boys too much or not showing enough attention, this was the laughed-out advice we started to give. But it wasn't for women simply looking for a man. Male consensus held that swallowing can help a woman keep a man she's got but will not help her get a man she does not. The guys unanimously agreed that swallowing without a title will automatically dismiss a woman from consideration for a relationship. And yes, they acknowledged that it's not fair.

"Life isn't," GVG noted.

I took the phrase for the partial joke I assumed it was until one night, I realized GVG was dead serious. I was walking to the car for a ride home with G and several of our mutual male friends. It had been a long Wednesday night celebrating a birthday on the rooftop of the Gansevoort Hotel in the Meatpacking District. Somehow the subject of swallowing came up (no pun intended), and I voiced my real feelings on the matter to the guys, which in a word was "Ugh!"

Avery, a friend of GVG's who had become like a brother to me, became visibly upset. "Not swallow?" he bellowed as if I was actually dating him. "What do you mean, not swallow?"

"It's disgusting," I shot back with equal venom. "You watch too much porn."

"Disgusting?" Another bellow. "My seeds are disgusting?"

I kissed my teeth like the Caribbeans on my Brooklyn block. "In someone's mouth or throat, they are!"

The look on his face was pure comedy. He was appalled that I could not fathom a woman loving his spunk. "Dudes swallow women's juices all the time. You think we spit it out when we're down there? You think we like to swallow when a woman cums in our faces? We commit to the act. A woman has got to commit to the act!"

The following weekend, I broach the subject Sunday night at Habana Outpost. The who's who of Brooklyn (and Harlem) are gathered at the casual Cuban restaurant on its outdoor benches waiting for the second showing of *The Warriors* to play on the brick wall via a projector.

"What's the obsession with all this swallowing business?" I ask the Pretty Boy crew, a traveling group of Uptown residents in their mid- to late twenties who stay perfectly fly at all times and always seem to be in Brooklyn. Harlem residents are always here; we only return the favor on special occasions.

"That shit just feels right!" is the general consensus. Dap and laughter all around. Apparently, they're not as deep as Avery and his friends.

From Twenty Four, the youngest member of the Pretty Boys, comes a bit more explanation: "Don't think about it in terms of what it can do for him, think about what it means in terms of the greater good for you. You swallow, and you can get anything you want." He wasn't speaking of material goods. More like romance, affection, and attention.

"Does swallowing feel better than sex?"

Twenty Four is in deep thought, trying to come up with the right answer. It's as if I can see the wheels turning as he recounts all his sexual experiences. Finally, he reaches a verdict: "Depends on the skills of the woman."

Eh . . . I'm not convinced about this swallowing bit. I offer an alternative, bringing up the skills of Italia Blue, an adult actress. She provides a good education, but whenever her mate reaches ultimate joy, she takes it, then spits the contents back onto the rod.

"That's the equivalent of swallowing, no? She took the mouth shot," I reason.

The guys are horrified. I get a flurry of "No!" and "Ugh!" and "She's gonna spit on me?"

Now it's my turn. "Yeah . . . what's the problem? Um, it's yours. You want women to swallow something you don't even want touching you?"

"That's disgusting, D," says one of the guys.

"But, um, it's not disgusting for a woman to swallow it?"

He shakes his head. "No!" he blurts definitively on behalf of the guys.

"Why not?" I challenge.

"It's just not."

"If men want women to do it, y'all have to give a valid reason. 'Because we want it' isn't enough."

Sensing that I'm not dropping the subject anytime soon, one of the other Pretty Boys takes a moment to ponder the question seriously. "Really? I'll speak for all men and say as long as a woman's down there, no real man's really complaining."

A WORK IN PROGRESS

I finally made plans to *go to* church instead of half-watching the live stream on my laptop while I clean my apartment or work on blog posts for the upcoming week. I'm not really a catch-the-spirit kind of girl when I attend. I usually sit through the service in silence, taking notes on my BlackBerry and Tweeting the best parts of the sermon for all of those attending Bedside Baptist. It's the right thing to do, since half my Twitter timeline does it for me.

But even I had to throw up a hand and let loose an "Amen!" when a fired-up Reverend Trufant said, "You may not be where you want to be, but thank God you are not where you were."

That quote was rolling around in my head on the train ride home and got me to thinking about all the things that I've learned about relationships and men since moving to New York. I've encountered my share of bull, and I've done my share of it, too. I don't regret any of it; I've grown and learned from most of my mistakes. I still have a long way to go, but I thank God every day that I am not where I began.

I broke out my BlackBerry and made a list of the lessons so I could track my progress. Most are very simple and very obvious but were very hard to get at nonetheless. They are all things that I wish someone had told me or the things someone told me that I didn't listen to. Sometimes I still don't.

1. If he doesn't call, he's not interested. Period.
2. It's impossible to fill an emotional void with a physical act.
3. If he says he's not ready for a relationship, he's not ready for a relationship.
4. Kings don't always wear crowns.
5. Wanting to have sex with you and wanting to be with you can be mutually exclusive ideas.
6. Wanting you to want him and actually wanting you can be mutually exclusive ideas.
7. If he has a girlfriend, leave him alone. If he leaves her for you, he'll do the same to you. If he stays with her and deals with you, he's a whore. Either option is bad for you.
8. A beautiful face (or body) does not make a beautiful mind.
9. Men don't read minds. If you want something, ask for it.
10. Men are insecure, too.
11. Just because he's a good man, that does not make him the right man for you.
12. It's okay to be alone. You'll be fine without him. Pinky swear it.
13. Sometimes things just don't work out, and it's nobody's fault.
14. You don't always get closure. Make peace with it anyway.

15. You have to grow, but you don't have to change.
16. Dysfunctional people love dysfunctionally.
17. Love with your heart; think with your head.
18. Just because you miss him, that does not mean you are meant to be with him.
19. Good guys exist, but perfection does not.
20. Learn to compromise, but don't compromise yourself.
21. Love is a verb. Having an emotion means absolutely nothing if it is not followed through with action.
22. Know that if he is the One, he will be the One.
23. When you feel as if you're forcing a relationship, you are. It's not working. Stop and look for the Next One.
24. Complaining about men will not somehow make men better. It will only make *you* bitter.
25. If you're single and can't find your type, go looking for him. There is nothing wrong with being proactive about what you want.
26. You don't have to be an angry woman to be a strong woman. Angry does not equal strong. It equals angry.
27. Good men make bad mistakes. That said, there's a difference between a moral failing and a mistake. Forgive mistakes. Get rid of moral failures.
28. Every man isn't out to get you or do you dirty.
29. If you're always complaining that men "ain't shit," ask yourself what's wrong with you that you keep attracting "ain't shit" men.
30. A bad break up is a valid excuse to break down, but not *to stay* down.

CHOIR BOY

I'm headed downtown to meet GVG for half-priced drinks near West Fourth Street, when I run into Choir Boy. He barely recognizes me, as I shaved my curls off yesterday. I was over doing my hair every morning. We strike up a conversation leaving an Obama rally in Washington Square, and I invite him to join me.

Choir Boy got his name because he doesn't smoke, doesn't drink, and is the nicest man on earth. Sticky sweet, always smiling. Total A. We initially met through mutual friends but never stayed in touch. We have a hi-bye relationship.

We walk the few blocks through the Village until we arrive at a hole in the wall where the music sucks but the drinks and company are great. GVG's friends are hysterical (and tall and fine). So over three-dollar cranberry and vodkas (gingerale for Choir Boy), a group of intelligent men and women discuss politics, the Black situation (all Black intellectuals' favorite topic), then move on to relationships.

I get a little hazy on the details of the conversation because for some reason, I am checking for Choir Boy. I always thought he was cute, but today he seems a little taller, his shoulders a little broader, his braces-perfect smile a little brighter, his laugh a little deeper. And the thoughts coming out of his mouth? Dude has sense, too! Why didn't I notice this before? Maybe because this guy has always been cordial but never once remotely expressed an interest in me (i.e., I'm in his Friend Box).

We bounce from there to Taj, a restaurant turned nightclub, because it's the only place we can think of to go. We walk in and find folks partying on Thursday evening as if it's two A.M. on a Saturday. The crowd is mostly suit-and-tie dudes who discarded their ties hours ago. This is a good look.

The group heads toward the back for a men's-room run, and I'm happily abandoned in a sea of tall men. I begin to check the room discreetly for available cuties, and I spot my ex, Evan, dancing with a woman right in front of me.

He spots me, too, gives me the I-barely-know-you wave. He was two-stepping when I first saw him, but as soon as he sees me, he starts getting low. Then he backs it up on his female companion. Then he turns her around so she can back it up on him.

I self-consciously run my hand over my freshly shorn hair. Is this his new girl? She's . . . cute. Taller than me. Thinner in the waist, bigger in the booty. Fluffy-haired.

I try not to watch them, but I can't help but look. They're two-stepping again, and he's holding the woman close, with his hand resting on her gigantic tush. As I look, he catches my eye and smirks. Is he gloating? I casually look away as if I didn't see him. I won't give him the satisfaction of letting him know he got to me.

Then, from somewhere inside, a surge of much-needed pride pops up. What is he gloating over? Despite his parting words, he's not the only man who will treat me well. Eff him for thinking he one-upped me 'cause he's rubbing up on some big-booty girl in a crowded club. So what if I'm alone . . .

Hold up! What am I talking about? I'm not alone. I walked in with three tall, broad-shouldered, well-dressed, well-educated, well-employed Black men. *Where are they?*

I look over my shoulder, hoping to see them emerging from the men's room in a pack. No such luck. I look right. No sign of them. I look forward, and there they are, parting the sea of bodies like a trio of Black Moses and bearing gifts like Wise Men—two Heinekens, a gingerale, and a white wine for me.

I run up to Choir Boy, giving him a big smile, grabbing his hand, and intertwining my fingers with his. "Quick," I say, pulling him down so I can whisper in his ear. "Pretend to be my boyfriend!"

He immediately wraps his arm around my waist protectively and pulls me to his side as if I'm his woman and he's proud to be my man. He doesn't even ask why.

"A guy I used to date is here," I explain, looking up. "He's dancing all up on some girl, trying to make me jealous." I nod in their general direction. The girl is winding on Evan now, and he's engrossed in her fatty.

The Boyfriend screws up his face, squeezes me a little tighter to him. "The dude with the chick with the mustache?"

I look over at her again. *Oooh!* I guess she is a little shadowy above the lip. "Um. Yeah."

Boyfriend turns around to tell the fellas what's going on. They peer over at the girl, and all are unimpressed.

"You have nothing to worry about," GVG assesses with a shrug. "You're much cuter . . ."

"But she has a fatty!" I declare. Big booties trump most everything else, right?

"And a mustache," Avery points out. I get a sense that I'm missing the big picture. "They cancel each other out," he says with a chuckle.

I have no idea what song comes on, but suddenly, I am being led to the dance floor by the Boyfriend. We dance a little two-step, and I tug on his tie when he comes close because it feels like the right thing to do. He has amazing rhythm. One song goes off, then another, then another, and we're still dancing. I'm biting my bottom lip to keep from breaking out in a huge, cheesy grin.

"Don't look at me like that," the Boyfriend says.

I'm blushing. I know I'm blushing. "Like what?"

He gives me a don't-start-no-trouble-you-don't-want-to-finish look. "Like that."

I tug his tie again, then spin off. I haven't even remembered to check on Evan and Phatty Girl to see if he has noticed me with my *may-an*.

A wack song comes on, and the Boyfriend pulls me to his chest, wrapping both arms protectively around me in a tight hug. Without meaning to, I nuzzle into that comfy space between his hardened man breasts and run my hands over the steel frame he calls his back. I fight the urge to purr in contentment.

He kisses my forehead affectionately and looks down at me, squeezing me tighter. "Am I a good boyfriend, D?"

I nod my head into the man breasts. And then I have an Alicia Silverstone–like epiphany, like the one near the end of *Clueless*. *I could like the Boyfriend!* He's a sweetheart, and he's gorgeous, and he's got rhythm, and he's got good politics and common sense and chiseled man breasts! Uh, why did it take me so long to notice him?

"Does that mean no?" He looks offended.

"Huh?" I pull back from my nuzzle and look up, realizing I've been caught daydreaming. "Oh, no! You're great. You're perfect!" I reassure him, patting a firm man breast for emphasis. "Of course, you're a good boyfriend."

"Good." He gives me another forehead kiss (damn that frontal lobe!) and releases me but keeps his arm around my waist . . . for show? I don't know anymore.

We chat it up with the rest of our crew for a bit, and then I finally remember that the purpose of the Boyfriend is to one-up Evan, who was attempting to one-up me. I look around the room discreetly, hoping to spot him.

The Boyfriend catches me searching, leans down, and whispers in my ear, "He left ten minutes ago." He kisses my almost bald head, squeezes me to him tighter, and rejoins the conversation with our friends.

An hour later, the Wise Men and I are in the Jeep headed back to the borough. Because of driver, height, and drop-off requirements, the Boyfriend is in the passenger seat and I'm behind the driver. It's postmidnight, and it seems Cinderella's ball has ended. The guys are discussing with great vigor their frustrations with Black women. Being the Girlfriend was fun while it lasted, but I'm back to being the Home Girl.

Now that the fun is over, I realize I am no better than Evan. I used a fantasy boyfriend as a decoy at a party to one-up him. I live a great life. A wonderful, fabulous, fulfilling life surrounded by great friends at great events in the greatest city (and borough) on earth. So why did I feel I had to impress him? Am I insecure about being single?

A commenter on my blog called me a serial dater once. She'd been following my dating chronicles for a couple of years before she reached her conclusion.

Is that what I am? And is that supposed to be bad? Isn't everyone who didn't marry their high school sweetheart or isn't in a multiyear relationship a serial dater? And if you're not a serial dater, how do you find the One? How do you even know what you're looking for in the One if you don't date to figure out what's out there and what you like?

If dating and meeting and interacting with a lot of people in the hopes that I meet someone I enjoy make me serial, then I'll be that. But I prefer to be thought of as a woman looking for meaning, one who doesn't settle for mediocrity. I'm not mediocre, so I don't expect mediocrity in return.

I zone back into the car conversation and hear that the menfolk have moved from discussing Black women who date interracially to the pivotal scene in *Crash* with Thandie Newton and Terrence Howard. The Black married couple gets pulled over by a white cop. The cop feels up the wife while the husband does nothing. I argue that in the given scenario, the onus was on the woman to defuse the situation and keep the husband from being killed.

The Boyfriend, or ex-boyfriend, is explaining that come hell or high water, it is a man's role to protect his woman, especially his wife. Yes, even at the risk of being arrested or getting beat or killed by cops. He wants to know, what kind of man doesn't protect his woman?

They still make this model?

We drop GVG off in Flatbush, then circle back to drop me off. I can't remember how the remaining three of us got on the topic of exes, but we did. The Boyfriend, who is American and raised in Brooklyn (rare), is explaining how he's never dated a non-Caribbean woman.

"What you got against American girls?" I ask from the backseat.

"Nothing. Just never dated one." He shrugs and never bothers to look back.

Just because I'm not the type to give up that easily, I throw out, "You should try one sometime. Might like it."

Now he looks back. "You think I should, D?"

I nod, bite my bottom lip, and look him directly in the eye. "Definitely."

He turns back in his seat, leans his head against the headrest, and unleashes that amazing smile again. "I think I will."

* * *

GVG calls the next day to say Choir Boy expressed an interest me. He wants to know if it is okay to pass my number and e-mail along. I tell him it is fine, and when I arrive at work a few days later, there is an e-mail in my personal account wishing me "Good Morning and Happy Monday."

For the next two weeks, Choir Boy and I talk, e-mail, and text regularly, but he never asks me out. The revelation hits me as I am logging off of my Outlook and AIM at work around eight P.M. Just as I am reaching for my purse, a text comes through from Choir Boy, inviting me to a party he is headed to *with his boys* in the Meatpacking District.

With his boys?

I text Choir Boy back that I won't be able to make it and head home to sulk. Another one—an even cuter one—bites the dust. I hit Penelope for advice, but she's too busy trying to decipher the actions of her own semielusive crush to indulge my passive ponderings. After talking her down off her own emotional ledge, I decide to text Tariq to blather about my romantic woe.

He's one of the few men around with whom I completely let go of all pretenses and let all my emotional shortcomings and insecurities run rampant. I can talk to him as if he's a girl, but he responds to me like a boy. I figure he's a better information source than Penelope, anyway.

In my semidepressed state, I lean against the kitchen counter to eat crackers and jelly. (It's better than a tub of ice cream.) I type: "So, he invites me out last minute to hang, talks to me on the phone for hours, e-mails and texts me all day, but has not asked me out on a date. Why not? He doesn't like me, does he? Sulk-sulk."

I hit send and reach for a knife to spread apple jelly (hard to find

above the Mason Dixon) on a saltine as I continue to think about
Choir Boy. And that's when I realize . . .

Ohmygod!

I grab the phone frantically, scroll through the sent messages,
and have my worst fear confirmed.

No! No! Oh, noooo! I sent the message to Choir Boy. Not Tariq.

I am mortified. He's gonna think I'm nuts. Or maybe he'll think
I'm grown-up and honest and don't play games. I dunno. This
could go either way.

I send off another text, triple-checking that it's headed to Tariq
before I push send, telling him the idiot mistake I've just made, and
forwarding the original text that went to Choir Boy. I need Tariq to
tell me how to get out of this one gracefully, if that's at all possible.

Trying to make light of the situation, I text Tariq again: "Tomorrow's blog title: How Texting Is Ruining My Life."

Tariq doesn't hit me back. Neither does Choir Boy. I can't bear
the thought of reading Choir Boy's response anyway. What if he
says something mean? Worse, what if he says nothing at all? My
mind is running in a thousand different directions that lead to a
decaying brick wall like the one those women encountered at the
end of Brewster Place. The nothing that Choir Boy and I already
had is now *officially* ruined.

Tariq, a true friend, finally texts me to say it's not the end of the
world: "It's a'ight. It happens, D. I would think she can't stop thinking about me . . . good sign for me."

A beam of hope edges through my dark cloud. "You wouldn't
think I'm a needy chick?" I type back to Tariq.

Before he can answer, an e-mail comes through from Choir Boy,
not a text. I take a deep breath and read.

Choir Boy apologizes for taking so long to ask me out. *Er?* Says
he hopes the delay didn't hurt his chances of getting to know me
better, and, furthermore, can he take me out on Monday night?

Can life be this simple? That you ask what you want to know and an answer is delivered just like that?

I text Choir Boy back, happily accepting his offer for a proper evening with me. I'm so pleased with myself that I sit on my counter and giggle like a gleeful toddler as I marvel at my profound discovery.

I asked what I wanted to know, and I got the answer. Better than that, I got the answer that I wanted to hear.

I text Tariq my new theory to approaching life: ask and you shall receive. Can life really be this simple?

He writes back thirty seconds later: "YES!"

THE CONFUSING KIND

I am out at a family-owned Caribbean bar in Flatbush with one of my friends, Bree, a Brooklyn native, when I spot a cutie.

I point him out to Bree, who knows him. Well. She says this has to be at least the third time I've met him, but somehow I overlooked him at those first couple of meetings. Surely I've seen him in a suit, she says. And surely he looked lovely, but I don't even remember him being in the room.

The evening I finally take note of him, he's strutting around in a T-shirt and jeans. He's over six, easy. And his back seems particularly broad, his waist quite narrow. And he's singing . . . he's happy, I guess. I turn around and look at this truly beautiful singing specimen and realize he's got the clearest brown complexion and the prettiest teeth and smile I've seen in a while.

How the hell did I miss this?

I lean over to Bree—a longtime friend of his—and ask for the run-down.

Bree: "Who? Marcus?" She leans forward to make sure she's got the right man. "You're so predictable."

Me: "Yes, I know. Now, about this one singing over here . . ."

Bree: "Good dude. Family man. Good character. I've known him forever. Was looking for a girlfriend last I heard." She shrugs as if there is a plethora of men who look as good as he does and fit this description.

So I turn around, smile big, enhance my below-the-Mason-Dixon accent, and make conversation.

After a hilarious evening, I end up catching a ride home with Marcus, who drops Bree off first. Turns out he lives up the block from me.

Marcus pulls in front of my house, and we continue chatting as he double-parks. It's late. I should get out of the truck and carry myself inside like the good Southern belle I am. But I can't. He's pure comedy. He has no self-censor button. It's like whatever he thinks, he says. It's crass, obnoxious, offensive, and amazingly delivered, all the traits of a good comedian. It's the funniest conversation I have had in I can't remember how long. And it's like a tennis match. No matter what I serve, he throttles it right back to me. (A very well known romance author once described good conversation as verbal sex. She was right.)

Somehow we get on the topic of exes and why neither one of us is seeing anyone seriously. He asks me what my type is. I hesitate, because I'm not trying to gas him by telling him that he is the epitome of my type—physically, at least. I try to change the subject. He's not budging. Eventually, I tell him my ideal: Chocolate (check-plus), over six feet (check), clean-cut (check-plus), pretty teeth (check-plus), cut up (check), funny (check-plus), and alpha male (loose definition: if you were a lion and you were in the jungle, all the other lions would listen when you roar—oh, this is a check, too).

Marcus laughs. Smiles. (Sigh.) And just before I think I will melt where I sit, he says in all humorless seriousness, "Well, you must be going crazy right now, then, huh?"

I am. But I'll never tell him that.

Marcus calls. I call back. We hang out once, He never calls after. I thought he was digging me, but I learn through the grapevine (i.e., Bree) that he's actually not looking for a "wifey," which he thinks I am. That is that.

We end up at the same venue at the same time again a couple of weekends later. Marcus sees me, comes by, chats me up . . . then flirts?

"Hey, D." He flashes his bright white, braces-perfect teeth. "You dancing tonight?" he asks.

Me: "I might."

Him: "If you're dancing, I'll dance with you."

Another flash of that smile. I am a sucker for a smile, and it's hard for me not to sigh where I sit.

Me: "Nah, I'm good. Thanks, though."

I brush him off—not to be mean but to respect the parameters he's defined. He isn't interested, so why the mixed signals?

Marcus chats for a few minutes more, then heads off for a destination unknown somewhere inside the bar. Through a series of events, Bree ends up asking him to take us back to our side of town. I'd prefer not to ride with him, but there's no way I'm taking the train home, and I'd have to wait forever for a car at three A.M. But Marcus and I are cool, right? There are no hard feelings. This should be no problem.

Marcus comes to the front of the room to tell me he's ready to bounce in ten. I wait fifteen before I gather my stuff and say my good-byes, because I know he's lying. Finally, he comes to the front of the bar, but he's chilling. I'm all ready to go, but I take a seat and wait for his cue. I'm at his mercy since he's driving.

He takes a spot three feet in front of me and then proceeds to bag a chick *right there*. Intentionally? Eh, I'm not sure. I admit, it stings. Like, dude made it pretty clear where he stood on he subject of me—which I respect—but this is a little inconsiderate, no? I have no right to say anything about this, so I check myself, enjoy what's left of the party, and ignore him.

So he seals the deal and says he's ready to go. Oh, and we're dropping Bree off first.

"Is that a problem?" he asks.

I cock my head. "Why would it be?"

He shrugs. "Just checking."

In the car, I take shotgun, Bree takes the back. Before the vehicle whips to Nostrand, Marcus begins to complain how there were no cute women at the party, and he was looking for some, too. *Er?*

I ignore him, because now I realize that hollering at the chick right in front of me was very intentional, and for whatever reason, Marcus is trying to push my buttons. After the last encounter with Evan, I will not give Marcus the reaction he is looking for. Bree has no comment for him, either. She and I start our own conversation . . . which Marcus interrupts to talk about how many women were after him tonight.

I don't get it. I'm in the passenger seat, trying to figure out what I did to dude for him to be so rude right now. He made it clear he wasn't interested. He didn't call. That's all the hint I need. I didn't call him, didn't harass him, didn't make a scene when I saw him again. I didn't say anything about it. Just moved on. That's what adults do, right? Then I wonder if I really have anything to do with how he's reacting. He could have always been a douche and I didn't see it till now. It's not as if we really got to know each other.

We drop off Bree in Bed-Stuy, and as soon as she's up the stairs to her brownstone and inside the front door, Marcus starts to complain about his shoulder. He asks me to massage it for him.

I'm done. Overdone. Outdone. "Jesus, keep me near the cross. Are you kidding me, dude?!" I dramatically throw my hands into the air for emphasis.

"Huh? Why?" He sounds baffled.

I regain some composure, because I'm giving him a reaction, and something tells me that's all he wants. As calmly as possible, I say, "I am not rubbing some man's shoulder."

"I'm *some man* now?"

"Ummm . . . what else would you be but *some man?*"

"I used to be Marcus."

I shrug and look at him blankly.

We pull in front of my house. And instead of stopping the car, he parks as if we're going to chill and chat. I'm confused. What do we have to say to each other? I promptly reach for the door and politely thank him for seeing me home.

"Where are you going?" he asks.

"Um . . . in my house."

"Why are you being so mean to me?"

"What? Mean?"

"You don't even want to talk to me now."

I thought when he didn't call, that was the indication that he didn't want to talk. Is it possible that he is this clueless? Either he's too dumb to know why I've fallen back, or he knows and he doesn't care.

Then I get it.

He doesn't care that I'm mean. He doesn't care if I dance. He probably doesn't even care about the chick he scooped right in front of me. And his shoulder probably doesn't even hurt.

He does care that I'm not interested anymore. A younger me would have mistaken all of his antics for a backward display of interest. I might have got giddy and thought something incredibly stupid, like *Oh, wow, he does like me. He's just fighting it!* But

I've discovered the difference between someone liking me (interest) and someone wanting me to like him (ego). This circumstance would be the latter.

In my most polite voice, I reiterate: "Thank you for the ride. I appreciate it. Have a good night." And then I get out of the vehicle and sashay upstairs.

Alone.

TEENAGE LOVE AFFAIR

The night I met Stars, I met another man. He was my physical type, and I was immediately attracted to him. We chatted, and I found there was a catch.

He had a girl . . . but he said they were on the rocks. I told him I don't deal with taken men. He told me I should take his number and call every so often to check up on his status. Eh . . . too much work. And does that not sound a little bird-ish?

I took the number, but I never called. The logic was, would I want some chick calling to check in on my man's departure from me? "Karma, karma, karma comes back to you hard," we learned from Lauryn Hill. Plus, there are certain people you just want to do things the right way with.

I ran into him again Saturday night at Josephine, a D.C. lounge catering to tastemakers and those who pretend to be such. I walked in with Tariq, who casually reintroduced us, and we—the stranger and me—had a dawning of recognition at the same time.

"Hey," I said. Blush. Giggle.

"Hey," he said. Grin, grin, grin.

I played it cool as we remembered out loud that there was a very mutual interest.

Finally, he said, "But you never called."

I shook my head. "You had a girlfriend." I gave a what-could-I-do shrug for emphasis.

He nodded, then smiled. "We were broken up. And she's moved out."

Word?

He made me promise to give him my number before I left. I don't know why I didn't give it to him right then. Maybe I didn't want to appear too eager? Silly me.

I left before I could pass him my card. I looked for him, please believe it, but he was nowhere to be found. So I texted Tariq and told him to make sure the guy got my number. Over brunch the following afternoon at Lauriol Plaza, a Spanish resty in Adams Morgan better known for its sangria pitchers than its food, Tariq assured me that he did.

I hope he calls. I *really* hope he calls (and is as amazing on the inside as he is on the outside).

SHIFTY NEGRO SYNDROME

He called. The next day.

For a month, we've talked on the phone, multiple times a day. Sometimes I scheduled my lunch break with his and sit at the fountain by Rockefeller Center and talk to him. I do the same thing after work before I head to the gym. I'm like a teenager. I've nicknamed him my Teenage Love Affair.

But now, I haven't heard from TLA in two days. I texted him last night, called this morning. No response. He usually calls me right back, even if it's just to say he's busy and can't talk.

I check my phone compulsively all day. Nothing. By the end of the day, I'm so wound up I'm debating not calling him ever again. I mean, if he wanted to speak to me, he'd call, right? I'm not trying to be that chick whom dudes laugh about like "Son, shorty's a stalker!" I read *He's Just Not That Into You*. A text and a call are enough. If he cared one way or another, he'd *call*.

After work, I skip an *US Weekly* party for Kanye West at Tenjune to go to the gym. I have to get some of my aggression out. I listen to Lauryn Hill's *Unplugged* as I run. Her lyrics make sense. I replay "Mr. Intentional." Bad, bad sign.

I go over my last conversation with TLA in my head. He called me before I ran my Saturday errands. We talked for thirty minutes. And as soon as we hung up, he called right back to say he was really feeling me. Then he didn't call again?

I do an extra fifteen minutes of cardio because I've still got energy to think. At least I didn't do him. I'd be devastated. I run the last mile—hard and uphill—to get my frustration out.

On the train home, I wonder what happened. Did he get back with his ex? Did he meet someone else?

I debate calling him again. I think of the possible outcomes. He could send me straight to voice mail. He could not answer and let it ring. He could not answer and I could leave a message. He could answer, act as if nothing's wrong. He could answer and give me a valid excuse for not calling. He could answer and then say, "I have to call you back," i.e., *if I'd known it was you, I wouldn't have answered.* I only have a one-in-six chance of getting the response I want.

I realize I'm driving myself crazy.

The next morning, I check my BlackBerry—I sleep with it under my pillow—before I get out of bed. No call. It's officially been three days. I rationalize why this whole "affair" ending is for the best. From great suffering comes great art. Maybe this heartache will inspire a great story for my blog. And I've been off my game ever since TLA and I started talking—posting on my site all erratic, daydreaming, talking on the phone all hours of the night, showing up to work exhausted. *This is for the best, D,* I tell myself.

I'm brooding as I get dressed. I miss him no matter how much I try not to, but that quickly turns to fury by the time I walk out the door. I step into the brick-cold weather and just get madder because despite giving into New York City culture and buying a North Face bubble coat, I'm still cold. Why did I let myself get so caught up so quickly? And what kind of games is this man playing?

Eff it. I'm calling. If for no other reason than to get the closure that will come when I curse out TLA. I don't care if he doesn't care. *I care*, and I want to know *why*! He owes me an explanation.

His phone rings.

And rings.

And rings.

He answers.

He doesn't talk so much as words just rumble in a drawl from his throat. I melt.

"Hello?" Even I'm baffled by how sweet my voice comes out.

"There it is! I've been waiting for you to call." He's smiling into the phone. I hear it, then I picture it. It's a beautiful sight.

"Uh, so why didn't you call me instead of waiting?" *Ooh,* I sound a little belligerent.

"I lost my phone. I didn't have your number written down," he half-explains, half-pleads. He must have heard my angst. "You didn't leave your number when you left a message, baby."

I feel like an idiot. I've wound myself into a frenzy over nothing. Nothing!

"But, uh, D, can I call you right back?"

Uh oh. I don't say that out loud.

By way of explanation, he offers, "I have a client on the other line."

I know what that means: *If I'd known it was you, I wouldn't have answered.*

I put on a chipper voice. I won't let him know how disappointed I am. "Sure! Talk to you later!" *Oops!* I didn't mean to be that happy.

I hang up and plan never to hear from him again. Now I'm mad that I called. I should have just let it be. I'm sure I'll bump into him in D.C. when I visit next month. I'll see TLA in the club, give a pleasant but brief hello, act like we're virtual strangers. I throw my phone into my bag and zone out for the train ride to work.

When I get off the subway in Midtown, there's a voice mail. *From TLA?* I immediately check my phone. "Hey," he says in his Barry White bass. "Just wanted you to have a wonderful day. Call me back, D. I miss your voice."

He wasn't ducking me. I'm crazy, I realize. I'm really crazy. I've mistaken life's ish happening for Shifty Man Syndrome. What if I hadn't called? What if I had really been on some hard pride, "eff that"? I would have totally lost someone I like over *nothing*.

I'm walking to my office, contemplating the exact level of my excessive crazy, when my BlackBerry vibrates. Two buzzes. Three? A call? I reach into my Louis.

It's TLA. Again.

"Hello?" I answer.

"Hey . . . I know you're at work, and—"

"I always have time for you," I say, cutting him off.

"D, I just wanted to talk to you for a sec. I wanted to tell you . . ."

He makes me promise not to tell anyone.

I lean up against the side of my office building, a big doofy smile on my face, biting my bottom lip as he says what needs saying. If my coworkers weren't passing me by, I would have screamed, doubled in half, jumped all over the sidewalk, and given Manhattan a morning show of just how crazy I am over TLA.

VIAGRA MONOLOGUES

TLA has called most nights for months now to tell me about whatever *eureka!* he had at work and also to make sure I post on my blog daily. He decides one night that he will contribute to my writing cause by offering an idea.

First up will be a confession: When he came to visit me, the time we went to a club to hear my boy spin . . .

"You mean Parler?" I interrupt. He's the New York equivalent of Tariq. On occasion, P and I seem to do couple-like things, but that's "just" my boy.

"Yes, him," TLA confirms.

That weekend, he continues, he popped a pill.

TLA was especially, uh . . . friendly that weekend, so I assumed he meant ecstasy.

"You were high?"

"What? No! Viagra!"

Pause.

Pause.

Pause.

"What?"

He explains that every once in a blue moon, when he wants to make a great impression or it's a celebratory occasion with a lady friend, he pops a Viagra or Cialis pill.

"Ummmm . . . So, babe, I mean, it, like, rises to the occasion on its own, doesn't it?"

He assures me it does. "Oh, yes, ma'am, Big Daddy has no problems in that area," he says. Then he reminds me of when he (insert verb here), and I (insert response here) on the (insert location here). I get a flashback and shift on my chair. "That was all natural," he points out.

"Oh . . . okay."

Although I'm currently pacified, he adds that he doesn't understand what I was initially so shocked about. A lot of men his age—twenty-eight—do it.

Really?

Before we even get off the phone, I send an e-mail to the Male Mind Squad inquiring about who's taken Viagra or Cialis, why, and, of course, the effects.

A well-meaning gentleman is among the first to respond: "This is a taboo subject for dudes, just like butt injections are for women. The difference is this regards sexual prowess. And if there is one thing the Black alpha male must have, it's an insatiable sexual appetite and that he can keep it up for ten hours straight. Anything less, you're not a 'man.' Dudes don't want women to know that they need an advantage. In fact, I'll be surprised if you get ten dudes admitting to have taken either pill."

He is right. I don't get ten confessions to the pills, I get way more from men all under thirty-five. And even the guys who don't admit to Viagra or Cialis cop to using various products to gain said "advantage" so they can live up to the Mandingo hype.

Other than the obvious (drinking liquor), I am told about working out beforehand to get the testosterone revving (pretty tame) and then the stay-hard pills you can buy at convenience stores and the numbing agents.

"Numbing agents?" I ask.

"I used those condoms that numb your penis so I wouldn't cum as fast," one gentleman explains. "I couldn't feel anything. It was literally like screwing a bag of hot ice. I would endure that just so I could guarantee that I did a *great* job the first time and she would come back for a second." He continued to use the numbing condoms until one day they didn't work in his favor. "If I have no sensation down there, how can I stay excited?"

The stay-hard pill taker had a more positive experience: "I recently found that the pills they sell in gas stations actually work, especially the Weekend Warrior and Rize pills. I've taken those within the last two months. Both chicks commented about how extra hard and stiff my penis was without me asking. I couldn't lose my erection to save my life, even after we had sex. I had sex four times in a row one night, damn near back-to-back!"

The men who confess to using Viagra or Cialis have some unique reasons:

"To make sure I leave a lasting impression for the long weekend."

"He is basically on call for a couple of hours, and the erection is very firm. They are a guy's best friend when trying to impress his lady."

"As I have gotten older, my body can't perform as long as it once did. I want to go more rounds than I am limited to now." (He's in his late twenties.)

"Alcohol is the only other special 'juice' that keeps a penis hard for a long time, but it takes an exceptional amount to do so. That's why these pills come in handy. They keep you hard without the hangover!"

Apparently, if a guy has broken out the Viagra or the numbing agents, he *really* likes you. The pills run about twenty dollars a pop, plus the price of condoms. So don't make the mistake I did and immediately assume a guy has to take it because you don't do it for him. In fact, you probably do it way too much for his longevity's sake.

"It is only used for special occasions or a special woman," another man says. "You just can't bring out the Superman any ol' time!"

I wondered if any of the men had tales of eight-hour erections or some otherwise insane story like Chris Rock's character in *I Think I Love My Wife*.

"I have only had positive experiences, and she did, too," says one guy. "Only thing was that my penis was still super-hard first thing in the morning, and it kind of hurt also."

I was beginning to think this Viagra thing might not be so bad after all, especially since women get a whole lot of pleasure from the deal, and there seem to be little or no side effects.

Then this little jewel landed in my in-box from "a strapping twenty-eight-year-old male." (I had to call him that to get him to agree to let me tell this story.)

My sister's a nurse and gets all kinds of samples from vendors, so I tried Viagra shortly after it came out. It was around my then-girlfriend's birthday, so I was planning on taking her out to eat and afterward bringing her back to my place to set her insides on fire.

My sister recommended that I take half a pill 'cause they were the extra-strength kind. Consistent with a typical twenty-three- to twenty-four-year-old mind state, I thought, If half a pill can make me last two hours, imagine what two WHOLE pills could do for me?

I took two pills before our date so I could make sure it had time to absorb into my system. I took her to Jezebel for dinner, and halfway through, she starts to rub on my thigh, causing me to catch some wood. But something felt different this time. Not to get into too much detail, but when a man's buddy gets hard, he can feel the blood pulsating, causing it to inflate. It's like you're inflating a bike tire with a hand pump.

Anyway, this time, the blood continued to pulsate even after it got erect. I had a boner that I couldn't get rid of. I thought about everything nonsexual I possibly could—baseball, work, jail, even my own damn mama. Nothing worked.

I tell my girl we need to go. "Why?" she asks. "We didn't even finish our dinner yet." I grab her hand and put it between my legs. We bounce with my jacket in front of my pants and head for my car. We get in, and now I'm getting scared 'cause it's starting to hurt, like how it hurts when you flex a muscle for a really long time.

I suggest to my girl that maybe if she tops me off while I drive to the crib, I could bust one off, and hopefully my joint would go down for a while. She heads me off for thirty minutes. She does it so long that her jaw gets sore and her throat dries out. I still haven't bust, and now my penis hurts even more.

We get to the crib and get straight to business. Being the soldier I am, I'm gonna put the pain aside and finish what I started. We ended up having a two-hour sex-athon. It was so bad that my girl had to tell me to stop after her fifth or sixth orgasm. Me? I'm dripping in sweat like a runaway slave, but I don't even have a friggin' drop of semen. I ended up just going to sleep. Woke up the next morning with a headache reminiscent of my college hangover days. But at least my joint went down.

Needless to say, I ain't fuck with Viagra since.

RED VELVET

I got a perm and no umbrella.

It's the evening of my birthday. It didn't smell like rain when I got out of my car, even though I knew it was in the forecast. Maybe I was too excited about being taken out on a date-date by a *may-an* to pay attention.

I met TLA at his condo a few minutes ago. I've been on plenty of dates, but I haven't had a "real" one in a long, long time. The kind where the man will drive you to your destination safely, look out for you for the night, and after, take you wherever you want to go. By my calculations, it's been a good seven years (roughly the time I've lived in Brooklyn) since that happened. I've grown too accustomed to the NYC kind of date, where you meet him at the location and you both jump on the train in opposite directions at the end of a great night, or, if you're lucky, he gives you cab fare.

I walk into TLA's house and am greeted by a big, wide, fine-looking, great-smelling man, who says hello to me . . . well, very warmly. I've never seen him dressed up. He doesn't have to wear a suit for work, and he doesn't really like to. But for my birthday, he has broken out a suit and some hard-soled shoes (fresh shine).

Just when we're about ready to go, I look out the blinds and realize it is pouring rain. Of course it is. It rains every time I see this man. It's as if we're living in *Love Jones* but without all the smoky cafés and stuff.

TLA doesn't have an umbrella. Mine is in my car. But nothing will ruin my birthday night. We're going out. I'm eating birthday cake—red velvet! My freshly done hair will have to be damned. I will get wet to go on my birthday date.

I steel up. Breezily announce that I am still good to go and there is no need to be late for our reservation. If he'll just give me a towel, I'll throw it over my head and hope for the best.

He looks at me as if I'm stupid . . . and starts taking off his clothes.

"No, baby," I plead, reaching to button him back up. "We can do that later. I still wanna go!"

He laughs, smiles at me like I am the cutest thing ever. "I'm gonna run to get the umbrella."

Huh?

This beautiful Black man undresses, redresses in basketball shorts and a wife-B, and runs out in the pouring rain to get the umbrella from my car. *Then* he runs to his car—still in the pouring rain—to swing it around to the closest entrance so I will stay as dry as possible. *Then* he runs back into the house, soaking wet. He dries off, undresses, and redresses.

He looks at me. "What? What I do? Hmmm?"

I'm staring at him as if he is a superhero and I am Lois Lane. My hair and good dress have been saved from destruction. "You're amazing," I blurt. I tiptoe up, grab his face, and kiss him. "Thank you, [insert nickname for him that I cannot say in public]."

"C'mon," he says, forcing himself to pull back. "We have reservations."

When he's ready again, he takes me by the hand and leads me out of the house. I happily follow.

TLA takes me to a fabulous Italian restaurant in the city. I let him order for me, and he picks out a wonderful dish, fettucine with crabmeat and shrimp. The only thing that is off is that TLA keeps checking his phone all night, texting someone, then apologizing profusely each time.

"Did something happen at work?" I ask.

"Um . . . no. I . . . just gotta take care of something," he says mysteriously.

I nod. "Okay." I don't even let my mind wander to some next chick. He's a man. He has man business to tend to. I keep eating my pasta.

The phone, on the table now, goes off again. He apologizes before checking it and typing back. I'm starting to get annoyed. I've been sipping on water. I order a glass of white wine when the waiter strolls by.

"I gotta run out. Okay?" TLA asks.

What? I think it. I don't say it. "Sure." I try to sound as nonchalant as possible. I am slowly seething.

He goes away for about five minutes, then returns. The phone doesn't buzz or ring again. It's back in his pocket. We have amazing conversation, and I eat until I'm stuffed, but I am still thinking about my birthday cake.

When the waiter comes by to run down the dessert options, TLA shuts him down before I can answer. Is he in a hurry to get somewhere? Did he make plans to do something after this? Maybe all that letting him order for me and lead me around has gone to his head. Red velvet wasn't on the list of items the waiter ran off anyway, I justify. No red-velvet birthday cake for me, I guess. It's the only thing that keeps the evening from being perfect. Oh, and his ringing phone.

I get a doggie bag, and TLA carries it with him as he runs to get the car in the rain and swings it around for me. All the way back to his house, we're laughing and joking in our own little world. I'm still annoyed about the phone, but I'll bring it up tomorrow, after my birthday.

Back at his condo, I kick off my shoes at his door. TLA runs ahead to the kitchen, then calls me in.

"I have one more surprise for you," he says when I'm walking through the doorway.

I'm beaming. "Really, what?" I stick out both hands like a little kid, waiting for my gift. I even close my eyes.

He laughs. "Open your eyes, silly girl!"

I do. And there is nothing there.

He reaches into my doggie bag . . . and pulls out a cake. A homemade red-velvet cake.

"Here," he says, placing it in my hands. It's still warm.

He gives me the backstory. That morning, TLA realized the restaurant didn't have red-velvet cake. He called a friend who bakes and told her the problem in a panic, then asked if she could whip up a cake.

Of course, it was an inconvenience. He pressed. He had to have it. She said she would rush home as soon as she could and make the cake. All of the texts throughout the evening were updates about the cake's status: "I put it in the oven." "I took it out the oven." "It'll be cool in 20." "I'm icing it now." "On my way."

I don't know what he said or did to impress upon this woman the importance of the night or the person he was entertaining. But this gracious, phenomenal woman, whoever she was, not only made the cake at the last minute, but then she jumped into her car and drove from Maryland to D.C. *in the pouring rain* to deliver it to

him while we were at the restaurant so that I would have red-velvet cake on my birthday.

The cake is amazing.

The night is amazing.

TLA is really friggin' amazing!

"You are the sweetest thing ever!" I blurt to TLA—not for the first time. I go up on my tiptoes for another kiss.

He has that look again, the one he gives when he's trying to brush off a compliment. I swear he would blush if he could.

FALLING BACK

TLA and I have been "dating" since March, which puts our situation somewhere around six months. We had a conversation awhile ago about not seeing other people and becoming exclusive. Last week, he invited me to meet his family for Christmas.

I

Everything was going swimmingly swell until I read the galleys of Steve Harvey's *Act Like a Lady, Think Like a Man* to prepare for an interview with the comedian-turned-author. Harvey said that when a man really likes a woman, he does three things:

Protect (√)
Provide (√)
Profess ( )

I'd never thought about a title with TLA. But I figured, *I do every-thing a girlfriend does, why hasn't he asked me to be his?* When I asked Harvey during the interview what I should do, he told me what I alreay knew, but wanted to avoid. It was time to have a conversation.

I brought it up when I spoke to TLA that night. I didn't ask in a way that would put the man on the defensive. It was more like a passing curiosity, like *Hey, we're so great together, why not?* I was expecting to hear something like *What? I'm already your man, what are you talking about?* Maybe the title was something he over-looked or thought wasn't important because I hadn't brought it up.

Him: "I can't focus on a relationship right now. I'm trying to fig-ure out how to grow my business and get my money right. Maybe go back to school. I need more time."

I recalled a conversation about marriage that I had with GVG once. He was explaining to me why he's mentally ready to jump the broom but just can't do it. He very much wants to commit, but he fears he doesn't have enough to offer a woman financially. He has a very defined idea of the type of woman he wants (he ran down the list, and it was basically an early Michelle Obama) and what he should bring to a relationship to give her the kind of life she deserves.

Before he'll step to a woman with any serious intentions, he wants to make his millions (or at least a good six figures), own a condo, have a reliable late-model ride, and a chunk in the bank.

I'd heard the same thing sitting at an *Essence* roundtable, too. I'd gathered a team of men and women to discuss "Why Don't We Get Married?" and one of the guys told me, "When I have a kingdom for my wife, I'll take one." That's what ran in the issue. What didn't make the cut was his detailed explanation:

A relationship stifles your ability to grow in your professional field. You're stagnated because you have to invest so much time in that relationship for it to be successful. If you have one hun-

dred hours in a week, at least twenty are going toward your woman. And that time could be used learning to grow a business or making more money. When I get to a point where I feel like I'm comfortable financially, then I'll be in a relationship.

The intent is honorable. It's noble. It's totally old-fashioned, and I'm totally in love with the idea (who doesn't just want the good life handed to them?), but frankly, I'm looking for someone to build *with*, not so much someone who offers me the keys to the mini-kingdom he's already built. A man wants to give me all? Really, I just want him to do like Mary J. Blige says and "give me you."

I didn't bother arguing with TLA. I was not entirely happy with the outcome of the Talk. But I liked him. And, well, except for not having the title, things were good between us.

A week later, I realize I've had a massive perception switch. Without thinking about it, I don't bother waking up on weekends to talk to him in the middle of the night when he gets off work from his side hustle. And I don't wait up late to speak to him most nights when he gets home late from work. When I'm entirely free, I call, and I answer when he does. Last minute, I change my plans to go see him one weekend and fly off to Atlanta instead. I figured if he makes noise about it, I can always politely remind him, "Uh, I'm not your girlfriend." There are advantages to being unofficial.

In the A, I'm sitting in 300, an upscale bowling alley, with Eddie, who's begun referring to a woman he's been dating for four months as "his wife." He's all "my wife" this and "my wife" that because he's convined she's "the one." (She wasn't. Long story.) That's when I realize I feel slighted by TLA. I'm good enough to kick it with, to unload emotional baggage on, but not good enough to claim? GTFOH.

II

Maybe it's the high of Stevie Wonder that makes me do it. Maybe I am just ticked at my "situation" with TLA and for allowing myself to be okey-doked. But listening to a man sing—live, no less—for hours about love and possibilities and hope can make a woman do unexpected things.

TLA was supposed to come visit me this weekend, but he had to work. He invited me to come to D.C., but the Wonder-Full party, an annual ode to Stevie Wonder's music, is at the Hammerstein Ballroom. For six hours, DJs Spinna and Bobitto only play music sung by or influenced by Stevie Wonder. Penelope and I never miss it.

Usually, Stevie Wonder calls in and talks to the crowd through the speakers. This year, he shows up and performs. I know by the lump in my throat when he sings the opening lines to "If It's Magic" that I am going to make the call: "If it's magic . . . then why can't it be everlasting, like the sun that always shines, like the poets in this rhyme, like the galaxies in time . . ."

He answers on the first ring.

"It's me," I say, walking down the street in the rain.

"Demetria?" he asks immediately.

"Yup."

"Hey." He sounds happy to hear from me.

"Hey."

He's silent for a moment. And I don't know what to say to fill the empty space. I only called because I wanted to hear his voice. I don't want anything.

"How are you?" Greg finally asks.

"I'm good, you?" I lean up against a *bodega* window, shielding myself from the drizzle beneath its canopy as I wait for Penelope to finish chatting with some guy.

"*Where* are you?" he asks.

Weird. "Um . . . New York."

"No, like, are you in the city or Brooklyn?"

What's he getting at? "Yeah . . . I'm by Penn Station. Why?"

"I'm in town for the weekend."

My stomach drops as if I'm going downhill on the Cyclone at Coney Island. *Thump thump* goes the traitor in my chest.

"Where?" I ask urgently.

"I'll come get you," he says.

Just like old times, I think. But I've learned how to take care of myself by now. "I'll come to you," I say. "Where are *you?*"

Penelope drives me downtown to 40/40 in her truck. I tell her who I'm meeting, and she says nothing while I fiddle in my purse for my makeup bag to freshen my face. She's heard the Greg chronicles. She's not his biggest fan. But she's respectful enough of my feelings to enable me.

She's double-parking on Twenty-fifth Street when she just can't help herself any longer. "Who goes to 40/40 on a weekday, much less a weekend?" she begins.

"P, stop," I caution. This isn't about the club. The layout of 40/40 is challenged, but on the right night for the right A-list party, it's just fine.

"I'm just saying. I don't even come here when Jay-Z is throwing a party, and you know how much I love Jay-Z. That's how wack this place is."

I roll my eyes. "I'll be back in ten," I say, popping out of the car.

The drizzle hasn't turned to rain, and I realize if it did, this whole reunion would be very Nina and Darius. Somehow I don't see us passionately exchanging "I don't know" and "I don't care" here on this New York street.

Greg spots me first. Years have passed since we've seen each other. He doesn't swagger my way. He walks. He looks the same, beautifully blue-black dark, square-shouldered, neon-white teeth, like Midnight from *The Coldest Winter Ever* come to life. There's nothing jaw-dropping about him, though, this time. He looks like a mortal instead of a god among men. I don't have to bite my cheeks to keep from smiling. I hug him, and, surprisingly, there are no butterflies.

"Your energy's different," he says when I let go.

"I don't know what you're talking about." My voice has its bass. It usually goes up a few octaves on its own for him.

"You're dating someone." It's a statement, not a question.

Do I bother to tell him about TLA? "I am."

"You're smitten." He smiles, but it isn't genuine. "I'm happy for you."

My smile probably doesn't reach my eyes, either. "Thanks."

He slowly steps close enough to me that I can feel the heat coming off his body. I take a big step back. Then another one. Surprisingly, that isn't hard to do. Greg doesn't react.

"Am I taking you home?" he asks.

"Huh?"

He repeats the question.

I tilt my chin to look at him quizzically, then shake my head without giving the question any real thought. I pull my sweater around me and keep my arms folded across my chest defensively. "I'm with my friend. She'll make sure I get home safely."

"Okay." He steps in again. My face is angled so I could move an inch in and kiss him without standing on tippy-toes. I can feel his warm breath on my lips. For someone who just left a bar, I find it odd that he doesn't smell like liquor.

"If you're so smitten with him, why are you here?" Greg asks. His voice doesn't rumble.

"I don't know." And I really don't. I didn't answer that way with an accompanying shrug to be dramatic.

"You should go, then," he challenges.

I nod. But before I step back, I stand on my tips anyway and crush myself into him. I remember how he used to leave at the end of the night or in the morning, and I would cling to him, wanting to feel him, to enter his aura. I remember how I clung to myself, holding me together when I thought I was ripping in two when he left. Our whole two years flashes through my head in twenty seconds, but the nostalgia isn't enough to send me back down this particularly rocky path even if he wanted to go there, if only for one night.

For just a beat, I wonder if I've done the right thing not telling him how he hurt me when he left. "Sorry" was good enough to forgive Dakar. I don't think there's anything Greg could say to make that better.

"Good-bye, Greg," I say. There are no heavy sighs, no pangs in my chest, no throbbing in my head, no yearning for more contact.

I purposefully don't look at his face in the second before I walk—not saunter—off. I didn't say it for a reaction. I didn't do it to make a point. And I don't turn back before I get into the truck to see if he's watching.

I open the passenger door and get in where Penelope is waiting.

III

After I got into the truck, he texts. "It was good to see you. You look good." When I don't write back, he calls. I answer, and when Penelope shoots me the side-eye of death, I tell him I'll call him later.

Since then, Greg and I have kept in touch. At first, it was a call once every other week, then weekly, then a couple of times a week,

then every couple of days. I reason that this is all harmless, especially since he lives out of state and is much farther than an Acela
train ride away. Oh, and he knows about TLA.

I am on the phone with Greg one night about six weeks after we
started speaking again. He keeps grunting. We aren't really talking
about anything, just sort of breathing into the receiver together
while we go about our lives.

"What are you doing?" I ask.

"Breaking down the bed," he says, as if it's most the natural
Tuesday night activity in the world.

"What are you doing *that* for?"

"It needs to be moved," he says.

"To where?"

"I'm selling it."

"Oh." Pause. "What are you going to sleep on?"

"I have two bedrooms."

"Oh."

The next week, I'm on the phone with him at work, recounting
a hilarious conversation with Zane about a sex calendar she did for
the magazine, when he cuts me off.

"D, I have something to tell you," he says urgently.

I get a feeling of what Christopher Moltisanti from *The Sopranos*
once eloquently described as "impending doom." I freeze, bracing
myself for the worst. *He's getting married. He got someone pregnant.
He's dying.* I don't say anything, because I can't.

"I'm moving back to New York," he says.

"What?" Pause. "Why? Why are you coming back here?" I've
gone from lackadaisical to hysterical in less than two seconds.
Classic signs that he's a B.

"O . . . kay. That's not the reaction I was expecting," Greg says.
He goes on to lay out the practical reasons, including a better-
paying job.

"Oh." It's all I can say.

"I just found out. You're like the second person I've told."

"Who was the first?"

He chuckles. "My mother."

"Okay." One-word responses are the best I can do.

"That's all you have to say?"

"Yes."

There's an empty silence as I stare blankly at my computer screen.

Suddenly, I have more than enough to say, but this isn't the time to say it. I regain my words finally and claim that I have work to do so I can rush him off the phone.

I've known for years that this was going to happen. But I thought he would return when I was head over heels in love, and I could tell him smugly, "Too bad, so sad, look what you missed out on when you left." But years have passed—where did they go?—and I'm in the same place I was when he left me. A little older. A little wiser, too, I hope.

IV

A month later, I'm sitting across the table from Greg one rainy Sunday afternoon at Café Lalo for dessert. It's quaint and very European, the type of place where movies about New York are filmed. Years ago, Greg talked about taking me here, and he asked if he could to keep his word. We're friends and adults, so we should be able to see each other . . . right?

As I'm forking Greg's pumpkin cheesecake into my mouth, I realize we're unintentionally mirroring each other's movements, both of us resting one elbow on the table and propping our chins up with the other hand.

This is the way we should have always been. For just a second, I wonder *what if?* And just as quickly, I bring myself out of the complete insanity crossing through my head.

Greg and I talk, mostly about TLA. TLA and I had our first fight a couple of days ago when I rushed him off the phone while I was out with friends. More and more, I'm starting to think I'm still not built for this relationship business and all of its obligations. Oh, that's right. I'm not in a relationship. Just dealing with the headaches of one.

I run down my frustrations to Greg, who listens, laughs where appropriate, and points out, "What real difference does the title make? You were happy before all this other shit came up."

I tell him about the advance copy of the Steve Harvey book. He shakes his head. "You're taking dating advice from a comedian?" he asks incredulously.

"You're missing the point," I counter. He thinks I'm good enough to act like a girlfriend with, but he doesn't want me actually to be one. If he really cared, he'd—"

"You don't get it, do you?" Greg interrupts.

I roll my eyes. "What are you going to lecture me about?"

"You're in a relationship, whether he calls it that or not. He doesn't want to see anyone else. Neither do you. From everything you've told me about him, he sounds like a good dude. If he says he needs time, give him time."

"I'm supposed to wait for him?" I shriek while accidentally clanging my silverware on my saucer. The women at the table next to us look over curiously.

"Relationships are about taking chances," Greg cautions. "You can't do everything expecting an ROI and when you don't get it right when you want it, think it's not worth it anymore. Be happy, Demetria," he adds, sounding exhausted. "Because you're not now. Behaving like a spoiled child because you can't have your way isn't going to get you in a relationship. You're ruining a good thing. And you're making yourself miserable trying to prove a point."

"I'm not miserable," I lie. He knows I'm lying. "How long am I supposed to wait for him to figure his shit out? Forever?"

He sighs as if he's disgusted. "I don't know. It probably won't be long, though."

"And what makes you think that?"

"Because you're an exceptional woman, and from everything you've told me about him, he's not an idiot."

"You think I'm exceptional?"

Another you-cannot-be-this-stupid look. "Just watch what he does, D. He's telling you he needs to get it together. See if he does that. If he does, work with him. Give him a chance to get on the same page with you."

"You don't think I'll make a fool of myself?"

He shrugs. "You might. That's what a relationship is sometimes. Would you rather have your ego and always wonder what if? Or would you rather try and see what happens?"

"Can't I have both?"

"You can, but how's that working for you?"

I'm watching him as he signals the waitress for the check, thinking about how far we've come and how we ended up here, back where we started as friends. For real this time.

"Thank you, Greg."

He looks up from his wallet, where he's reaching for a wad of cash. "For dessert?"

"No, for caring enough about me to be honest with me."

"You wanted me to lie?"

"I'm glad we can be here again." I go to place my hand over his on the table, and he pulls his back.

After dessert, Greg drives me downtown to let me off at the same stop he used to come to many years ago when we first met and I lived by the World Trade Center. The irony isn't lost on either of us. Since it's before ten, we both agree I should take the train home.

We're friends, but him crossing into Brooklyn might not be the best idea. We still have our chemistry and we'd rather play it safe.

Penelope texts when we're on the West Side Highway to ask where I am.

"Leaving the city," I write back.

"The city? On a weekend? You don't leave Brooklyn."

"I'm with Greg."

"WORD? On a date?"

"No! We're friends."

"I'm your friend. I've NEVER hung out with you in the city . . . on a WEEKEND."

I don't text her back. So she calls.

"Uh, isn't this what happened when you guys first met?" she says, skipping pleasantries. "You met him and then hung out for eight months before he even kissed you."

I roll my eyes, wishing she could see me. "Something like that." I realize this sounds worse than it is. Before I can explain, she beats me to the punch.

"Still just friends, huh?"

"Just friends," I insist.

"Riiight . . . "Did you ask him about—"

"P, I'll call you back," I say. (I haven't gotten around to that yet.)

Greg pulls up next to the subway station, and we sit in the car for a moment. The engine idles, and so do I. I'm trying to get up the nerve to address the bedazzled pink elephant in the room.

"Why'd you leave me like that?" I finally ask. I don't need to give the details. He knows what I'm talking about.

He sighs heavily, fiddles with the key ring for a moment. He had to know I'd ask someday. He doesn't have an answer ready? "It's complicated," he says, censoring himself.

"This isn't a Facebook status," I quip.

"You really want to know?" he challenges.

I nod. I'm a big girl now.

"I didn't know what I was walking into to bring you with me. And you had so much going for you here . . ." His voice trails off, and he shakes his head. "It was the right thing to do."

"You can't believe that. You can't," I say. I'm choking back tears already, the same way I did on the steps of the museum. I thought I could handle this conversation. I guess not. "I would have given up everything."

"I couldn't ask you to do that," he explains. "You had to accomplish what you came here for. All you ever talked about was getting on a masthead. That wasn't going to happen for you in South Carolina."

I can't hold back anymore. My tears slip down my cheeks. He pulls me to him, across the armrest, and embraces me hard. "It would have been selfish to ask you to go. You would have said yes, and you wouldn't have lived your dream," he says into my hair. "And you would have resented me for it at some point." He says this as if it's a matter of fact, not opinion. "I told you I was coming back. And I'm here. I'm not going anywhere."

The weight of his comment, well, weighs on me. I wipe my face and suggest that it's time for me to get on the train. He gets out of the car to walk me to the steps, and I hug him good-bye tightly.

At the bottom of the stairs, I look back up to see if he's still there. He is. As he promised he would be.

"Now it's you who's running from me," he says with a smirk.

V

The next week, Greg picks me up from the airport when I return from a business trip in New Orleans. The next night, he asks me to dinner. The following day, he stops by my job that morning and meets me at a party that night. The day after that, he takes me to dinner. The next day, I head to D.C. for Congressional Black Caucus weekend.

I asked TLA to be my date for CBC, which is like Freaknick for bourgeois adults, except barely-there clothing is replaced with cocktail dresses and ball gowns. Technically, the weekend is a legislative conference where Black intelligencia converge on the nation's capital to discuss the problems plaguing the Community. But unofficially, it is a weekend full of VVIP parties, cocktail hours, receptions, and banquets for the well-connected and their plus-ones.

As it worked out, TLA couldn't hang out with me. He had to work parties, not attend them. I respect his hustle, but I'd rather have him by my side. I ask Aliya to join me instead. We spend the entire weekend on a cutie run, replenishing the files of men I keep under my work desk.

Day One (Thursday night): Ibiza, the Park, and Lotus.

Day Two (Friday): A presidential debate party at Bobby Van's, followed by a black-tie party at Love.

Day Three (Saturday): A quaint VIP BBQ on the W rooftop, a Coca-Cola party at the Women's History Museum, then the annual gala that night, where would-be President Obama gives the keynote address. That's followed by after parties at the Newseum (the writer in me loved this) and finally the annual Chief of Staff party at the French Embassy.

Day 4 (Sunday): I see TLA.

We go to dinner at Timbuktu, a seafood spot just outside Baltimore with the best damn crab cakes, period. This has become "our spot,"

and while we eat, I suggest we go to the movies to see a Black film
that opened this weekend. He can't/won't go. He's seen the movie
already, but even bigger, the Redskins-Cowboys game is coming on.

I'm from D.C., so I know what a rivalry this is. But the idea of
being cooped up in the house while I'm sort of on vacation bores
me to tears. I make plans to go to the movies with my mother instead.

When I get back to TLA's apartment, he's annoyed. He feels
"a way" about me going to the movies when I've been in town all
weekend and have barely spent any time with him. I gently remind
him with my most valid excuse that it was CBC weekend. That
I live for this every year and I invited him to go with me and he
couldn't.

"You saw me when you were done doing everything else!" he bellows. "When did I start coming second?"

I take a deep breath before I say something that cuts deep and
will leave this whole situation in complete shambles. "I really like
you, but you can't expect me to treat you like a priority when I'm
an option," I say evenly.

"An option?" He looks at me crazy. "You're not an option. I told
you, I'm good. I'm not chasing other women."

"So what's the problem, then?"

"D, I told you." He then recounts the same reasons he listed
before. He needs to get his money right, formally launch his company, go back to school, blah, blah, blah, take his time. "I can't
focus on a relationship right now. I just can't."

"Look, we'll figure this out," TLA says, filling the silence. "I
know where you're coming from, and I'm not stringing you along. I
just need to work on some things, okay?"

He pulls me up from my seat on the couch and to him.

I don't know if I believe him or I just want to. I nod into his
chest. "Okay."

VI

Me: "Hey."

Him: "Hey."

Me: "What are you doing after work?"

I haven't seen Mr. Ex in almost a week. I . . . miss him. There, I said it.

Him: "I don't know. Probably going by home to cook for my mother. Why? What's up?"

Me: "You're such a good son."

Him: "What are you up to, Demetria?"

Me: "I wanted to see you."

Him: "You want me to bring you dinner?"

Me: "I'm going back to Brooklyn."

Him: "Okay."

Me: "You're going to drive from Harlem to Brooklyn on a weeknight?"

Him: "Do you want me to bring you dinner?"

Me: "What are you making?"

Him: "Lasagna."

Me: "Your mother's not a vegetarian. I don't eat meat."

Him: "Do you want me to bring you dinner or not?"

Me: "Are you going to bring me meat lasagna?"

Him: "Would I do that?"

Me: "No."

Him: (Laughs.) "So why would you ask?"

Me: "I don't know."

I'm being intentionally difficult.

Him: (Sigh.) "Do you want me to bring you dinner?"

Me: "I'm going back to Brooklyn."

Him: "Woman, is that a yes or a no?"

Me: (Laughs.) "Yes!"

Him: "I'll call you when I'm on my way."

Four hours later. I buzz Greg into my building. I open my door to find him in a zip-up knit cardigan. Nothing says domesticated man quite like a cardigan. I think it's because of *The Cosby Show*.

He has a towel-covered dish. The wonderful aroma immediately overwhelms my foyer. I follow him to my kitchen. Greg places the dish on the stovetop and unwraps it carefully, the way old people do Christmas presents so they can reuse the paper.

Years ago, he started promising to cook for me, and more than a thousand days later, he hadn't. I teased him about this all the time, usually while sitting across from him at a restaurant. I can't wait. I reach over, hastily peeling back the foil, and peek.

"Sorry if the top is a little dark. I wanted to make sure it cooked all the way through," Greg apologizes, leaning in the doorway.

I look up. "Cheese always browns fast," I offer, dismissing his disclaimer. It's perfect because he made it.

He's looking back at me. "Zucchini, squash, and peppers. That's what's in there."

I'm trying to hold back a big, silly grin, but my mouth won't stay in a straight line. I had the same problem around him when I was twenty-one. My lips are pursed instead.

"You really made me veggie lasagna?" I squeal. I give up and beam so hard my eyes are like slits. I bite my bottom lip in an attempt to dignify myself, but it's no use. My smile breaks through. Thank God I had braces.

"Hold up. You made your mom eat veggie lasagna?"

He's beaming back as he shakes his head. "I made you a separate one."

I'm still smiling. "Oh."

"Taste it."

I dig a fork in as he watches me, anticipating my reaction.

It's good. Really good. I tell him as much.

"I know," he says, before leaving me in the kitchen.

I make us plates and plop onto the couch, where he's made him-self comfortable. After we eat, we end up in a spirited debate about whether Jay-Z had more creativity in his heyday than Kanye West does now (I argue for Yeezy), and then we talk about everything and nothing until I find *The Wire* reruns on HBO.

At some point, I doze off on his shoulder. When my alarm goes off at seven A.M.; I'm on the couch with a pillow under my head and a comforter over me. Greg is gone.

I have that armor-of-love feeling, the same one I had in my early twenties. But what does it matter? This isn't a TV show or a movie. The guy who breaks your heart doesn't one day magically become an attentive boyfriend, then a doting husband. He's a heartbreaker, and that's all.

VII

TLA calls me the next morning at the office. He likes my work voice—professional, breathy, and intentionally vague to keep my coworkers out of the loop about my personal life.

"What's up, sista?" TLA asks.

"Nothing. Chillin. Just working." TLA's version of "figuring it out" is acting as if nothing is wrong. He hasn't addressed the (lack-ing) status of "us," and as much as I'm trying to ignore it and "just be happy" with this whole thing, like Greg suggested, I'm not. And that's making me distant and aloof.

"Oh, all right. It's crazy today?"

"Like every day," I say. Ten minutes ago, my *Essence* Single Man of the Month called to say he's in a relationship now, he won't be at the photo shoot tomorrow, and could I please not run the article? Now I'm scrambling to find a single bachelor who can have his picture taken in twenty-four hours.

When I'm done rambling, TLA mentions an upcoming wedding he's in, in New York, and that he still has to get fitted for a suit.

"When's the wedding again?"

He gives me the date. "It's cool if I stay with you, right?"

"Sure." I make a mental note that he didn't invite me to go.

Awkward silence.

"Hello?" he asks. "D, you're going to the wedding with me, right?"

I guess I could have assumed, since he mentioned it and was staying with me, that I was invited, but I prefer a formal "Will you go?" when a man wants me to go somewhere. That said, I'd hoped that TLA would ask. I'm still not gung ho about marriage, but I love weddings.

I smile. "Yeah, sure. I'll go."

"Okay."

Pause. "Well, get back to work, then," he says.

VIII

TLA is pissed. I'm brooding. I've spent most of the day lying in the bed with my covers pulled to my chin. My BlackBerry is off—I was tried of fighting on BBM—as I stare at the ceiling.

Something needs to be said beyond these irate messages we've traded back and forth half the day. They aren't solving anything.

I've been lying here all Saturday afternoon thinking. He and I have to talk. Even though now's probably not the best time.

I didn't make the wedding. Or the reception. TLA was supposed to stay with me last night; he never showed up. He went out with the groom and friends for the bachelor party, which he said he wasn't going to do. He was only going to be in the city one night, and he said he'd spent it with me.

At one A.M., I texted him a not-so-pleasant message for standing me up. He texted back with a flurry of his own, then called me *after the wedding* to invite me to the reception, which I refused to go to. He doesn't even feel obligated to keep his word to me now? And he wants to break his word but still have me keep my end of the deal? Where they do that at?

I cut my phone back on to call TLA. I don't know if we're fixable. I don't even know if I want to fix anything. If we're done, then that's what it is. But I need to say that. Broken I can deal with. Living in limbo is driving me crazy.

I find a voice mail waiting. Who leaves messages these days? Just text and type out what needs saying.

"Uh, D. This is Parler. I spun a wedding today and ran into [TLA]. Um, you need to talk to your boy. I don't know what happened between y'all. But he is messed up. Just thought I'd give you the heads up."

Oh, Jesus. What'd he do?

Later the full story will come out. Apparently, TLA took the liberty of cursing at the DJ, my boy, about me. "Tell her I was here! Alone! Without her! And she should have fucking been here!" he slurred somewhere around his third double shot of Henny. His friends stopped him from enjoying the open bar shortly after that.

I dial TLA's number.

"You still have an attitude?" he answers on the third ring.

I ignore the urge to say something bright. Someone has to be level-headed right now. And since I am woman, by default, keeper of the flame, and haven't done it so far today, I'll start. "We need to talk."

"Yeah, we do," he says, revving up. "Let's talk about how I invited you to be with me at this wedding, and I came to New York to see you, and I wanted you to meet all my friends. I sat alone with an empty seat next to me all day. And I wanted you to see me in my suit, and you didn't even show up, Demetria! Let's talk about that,

888

huh? And everyone telling me how miserable I look and everyone asking me what's wrong? And where you are, because I told them you were coming and you weren't here! You want to talk about that?"

"You're not going to blame this on me," I say evenly. "You didn't keep your word. This isn't my fault. You know that."

"I can't do anything about the wedding," he says. "It's done. What do you want me to do?" He sighs heavily. "Come here. I miss you, D. Can you come here? I'll pay for you to come here."

He's a mess. Still. I'm not sure if it's the liquor, his emotions, his sign—Cancer, like me—or a combination of all three.

"What time is it?"

"Are you coming?" he pleads.

I'd already thought about what to wear. "I'll be there in an hour. I'll hit you when I'm outside, okay?"

I call TLA from the hotel lobby. Five minutes later, I hear the *ding* of his elevator arriving. I've turned around for every *ding*. This is the sixth one. He's emerging from the back of the carriage. He's still got on his suit, and he looks amazing.

"Hey," he says, swaggering up to me.

"Hey." I smile up at him. "You look very handsome."

I didn't know what to expect when I got here. I came prepared for anything from a screaming, make-a-got-damn scene fight in the lobby to a postreception sit-down with his friends and their wives, where I was viewed with scorn as the outsider who mistreated their boy. I put on a DVF wrap dress for the occasion. It's an all-purpose outfit.

"I'm glad you came," he says.

"I'm glad I'm here." And I mean it.

We're both staring at each other like Larenz Tate and Nia Long at the end of *Love Jones* when they've finally put their differences aside to focus on what matters most. I imagine that, like me, TLA is wondering either where do we go from here? Or how did we get here? Then the groom—I assume such because he's wearing an all-white tux with tails—walks up and introduces himself to me.

"I'm so glad you came," he begins. "I want to apologize for my role in the confusion last night. I take full responsibility. It's my wedding day, and I was demanding."

This man just got married. He should be somewhere with his bride. And here he is apologizing to me, some woman he's never met. I try to interrupt him several times to congratulate him on his wedding and get him back to the important matters at hand—like his wife, wherever she is. But there's no stopping him until he's done saying what he feels needs to be said.

"He's been moping all day. Thank you for coming. My boy really likes you, and I hope y'all can work it out."

TLA looks sheepish. I don't know what to say, so I laugh awkwardly. I'm embarrassed that our confusion is spilling into other people's lives. "Well, thank you for telling me," I say to the groom. "And congratulations again on your marriage."

"Black love. Believe in it!" he boasts, raising two fists above his head like Rocky when he reached the top step at the Philadelphia Museum of Art. The groom heads for the hotel bar.

"Wow. That was a lot," I say when he's out of earshot.

"I didn't tell him to do that," TLA says. "I am so embarrassed."

"Don't be. He's funny."

"You want to sit outside so we can talk?"

I nod.

He takes my hand and leads me to the courtyard. We sit on the benches, where there's a gentle breeze and an obscured view of the Brooklyn Bridge. I put my big Louis bag between us to create a barrier as I sit, and TLA promptly moves it to his side of the bench, wrapping his long, wide arm around me to pull me close.

"You good?" he asks.

I nod into his shoulder.

We sit in silence for a few minutes. We don't know what to say, but we know the argument's over.

"How did we get here?" he finally wonders aloud.

I shrug. I know the answer. It's totally me and my obsession with a title. But I'm assuming the question's rhetorical.

"Can we get back to how we were?"

I lean back and look him in the eye. "I don't know."

"Do you want to get back to how we were?"

"I don't know how," I say honestly.

"I'm not asking you to do anything but to be you again." TLA says. "Just don't treat me like I'm your enemy. I don't want you to wait for me, if you want to see other people. If somebody else . . ." He clenches his jaw. "You're gonna do what you're gonna do, D," he continues. "But just give me a chance. You deserve the best, and I need to be able to give it to you in order to be your man."

I nod again. I've decided to try. Because I see him trying. I've riled myself into thinking I'm being set up for a fall because it's happened before. But he's not the guys before him. He's TLA. And he's telling me what he's working on, and I'm seeing him in action. I haven't been listening, worrying so much about what Steve Harvey says I should have and what I'm not getting instead of what I am. And as Mr. Ex pointed out, I've been miserable the whole time I've been trying to fall back. "Okay."

He screws up his face. "That's it? Okay? I'm trying to tell—" he begins passionately.

I place my hand on his cheek, quieting him. "I'm saying okay," I squeal. "I'm here, okay? I'm good, okay? Okay?" He's looking at me as if he doesn't believe I'm saying it.

Then he nods, trying to stop himself from smiling, but he can't. I laugh 'cause I know that feeling. "Okay. And I'll come up here more often, too, and I'll TiVo the games when you come down and take you out to do something more exciting. We can go to the harbor or the city or-or wherever you want to go."

He kisses me then and cuddles me even closer. Eventually, I recover a sense of decorum and realize his hand is gripping my thigh. I remind myself—and him—that I am a lady and we are in public. He apologizes for getting carried away.

We go inside then and join some of the other groomsmen and their wives—TLA's the only unmarried one—at the hotel bar. We're not technically a couple, but I feel like one because we're finally on the same page again.

IX

TLA never asked me to be his girlfriend. Maybe because I didn't give him the chance.

After continuously listening to him explain how he needed to get his life together, I started to think about how my boy once thought about the woman who wrote him an e-mail explaining all the ways she wasn't good enough. The logic went: If he doesn't think he's good enough, and he knows himself better than I do, then why do I still think he is? We stayed in touch after the wedding—mostly three-minute phone chats with pleasantries and no depth and an ongoing BBM chat where he asked me once a week, "What's up, miss? How's everything?" I was always happy to hear from him, but I couldn't shake the feeling that I was settling. Eventually, we fell off each other's radar.

Or so I thought. We'd gone a few seasons without actually talking when he finally picked up the phone for our first real conversation in many, many months. It was nine-thirty in the morning, and I was running late, but I made time to speak to him when his name popped up on my screen.

"You sound frantic. Bad timing?" he asked.

"Something like that," I said, running into the bathroom for my toiletries. "But what's up? It's good to hear from you. How are you?"

TLA wanted me to know that he'd landed a new job, paid off his student loans, and was reenrolling in college. Oh, and to wish me a happy thirtieth birthday.

"You got big plans for your big day?" he asked.

"Uh . . ." I paused mid-reach into my closet for a third pair of rhinestone flip-flops. "Yeah, I do . . . why?"

"I just wanted you to know that I got my life straight and I've always cared about you, Demetria."

Whoa! What?

"I'm packing. Can I call you back?" I can't do this right now.

"You're coming to D.C. for your birthday?" he asks excitedly. He sounds the same way I did on the steps of the museum when I thought Mr. Ex was moving to Brooklyn.

"Uh . . . no. I'm going to Mexico."

"Girls trip?" he asks hesitantly. Why do people ask questions they don't really want the answers to?

"Nah . . . I'm going with . . . my boyfriend."

My buzzer, well, buzzes right then, alerting me that Nathan is at the front door. He's coming upstairs to get my bags to take them to the livery car that will take us to JFK.

"My ride's here," I tell TLA. "I gotta go."

Nate and I ride in silence in the cab. He's sipping his coffee to get fully awake; I'm lost in my thoughts. My mother was right. They do always come back. I guess that means I'm at least a half-way decent woman. I smirk to myself as I stare out the window like Diana Ross in *Mahogany*, but watching Brooklyn's monuments pass instead.

ACKNOWLEDGMENTS

Above all, I'd like to thank my parents for raising me in a home filled with books, art, and music. It was inevitable that I create something. Thank you for believing in the dream, especially when it became apparent I wasn't letting it go. (Sorry about law school.)

To my editor Malaika Adero, her assistant Todd Hunter, my book publicist Adiya Mobley, and my publisher Judith Curr: thank-you for the opportunity, the encouragement, and treating "my baby" as if she were your own. Marie Brown, thanks for holding my hand and offering your unparalleled wisdom. Michelle Huff, my personal publicist, you brought sanity back to my world. Thanks for what you've done and what's to come.

Jess, Kev, Hov, GVG, E. Isis, Parler, Erik, Nicole, Kristi, Rich, and Toya (and my other friends): there are no words to express how grateful I am to have you all in my life. Thanks for never letting me hit the ground.

CBW and "Greg": *Thank you.* For everything. There are too many reasons to list.

Angela Burt-Murray, thank-you for believing in me and leading by example. To the entire *Essence* team, including Sheryl Tucker, Dawn Baskerville, Lynya Floyd, Emil Wilbekin, Karen Williams, Cori Murray, Kenya Byrd, Tanisha Sykes, and Rodney Trice: thank-you for your unwavering support and guidance.

To my mentor and former professor, Gary Belsky: Thanks for pointing the way when I stumbled off the path.

My "children": Lenise, Alize, and Niema: Thank-you for helping me see the world again through twenty-something eyes.

To the Belleionaires: We did it! Thank-you for every kind word (and every criticism, too).

To my cousin Andrea, who I've never met: you live within me. Thank you for igniting my passion for this big, beautiful, and wonderful city. And my cousin Noelle: I'm here, waiting on you to join me. When are you coming?